Endorsements of *Doubting God's Goodness* (previously titled *Interrogating God*):

"As thoughtful and thought-provoking as it is inspired and inspiring . . . an extraordinary and unreservedly recommended addition to church, seminary, community, and college/university library Christian Studies collections."
— Midwest Book Review

"During my 50-plus years as a priest and pastor I have been asked the very same questions with which John Spencer wrestles in this engaging book. The answers he shares to these questions come directly from Holy Scripture. We may not like the answers, because they challenge some of our preconceived notions about the goodness and love of God for the world He created. This book will serve as a good review for clergy of what they learned (or should have learned) in seminary; but it will also be helpful for the thoughtful Christian who struggles to more fully understand God's great love for us."
—The Very Rev. Geoffrey A. Boland,
Vicar General East of the Missionary Diocese of All Saints

"You will finish *Doubting God's Goodness* challenged and enlightened. If you're already a believer, prepare to be emboldened and educated. If you're struggling with doubts, prepare to be encouraged."
— Michael Miller

Doubting God's Goodness

Doubting God's Goodness

Hard Questions, Real Answers

John R. Spencer

Doubting God's Goodness, Hard Questions, Real Answers
© 2020, 2025, John R. Spencer
All rights reserved.

Second Edition, January, 2025
DeerVale Publishing,™ Trempealeau WI

(Previously published as Interrogating God, Seven
Questions That Cause You To Doubt His Goodness)

DeerVale Publishing thanks you for supporting Copyright of intellectual property by purchasing only authorized copies of this work.

No part of this book may be reproduced, scanned, stored in a retrieval system, transmitted or distributed in any printed, electronic, or audio form without the written permission of the author or his authorized representative.

Unless otherwise noted, Scripture quotations are from the ESV® Bible (The Holy Bible, English Standard Version®), copyright © 2001 by Crossway, a publishing ministry of Good News Publishers. Used by permission. All rights reserved.

Contact information:
www.deervalepublishing.com
Email: deervale@mtco.com

The author and publisher have provided accurate contact information at time of publication. Neither the author nor the publisher assumes any responsibility or liability for errors or changes after publication, or for any third-party websites or their contents.

ISBN 978-1-7365689-4-1 (Print)
ISBN 978-1-7365689-5-8 (eBook)

Cover design by Images In Ink

Cover photo: Nathan Cowley
Back cover photos: Hilary Clark, Mahdi Gh, Gerd Altmann,
Nathan McBride, Jacquelynne Kosmicki, & Mstudio

Dedication

For Mimi, Lee, Benjamin, and Allison

Preface

Most of us — perhaps all of us — have at some time had this experience: in the midst of some dark moment or great tragedy, we have asked our wise teacher, or priest, or pastor the question, *"Why did God let this happen?"* Or maybe it was more personal: *"If God is so loving, how could he do this to me?"* Then, as a response, we have heard something like, "Well, there are just no real answers . . . ."

Not true. There are. They are answers though that we just don't want to hear — especially in those dark or difficult moments. This book offers some of those answers. The questions are hard, so the answers are sometimes hard, too.

I've had the opportunity of some very unique experiences in life, working in a variety of professions like law enforcement, social work, teaching, and over twenty years in pastoral ministry. Dealing with many chaotic events, traumas, and tragic deaths has given me a different perspective on these questions.

What I offer here was not written from the shelter of a polished-marble academic hall or an ivory tower, but from life's murky trenches. I hope it will not just be "information" but will perhaps comfort and support you in coming to terms with some difficult time that you or someone you know may have experienced, or may be going through right now.

One

The world we enjoy each day is a beautiful, magnificent place — in many ways, a glorious place. But if, like me, you believe in a good, loving, and sovereign God that rules over this world, your gut wrenches every time you listen to "the News" and are confronted by the evil and wickedness that surround us.

Evil, wickedness. Both are words we avoid, thoughts and ideas we would just as soon ignore or bury deep out of sight. Yet both provoke difficult questions about who we are as people, and about this world we live in.

Pause and reflect on what those two words mean to you. Only if you stare them in the face, *and see them in the mirror,* will you understand the full weight and purpose of what I will talk about in the pages that follow.

Tragedy Close At Hand

We are confronted with the stories every day.

A four-year-old child at play runs carelessly into a suburban street one bright, sunny afternoon and is struck and killed by a car whose drunken driver could not react in time.

A sudden earthquake strikes a mountain village in China and kills thousands of residents: men, women, tiny children.

A smart, talented young teen beloved by his family hangs himself after school one day. Like lightning from a blue sky, with no warning signs and no explanation, his death leaves devastated parents and siblings to grieve for years.

A young man with serious mental problems walks into an elementary school early one morning, a semi-automatic rifle in hand, and guns down dozens of innocent, helpless children and staff.

A young college student goes jogging one morning on the country lane near her rural Midwest home. She is suddenly assaulted and stabbed to death by a man who has been stalking her.

I could make the list much longer. Events like these — all true — can strike us with horror and confusion, unless our hearts have become completely hardened to death and tragedy. If you are like me, you sometimes avoid "the News" altogether because of stories like these. When we read or listen to reports such as these, we are assailed by the unavoidable question, "Why?" And if we have a relationship with the one we believe to be a caring and loving God, we must face a much more difficult question: "How could God allow something so awful to happen?"[1]

If we are to claim faith in a just and loving God, these questions cannot simply be sidelined or ignored. Unless we hide in the false armor of a shallow, unreflective faith, we must grapple with the reality that God allows menacing evil to rear its head all too often. The kind of tragedies I just described strike deep at our heart. They seem so unnecessary and pointless, the questions just multiply. Why would God allow so much evil in the world? Why is there evil at all? Wasn't this all somehow avoidable?

Questions like these have plagued the human race for all of history. When I was in fulltime ministry, people asked me such questions over and over; and I readily admit, I have asked them myself.

Just out of college, I went off to seminary to study theology and prepare for ministry in a local church. I learned all the technical terms regarding evil. What I did not find at seminary were any real answers to these common questions about evil. A professor would say, "Evil exists, of course. But God is sovereign, his ways we can't understand." Another would assure me, "Suffering is real, but it's not our place to question what God does."

The problem was, these responses were completely useless once I left the seminary and began actual ministry. Worse, they seemed *to blame God* as the direct cause of all our suffering. In the parish, confronted not just with real suffering and sometimes ghastly deaths, I was not equipped to respond. I could only lamely offer what I had been taught: "God is in charge; he knows best," a trite answer that vaguely echoed the title of a popular television show. While that answer embodied a whittled down version of the truth, it helped no one.

Throughout those early years of ministry, I faced many tough questions about evil. A suicide in the community always provoked the worst questions — those I was least equipped to answer. My answers rang hollow; I was left feeling the same. I left active ministry after only five years, discouraged and not feeling up to the task.

While at my second parish, I had served as a volunteer police chaplain and reserve office for our small community in Colorado, and not long after leaving parish ministry I was offered a fulltime job as a police officer. The awful realities of suffering, death, and evil now became even more apparent — and unavoidable. I thought I had met evil before, but I had met very little first-hand. From behind a badge and uniform, I discovered the ugliness of evil and the underbelly of human wickedness in a hurry.

The details of just one example will suffice. Not many months on the job, on a quiet Sunday evening, I was first to respond to the scene of a terrible car wreck. A young woman, a cocaine addict and publicly-known prostitute, had been caught by her boyfriend with another man. The woman fled in her high-powered sedan, careening down city streets at over 70 miles an hour, flying through stop signs with her boyfriend in pursuit. A car with five family members heading home from church that evening pulled out from a blind residential intersection and was slammed broadside by the woman's car which was moving at 55-60 miles per hour. The family's heavier station wagon was literally lifted off the pavement and thrown onto its side into a house nearly 50 feet away.

The father, mother, and their eight-year-old son in the front seat of the station wagon were killed instantly. Their two young daughters in the back were thrown around like ragdolls, one landing on her parents in the front, the second ejected through a window.

I arrived to find the injured fourteen-year-old daughter screaming hysterically, trying to claw her way out of the overturned station wagon. After rescuing her, I found her eleven-year-old sister on the porch of the house in shock, disoriented, shaking violently, her face cut and bleeding. As other responders arrived, I crawled into the car to check the family, but it was clear immediately that both of their parents and their little brother were dead.

The ambulance rushed both girls and the woman who had hit them to the hospital. When I got to the emergency room to check on them, the younger daughter looked up and recognized me. Her first words were, "Where are mommy and daddy?"

The woman who had killed their parents and brother was tried but was let off on a technicality in the vehicular homicide law. She skated free, without so much as a traffic ticket.[2] I remember feeling despair after the trial ended, but I had to learn to deal with such things yet keep doing my job.

Just a few years later, my sister Mimi, one year my junior, was diagnosed with cervical cancer at the age of 35, shortly after the birth of her second child. I was shocked by how unfair it seemed! The specter of evil now reared its head attacking someone very close to me. But then came good news: Mimi was treated and declared "cancer free." Our whole family was grateful and ecstatic.

About 18 months later, though, Mimi was admitted to the hospital with a collapsed lung. A chest X-ray, by chance, revealed a large tumor on her liver. She had suffered severe aches and pains throughout her body for over a year, but a half-dozen specialists had assured her she did not have cancer again.

Suddenly, she was in the hospital dying. The "cured" cancer, undetected by incompetent doctors, had spread to nearly every organ of her body and was inoperable. A tumor on her spine paralyzed her lower extremities. She was so weak that chemical or radiation treatments would simply kill her faster.

I flew out to see her. We cried together as I prayed with her in the hospital. I cried when I left her for the last time, and on the plane home. Several weeks later, she died.

I cannot fully express how I struggled with God. This did not just test my faith — it nearly uprooted it. My heart kept demanding an answer, but God seemed silent. I rarely in those days opened my bible, though several were at hand. What was the point? Our "baby sister" Mimi was gone. The youngest of us five siblings, we all expected she would outlive us by years. She was the first to go.

I was angry at God. What was the point of her life being cut so short? What possible purpose could this serve? The wake of her death left her distraught husband with their seven-year old son and tiny, two-year old daughter. He worked fulltime — in the home and out — and raised both children on his own. The loss was deep. He never remarried.

"Why, God?" That's all I could muster. My faith held, but my theological training utterly failed me. There seemed to be no answer. If there was, I had never found it. All I could think was that evil had attacked her, and it had won.

A Turning Point

After over twenty years in secular professions, I returned to active ministry in a small, rural church. Nothing had changed. The tragedies and suffering had not gone away. Nor had the many questions from those suffering terrible illnesses, or facing the death of a spouse. The difficult questions peppered me in counseling sessions, bible studies, in people's homes.

What I realized was that certain common questions kept coming up over and over, like a record stuck on a scratch.[3] The more I heard these same questions the more I struggled myself, because I still had no solid answers to offer.

Out of deep frustration, I started to dig for answers. If God allows so many tragedies, there must surely be reasons. God is not a bumbling idiot, and he gave us real intelligence, so it must be possible for us to find the answers to these serious, troubling questions.

I turned — finally — to the one place that should have been my obvious starting point all along. I dug deeply into Holy Scripture. I read, studied, reflected. I began to see answers, and began to sift them. To my astonishment, the answers to so many difficult questions *started to fit together* and make sense.

To say this, though, is not to suggest that the search — or the answers — were easy. The truth is, when it comes to living our faith, many Christians never leave the wading pool. Take a good breath. Because I'm about to push you into the deep end.

The Questions

Our questions about evil and suffering are difficult and complex. They get more so as we get older. In order to be focused, I have boiled them down into what I call "the seven deadly questions" that cause us to doubt God's power, or his goodness. Theologians speak of "the seven deadly sins" that hurry us straight to hell. These seven questions — if not answered — can do the same thing.

Some of these questions are nearly universal. They crop up across generations, and nations, and various religious faiths. They arise in both war and peacetime; they trouble both young and old. And yes, some of these questions trouble atheists as much as they do theists (those who believe in God). In fact, I suspect that some of these questions, ignored or left unanswered, are what drive some people to become atheist in the first place, and they can drive believers to despair and disbelief. These, then, are the seven questions I will focus on:

1. If God exists and is really good — and loving — why would he allow so much evil in the world?
2. Why doesn't God intervene to stop specific evil events, like a terrible school shooting? If he really is almighty (all-powerful), why can't he just prevent them?
3. If God does not stop a specific evil event, doesn't this lead to the unavoidable conclusion that God is not all-powerful, and is simply too weak to stop tragedies?

4. If God allows something terrible to happen to me personally, doesn't that show he really doesn't love me or never cared about me in the first place?

5. Why do we have to die? This (surely) universal question encompasses several related questions: We are obviously designed to live, so why death? Christians in particular will ask, "Didn't Jesus Christ promise us 'eternal life'? Didn't he supposedly 'overcome death'? Why, then, must we still die?"

6. What about hell? How could a loving God condemn anyone to an eternal hell?

7. Why doesn't Jesus just come back — today — and stop all this evil, and death, and destruction? He promised to return. Why is he waiting?

The Answers

The following chapters will set out answers to each of these questions for you to consider. You may not like the answer. You may declare it "too simple" to be believable, forgetting the principle of Ockham's razor.[4] But actual truth often comes dressed in the sheerest simplicity and it is only our intellectual pride that demands something more difficult.

On the other hand, you may find each answer believable, simple and true, but you still may not like it. Remember, we are dealing in several instances with questions about the mercy, goodness, and love of God in base relief against his essential integrity, holiness, and justice. I don't, and won't, apologize if some of the answers initially strike readers as "unfair." I will offer no moral discounts, no half-price sales to salve your conscience. My goal is to give clear answers that not only square with Scripture but with our common experience.

We often hear the quip that "Life isn't fair." Actually, it is. It is ultimately fair from God's point of view. Yet when caught up in the midst of life's tragedies, we may be hard pressed to believe that, especially when we find ourselves on the receiving end of what we feel would only be fair if it happened to someone else.

Please remember what I have shared about my personal experience. This book is not an academic exercise. These seven questions are not "straw men" that I have set up on an intellectual fence rail just so that I can easily knock them off. To the contrary, they are deadly serious questions that I have personally faced over and over. When in law enforcement, death investigation, social work, and corrections, I have investigated and handled some of the worst crimes imaginable: the murder of a drunken but innocent man during a quarrel over a few dollars; the brutality of men who in unprovoked rages severely beat their wives; the repeated sexual assault of a five-year-old girl by her mother's "boyfriend" — and by that boyfriend's father; the conspiracy to assassinate an up-and-coming black political candidate by a group of white supremacists; a fifteen-year old Hispanic boy shot execution-style by a gang leader for failing to follow orders; a twelve-year-old oriental girl beaten to death by her father because she refused to obey his rules. I've also dealt with multiple suicides by very sick elderly individuals, as well as by perfectly healthy teenagers.

I could go on.

Why does God allow it all? This is what we must uncover. As we do so, we will find that God is not oblivious to our suffering, and he has an overarching purpose for our lives toward which he is leading us, if we will agree to follow. My goal will be to shine the light of Christian Scripture and experience on each question.

To the reader who is not a Christian, I urge you to take heart and read on. You will find that much of what I share will ring true regardless of where you stand in matters of spirituality. It may test your limits. For I believe that apart from a deepened understanding of the spiritual realm and its constant interactions with what we so casually call "the real world" there is really no valid or comprehensive answer to the dilemmas created by the reality of evil.

If you have grappled with these questions, you want answers that are true and reliable, answers that can help reset your course in life. Do such answers exist? Yes. But it takes serious mental and emotional energy to discover and digest them. Just reading this book will not — and should not — satisfy you. You will need to take the answers I share and test them through the course of your own experience.

This is not a book of simplistic answers. It is an effort to chart out authentic answers that will offer hope and courage when we confront evil. These seven questions are about life and death, including the eventual reality — for each of us — of our own death. They demand real answers. Platitudes don't help, and in the final run, evasions are impossible.

To uncover those answers, we need to shine light into the darkest corners of existence where evil thrives. It will feel like digging in a dank, dark mine. I learned that the hard way. The good news: it is a goldmine. The digging requires patience, and a light source. That light comes partly from Scripture and Christian experience. But we are asking questions about God, so ultimately only God himself can shine clear light on what seems gray. Be patient. He will.

You may become frustrated and tempted to give up digging. Don't. Know that your search is a common human quest, and the answers *are* worth finding. Life can change as a result. Mine did.

Endnotes

1. Some, who hold to a radical philosophy of divine determinism, might ask this question in a more insidious and cynical way, "Why did God *cause* this to happen?" I address that issue in detail in Appendix B on Calvinism.
2. Only a few months after the young woman's trial, I stopped her for running a red light in an elementary school crossing — one block from where the fatal accident had happened. She paid roughly a $30.00 fine.
3. Younger readers may have to ask an elder what this means.
4. "Ockham's Razor," sometimes called "the law of parsimony," is the problem-solving rule that "Entities should not be multiplied without necessity," that is, we should avoid adding unnecessary assumptions into a question. A common expression of this rule is that "the simplest explanation to any question is likely the correct one."

Two

"Life is just a mystery." How often have you heard something like that when evil or tragedy rears its head?

If you are like me, you have listened to tedious, hopeless words of a preacher droning on at someone's funeral that "Suffering and loss are just beyond our understanding, we must just not worry over them." How often have you been told, "It's all right. Don't let these things bother you. God knows best."

I always found such statements irritating as a young man. They simply dodge our deepest questions about evil. I really wanted to know: why must I face so much pain and suffering in life? Why does evil seem to run wild at times? Can it not be stopped?

In the chapters that follow, I will tackle the "seven deadly questions" raised in the first. To do that intelligently, we must lay a foundation. All seven questions essentially deal with three things that disrupt or ruin our peace in life: evil, suffering, and death. So, to answer our questions, we must begin with a look at the nature of the three "disturbers of our peace."

What Is Evil?

First, what do we mean by "evil"? The word is commonly used, but do we all mean the same thing when we use it? Or is it one of those words that means whatever the speaker wants it to mean? Is it merely the opposite of "good"?

Let's go deeper. Is evil something specific, or does it refer to a variety of events, feelings, thoughts, or decisions that trouble or upset us? Is evil *anything* that is "bad" or "wrong," or is it something more insidious? Indeed, is it a "thing" at all — an actual reality — or merely an idea *about* other things?

In our present day, I don't believe there is any single, commonly agreed meaning of "evil." English, to begin with, is a lazy language that is not always consistent in the use of words, and there is a lot of verbal slush in our culture in how words are thrown about. What, for example, is the present common definition of these words: "love," "sex," "marriage," or "perversion"? You see the problem immediately.

We face the same problem — really more so — when we try to define words like "good" and "evil." We live in a largely post-Christian time when traditional definitions and biblical understandings of the world and human beings have pretty much evaporated. So I never assume that when someone asks a question about why God allows evil that the person and I mean the same thing by the word "evil." Even less so, in our religiously pluralized society, can we assume that we even mean the same thing by the term "God."

For our purposes here, though, I am going to rely on commonly agreed definitions of "good" and "evil" as they have been understood within the Christian framework for two millennia. There would be other ways to proceed, but I am afraid they would only lead toward greater confusion rather than greater clarity. There are still a good many Christians running around, and because the underlying basis of our societal morality and common law in western culture is so deeply rooted in biblical thinking, this will be the safest approach if we are to agree about what "evil" means.

In the biblical understanding, evil contrasts with good. In one sense, it directly opposes good. What is "good" is what conforms to God's desires and direction for our lives. "Evil" runs afoul of God's will. Most simply put, evil is any thought, or desire, or decision, or action that runs contrary to the known will of God, to the extent that he has made his will known to us.

Good, therefore, tends to be essentially God-centered; evil derives from an act that is purely self-focused and self-centered, where we seek to impose our will over God's creation (which includes our own being).

One traditional understanding of evil suggests that it is not a "reality" or "thing" in itself, but is instead the *absence* of some good. This is called the "privation" of good (as in "deprivation"), acting in intentional opposition to a known good.

An example will help. If I know that it is important to feed my family but I choose to go out on payday and blow my entire check buying drinks for my fellow workers, leaving my family hungry at home, that is evil. Yes, my coworkers get tipsy and feel good (or not) for a few hours, so that is a modest good; my family, however, bears the brunt: the pain of hunger and the absence in the home of one they love (perhaps). If I spend my entire earnings trying to please my coworkers and ignore the more important and basic needs of my own family, my action is evil because I am depriving the more important persons in my life of something I ought without question to be providing. Privation: the good of feeding my family is absent; the vacuum created (the privation) is a manifestation of evil. It is, in fact, sinful. God has commanded us to care for ourselves and our families; he has nowhere commanded us (as far as I am aware) to get our coworkers drunk on Friday night.

We could look at other examples, but can hopefully agree on this much: any thought, feeling, decision, or action that operates in such a way that it denies a good outcome, or destroys or depletes any good, is evil.

We can also distinguish varying degrees of evil in relation to good. As with good, evil manifests itself in relative importance depending on the setting and circumstances. If I argue with a coworker and strike him in anger, this is evil of a relatively mild form — not taking into account a deeper evil resentment toward him which I might harbor in my heart. If, however, I take a knife and go out and brutally stab the same coworker to death in a dark alley one night, my action is, by magnitude, a much greater evil. It not only causes harm, it is more wicked because it is surreptitious, premeditated, hateful, and takes a life. The love and respect I owe him as a fellow human — the good he is due — is destroyed. Evil fills the void. Evil, in a sense, *is* the void.

If we understand evil in this way, we notice something that is central to our discussion of the seven questions. Although we generally (and quickly) leap to blame God whenever tragedy occurs, the plain fact is that nearly all of what we call "evil" is the direct consequence of human thought and behavior. Yes, there are things that we call "natural evils," like a killer tornado, or severe illness. These are sometimes (wrongly) called "an act of God." Insurance companies like that term. We will examine these natural evils — which are actually *un*natural — in a later chapter. For now, let us simply admit that if we stop and reflect on "the News" each day we instantly recognize that most of the evil we react to are events perpetrated by human beings.

Even such a thing as the massive bridge collapse in Minneapolis several years ago is an example of this. The insurance companies may have categorized it as "an act of God," but the reality is this: that bridge collapsed either because it was improperly designed, over-stressed for its designed limits, or poorly maintained. Odds are good that it was a combination of all three factors. And all three were the direct result of human actions and decisions. If you lost a loved one in that collapse, you may have heard someone say, "Well, it was his time," or, "God decided to take her home." Nonsense. Some fool(s) underbuilt or overstressed that bridge. Some governmental officers failed to ensure that it was properly inspected and maintained. God didn't take those victims home. We sent them.

Suffering

Once we understand the nature of evil, it enables us to understand what we commonly call suffering. It is not hard to describe or define. Every kind of suffering is the fruit of actual evil or evil intention, and it results in the loss of something good. Except for the presence of evil, there would be no suffering in the world at all. Anything we experience that injures or hurts us results in some level of pain, and over time becomes suffering.

Whether it is mental, emotional, spiritual, or physical suffering, the pain we experience is not "natural" or "normal" in origin; it is a direct consequence of evil playing itself out in us, or around us.

Depending on the source and magnitude of the evil, our suffering may be greater or less, but all suffering is distressing. It always robs us of peace and contentment, at least at first. Invariably, our one desire amid suffering is simply for it to stop. Who has not been confined to a sick bed and wilted with the frustration of "When will this ever end?"[1]

That is the nature of suffering: it is so often ill-defined and indefinite. We can't always tell why we are suffering, we often don't know its source, and we can't predict when — or if — it will end. Why must we go through this? It feels mysterious. But more mysterious is death. For if you ask anyone, "What is the worst possible thing that could happen to you?" you will likely hear, "I might die."

Death

Physical death is real and we all live under its cloud, "the shadow of death," as the Psalmist put it. It's no good to simply whistle past the graveyard, limping along through life in the vain hope that we can escape the one thing that is as certain as taxes.[2] And our "gut response" is to feel that since God imposed this universal death sentence on us as a race, it must prove that he cannot be good, or that he does not actually love us.

In both reactions we will be wrong. To grasp why I say this, it is important that the reader have a realistic — and accurate — view of death. Death is not just some "normal" process of "passing over" or "passing on." Such euphemisms are attempts to minimize its awful reality. Death is not normal; it is abnormal and ugly. It is the tearing of our spirit from our body, the destruction of the wholeness of who we are as a human being. The only decent thing we can say about death is that the "event" of dying is short-lived and therefore the pain of that moment is only temporary.

Yet as horrible as Death is, if we are to fully answer the questions I have laid out we must understand something else:

contrary to all common wisdom, death is *not* "the worst possible thing" that can happen to anyone. There is something far worse, and it is directly related to our seven questions.

Something worse than death? What could possibly be worse?

To understand the answer, we must start from a central biblical truth about this mystery called human life. It is this: we have all been created to live forever. The germ of this truth, as we will see in course, is in Genesis, the first book of the Bible. There we learn that everything God creates is in its origin good. Because of this, God does not intend to permanently destroy any human life he creates. Each of us is an "eternal" creature made in the image and likeness of the eternal One, God himself. So, if you are ever asked how long you expect to live, the only really correct answer is, "Forever."

"But we must all die," someone will protest. Yes, we will all undergo physical death, the end of our present physical organism. But that is not the complete cessation of life nor a complete destruction of the person. It is, instead, a transition to something else, leading eventually to a new, future creature.

If you examine both religious and scientific studies of death, you discover ample evidence to show that the spiritual core of a person survives physical death. Not only have many people experienced the presence of the spirit of a departed person in close proximity (I have), but other evidence suggests that an invisible but real "something" of each person leaves at death. Indeed, this common experience is where the description of someone "departing this life" comes from. In today's lingo, most call what leaves and survives "the soul," though in biblical terms it was usually referred to as the person's "spirit."

Please do not misunderstand. By pointing out that some part of us survives death, I in no way mean to minimize the ugliness of death. Death is very real, a very painful part of life. I have seen a great deal of it, from the merely gross, to the gory, to the utterly disgusting. Death is a horror, it is not natural, and it is not what God first desired for us. And I promise, I have no eagerness to face it myself. As Woody Allen reportedly said, "I'm not afraid of death, I just don't want to be there when it happens."

Why it happens — indeed, why it *needs* to happen — we will discover. But to understand the answers to our seven questions we must realize that physical death is not the worst that can happen to us.

Having said that, there is no doubt that on the most basic level the death of our body is catastrophic. And sadly, as I have hinted, some people wrongly believe that it is the absolute end of personal existence. They recognize no difference between the human body and spirit and believe that both simply cease to exist, together, at physical death. What goes in the ground is "as dead as a doornail." That person is done.

I don't hold that view but a good number of people do, especially in this day when what I call "pop atheism" is on the ascent. For if a person dismisses God from their life's equation, the result of the equation becomes less than zero. Life will seem to have no ultimate purpose, so there is no expectation *or desire* for survival. For that person, only the barren emptiness of a spiritual vacuum remains. Under the oppression of such a view, life is seen as utterly meaningless: a random, accidental birth, followed by a haphazard and apparently pointless life, followed by another random event we call death. The person may stand heroically against the devastating gloom, but bravery does not lessen the darkness. This is the stuff for which the word "grim" was coined.

While few people formally hold such a grim view, I would wager that virtually everyone you know thinks and acts as if physical death *is* the worst thing that can happen to them. Millions (now billions) live their whole life under this lurking, malevolent fear of death, squandering along the way their hopes and joys, the two very things that make human life worthwhile.

It is important to understand this widespread anxiety for it moves us toward a glimmer of a different kind of death that is truly worse: *spiritual death.* While so many people sit through life worrying about their eventual physical demise, a deeper danger lies in the fact that their inner, spiritual nature — which will survive their physical body — often begins its own death years ahead of their body.

"Nothing can be worse than physical death," some may react. Let me challenge that common view by explaining why spiritual death is not only worse, but infinitely worse.

Spiritual Death?

Because there is such a lack of understanding of spiritual realities today, many people may not grasp what "spiritual death" means. It is simply this: the God-created spiritual core within each of us is what gives us actual life. It is the life of God living within each of us. This is pictured in the Bible when God blows his own "breath" — in Hebrew, the word is also the word for "spirit" — into the man he has created.[3]

Thus, from a biblical understanding, this inner spirit from God is what sustains us in life. If it is cut off from its source, the whole person will wither and die. To use a metaphor, our spiritual essence is designed to be tethered by a spiritual umbilical cord directly to God throughout our existence. That connection is not only our source but our means of spiritual nourishment. If that cord ever gets cuts, our spirit will figuratively bleed to death. This sounds odd or fantastic to one who has never experienced their true connection to God. But for those of us who have at least once tried to cut ourselves off from God, the experience of spiritual decay and death is very real.

What I have discovered through my own experience and the experience of others is that when this "tether" between maker and creature begins to fail, our spiritual nature begins to shrivel. It is much like our physical body. It we don't feed, care for, rest, and heal our body, it will die sooner rather than later. In the same way, if we deny our spirit its spiritual sustenance, nurture, care, and rest, it too will shrivel and begin to die.

There is a key difference, however. When we begin to approach *spiritual death,* the "dead" spirit does not cease to exist. With physical death, our organism decays and is eventually completely gone. Not so with spiritual death: the "dead" spirit lives on but becomes dormant, weak, and often hopeless.

Because we are created as eternal beings, when we suffer spiritual death our spirit does not entirely disappear or "stop." That is precisely the problem. This death is not a one-time event, it is more like a permanent weakness and paralysis. That is why it is *infinitely* worse: it may be of infinite duration. Our spiritual nature cannot die entirely, for it is given by God himself who ultimately possesses it. It can, though, become so weak and atrophied that it is incapable of enjoying life, and can no longer properly serve the body with which it was made. It becomes so sick that it can desire comfort yet relish despair.

We all fear physical death to some extent, yet many people seem utterly oblivious to this danger of spiritual death. What happens if our spirit is intentionally cut off from its source? Here is the disconcerting reality: it cannot cease to exist so it will end in an unending existence of isolation, despair, and anguish. This is what the Bible calls "hell." The essence of spiritual death is that it destroys the fullness of personal life that God wants us to enjoy. It is not the "end" of our spirit's existence; it is the end of all joy and happiness and contentment with life. Physical death is (fortunately) a one-time event; spiritual death can become a never ending event. It results in a pain that rebukes healing. It is the ultimate prison, a personal starvation, a self-inflicted hunger strike against the one who sustains us.

This is why I say that spiritual death is far worse than physical death. Spiritual death is not some future threat of misery. The terrible truth is, many people undergo spiritual death at a very young age. Some will consciously know the process of spiritual decay is fast overtaking them, but take no hand to stop it. Many older souls feel this slow death on a daily basis and will admit this, if asked. It is what some call "hell on earth."

This, I insist, is what we should most fear. Physical death is transitory, and by God's gift will be overcome. Spiritual death by its very nature becomes a matter of permanency, in rebellion against the life-giver. It is not a death you will likely recover from, for once there, you do not realize you *are* there.

The question becomes, if we begin to undergo spiritual death, will we try to nurture our spirit and thrive again? Will we seek to reestablish a purposeful connection with God, or attempt to live on separated from him? The answer is literally a matter of life or death.

Why Does This Matter?

It may now be clear why I have called our seven questions "deadly": these questions relate to doubts about God, and those serious doubts left unanswered fester and can lead to spiritual death.

I compare it to an addiction: you creep into it, unaware. Like any first hit, or buzz, or booze, it often feels sort of freeing — at first. You become "your own." You sense you are disconnected, but misconstrue this for freedom. Eventually, you have little real use for others, in particular little use — or no use — for God.

There can be many contributing causes. A person may fall into disillusionment, or depression. A woman may simply decide "God isn't real" and cut herself off from the one source of spiritual nourishment. A man may try to fill the void with food, or pleasures, or sex, yet find that nothing satisfies. He may get angry with God over some event that seems outrageous if God is indeed loving. As a result, doubts mushroom and cut the one umbilical cord that was never meant to be cut. God made us for connection and communion with himself. There is no substitute, though many have searched the universe for one. God is not just the source of our spiritual nature, he constantly holds us in life. If we reject him, spiritual starvation is the result. Like all starvation, it may not seem very painful at first. Again, it may feel like freedom but it leads to the ultimately slavery: to oneself.

When this happens, we become spiritual zombies who may look lively at times but are hollow and festering inside. In the culture of spiritual decline in which we find ourselves, it is no surprise to me that one of the most popular television programs of recent time is "The Walking Dead." It is an all-too-apt symbol of our actual society.

I have said that once a person is spiritually dead, he may not even realize the fact. Can someone come back from this death? Yes. Because God, the source, has not left. We can turn and retreat from spiritual deterioration at any point, but only by turning to God. His Holy Spirit is the only cure. And he is patient. He did, after all, make us and knows our heart. But the danger remains. Once we reach a certain point, we may no longer *want* to turn back to God. We can too easily become stuck between the rocks of self and bitterness, and from this there may be no desire to come back.

Many of us, even young people, will recognize moments in our life when we have experienced a degree of spiritual death or have started down that path. If not, consider yourself deeply blessed. But many readers will understand exactly what I am describing.

To live in such a deadened state will over time bring much more pain than physical death. Physical death is quick, it is subtle; spiritual pain can seem unending. The root, of course, is evil dwelling in us. Like all suffering, spiritual death is a direct working out of evil in our own heart turning away from God, putting our self in his place. It can wound our heart unmercifully and it can lead — here's the irony — directly to physical death, that of suicide.

Yes, spiritual death is far worse than physical death. It is the worst possible outcome of any circumstance in life. Some people chronically worry about some terrible disease striking them, when all the time they are unaware that a deeper spiritual sickness has already infected them.[4]

Facing Doubt

Unresolved doubts invariably lead to spiritual disease, and ultimately spiritual death. If we neglect this fact, nothing else will matter much. Don't ignore doubts. Deal with them head on. That is the purpose of this book.

There are real and reliable answers to our most troublesome questions about suffering and evil. As we dig you may find, as I did, that sometimes those answers literally stare us in the face. It is, in fact, sometimes too much like looking in a mirror. For the one place none of us can deny evil is when we find it in our own heart.

But remember, God knows that heart. Though we may at times doubt him, he is not unjust, or unfair. And what may seem wrong or unfair to us in the moment, in the heat of the day or the night of our bleakest spiritual darkness, will look different in the warming sunrise of an entirely new world. Time is God's great revealer of truth.

Endnotes

1. I will deal at length with physical illness in a later chapter. I will simply note here that I have known people who experienced severe pain and suffering over a long period of time and, interestingly, the longer the suffering extended, the more content they grew to endure it. I don't presume to know the physical or psychological mechanisms that may come into play, but my observation has been that those who were most deeply grounded into the spiritual realm were most able to endure long suffering.
2. One of the real problems with the popular "rapture" mythology (but *only* one) that some Christians have foolishly believed is that it thrives on this universal human wish that we can somehow escape death.
3. Genesis 2:7.
4. While I may be expressing the idea of spiritual death in different terms, it is by no means a new idea. It is grounded in the biblical understanding of humanity and our inborn relationship with God. If you look, you will see that many biblical personalities suffered from this common human disease. Look, for example, at David after he arranged for Uriah to be killed in battle (2 Samuel 11-12) in order to steal Uriah's wife.

Three

Evil, suffering, death — and yes, even worse, spiritual death. These are the ills that plague us, and they provoke all of our seven "deadly" questions.

In answering those questions, I want to start not with the first but with the second, for this reason: the answer to the second question contains a key truth that is absolutely central to our understanding of God, his relationship to our world, and his relationship with each of us. More importantly, the answer to the second question will provide the foundation for answering both the first and the third.

The second question is, "Why doesn't God intervene to stop specific evil events, like a terrible school shooting? If he really is almighty (all-powerful), why can't he just prevent them?"

The Core Of The Question

This is really a question about God's power. In the previous chapter, I said that evil is anything that runs contrary to what we know to be the will of God. Evil runs against him; and it seeks to destroy whatever is good and right. In fact, what we call "sin" is evil because it is a thought or action that runs directly contrary to God's will.

But this raises an obvious question: if God is truly "all-powerful," how *can* anything go against his will?

The answer, from a biblical perspective, is really quite simple: there is a vast difference between what God *can* do and what he *chooses* to do. Moreover, there is a crucial difference between what God will do (his direct action) and what God will permit others to do.

These are absolutely crucial insights and the answers to several of our questions hinge on understanding both distinctions.

A conversation I recently had with a friend will illustrate why these insights are important. My friend said flatly that God was to blame for all evil. I asked why she thought that. Her answer: "He allows all this terrible stuff to happen, so in the end it's his fault."

It took me some time to get her to consider what she was saying: she was implying — wrongly — that if God does not prevent some evil then it must be his *actual desire* that it should happen.

This is simply wrong thinking. We can see the error if we merely consider our own thought processes and actions. Like God, we each possess a mind and a will. But just because I want something to work out a certain way does not mean that I will impose my will on someone else to make it happen that way. For example, I may want my teenage son or daughter to live a wholesome and safe life. That is my will, my desire. Do I have the power to impose it? To some extent. *Will* I impose my choices on his or her life? I may try. Will I be successful? Never entirely, because they possess their own mind and their own will and, like it or not, regardless of my views or feelings, their choices and desires will govern their lives. If I am wise, I must learn to accept their choices and allow them to lead their own lives.

Now, my child may make choices that will injure himself and mess up his life, choices that run completely contrary to my wishes. I can do my best to dissuade him but, in the end, he will make his choices and live with the results.

Here is the reality: as the parent, I have a lot of power to interfere, to try to influence my child's decisions. But does that mean I will exercise my power to its full extent? Not if I am smart. At some point I won't be around. So, like it or not, I must let go and allow my child to live his or her own life.

When we consider how we ourselves relate to those we love most dearly, it is not hard to understand why God may allow us, his children, to do things that may run directly contrary to his will. He desires our happiness and fulfillment, but he has implanted in us a mind and a personal will, the ability to make real choices. As a result, he may allow us to do things that run not only against his will but against our own interest, even when he realizes those choices may harm us. Does he have the power to interfere, to stop us? Of course. Will he? That is a different question.

If we want true answers to our seven questions, we must begin from this key point: in fulfilling his own purposes for our life, God may let us choose to do something that is contrary to his will, not because he doesn't love us, but because he does.

This gets sticky. So let's move carefully.

God's Purpose For Us

God does not give us commandments because we are unable to break them. His desire is that we obey them, but that doesn't mean we will. We know this truth from first-hand experience: we do break them. Unless we are blatant liars, we know we sin. We do things that run directly against what we know God desires. Even the conscience of a pagan knows this truth to some extent.[1] We choose things that mess up our lives, and God allows us to do that. Why? God certainly has the power to stop us. Perhaps sometimes he does stop us. But often, he doesn't.

This reveals a central but disconcerting point about God and our relationship with him, and it is key in enabling us to answer our seven questions: God never desires evil, nor does he ever directly cause it, but he does permit it.

"Why doesn't God intervene to stop specific evil events?" we have asked. Here is the frank answer: because he chooses not to.

I warned that you might not like some of the answers. But don't throw the book aside. There is more here than meets the eye. This "simple" answer, the simple truth that God may choose *not to intervene* in a particular evil situation, is grounded in three distinct but closely related truths which we must also understand. These truths have to do with his own nature, and with our own nature — what God created us to be.

God's Power

First, God is by nature all-powerful. Being "almighty," he does have the power to stop any specific event. He has no limit on the exercise of his power *as he chooses*. But for his own reasons, as a matter of his own will, he may choose not to act in a given circumstance, or not to exercise his power to its fullest extent at that moment. Relate this to your own experience. You may have the power to stop another person from doing something, but that doesn't mean you will. Many lessons are best learned the hard way. I may, for example, decide it is better for my child to learn the hard lesson than for me to jump in and protect him from some short-term suffering.

Second, one reason why God may elect not to act in a given situation is that every time he does intervene directly in human affairs, he is directly interfering with his own design of our world. He is the one who gave you and me a mind and a will. Every time he overrides those, he is interfering with his own original plan that allows us to make real choices.

Third, if God *does* intervene in a particular situation, he may thereby deprive us not only of the responsibility of our own actions but also of their due consequences. Those consequences may be very unpleasant but they may be something we need to experience in order to learn, and to become more mature and loving.

Now, review those last three paragraphs, for it is absolutely essential that you not read any further until you have grasped these principles. God is all powerful. There is nothing — nothing — he cannot do, if he chooses. And the fact is, God does at times "intervene" into human activity, of his own volition or in response to prayer.[2] This is why we have events called miracles. I have just read of a man whose large, malignant brain tumor suddenly disappeared in a matter of hours (verified by his doctors). The man said it was in response to the prayers of many friends. His doctors could not explain so could not argue. I myself once prayed for a young woman during a healing service who had just seen X-rays of her own brain tumor, which was rapidly growing. When she reached a specialist a few days after the healing service, the tumor had collapsed and was dis-integrating.

Does God act? Yes. Does he act as we wish? Sometimes. Does he always? No. Part of the answer to our question then must be, "Why not?"

Here is a truth that is often missed. The reality that God is all-powerful does not imply — nor require — that he always and at every instant *exercise* his power, or exercise it to its fullest extent. We may want him to step in, to exercise his power in a certain way. That does not mean he will. I have, for example, also prayed for people who were gravely ill who not long afterward died. Did God fail to act in those cases? Does this mean he was suddenly weak? Or did he restrain the exercise of unlimited power — which might have kept one person alive a bit longer — for some very good reason that I could not see?

In that instance, God chose to restrain his power. This is crucial for us to see if we are to arrive at answers to our seven questions. So, reflect on these points carefully.

If God chooses not to act in a given circumstance, it is absolutely no indication of either power or weakness. It is, instead, a clear indication of him exercising his good judgment where he can see ultimate outcomes that we cannot. He will, I believe, always do what best accords with his overarching will and purposes for us, even when we cannot see the reason, or his broader purpose.

We can see this paralleled, too, in our own experience. We know that we make choices not to do something even though we have the complete power to do it. Indeed, I have found it sometimes takes much greater strength to resist some pressing decision, or to refuse to act when cajoled, then it does to simply give in. Greater strength is required to hold back when someone provokes you to your face and you feel the urge to give him his due. This is always the case when we face any temptation. It takes much greater strength to resist the sin than to give in. (I am not, by comparison, suggesting that God can be tempted; I use this only as an illustration from the human level.)

We must also not lose sight of the second principle: God may not act in a given situation because to do so may override and conflict with his design for creation. In creation, God set in motion certain powers and forces, not least of which are the powers he entrusted to humankind. When he intervenes, he is to some extent, for that moment, obstructing the processes he himself put in place.

If we simply consider our own experience, we will see that when it comes to restraining evil or interfering in an event which might cause harm, we can find ourselves in a position very much like God. Just because we may have full power over some situation does not mean we will, or should, step in to stop things. There are often complex circumstances at play and we may have a very sound reason to hold back and not interfere — even if someone might suffer painful consequences. It may be our child, or our student, or our coworker. But we may see that wisdom says "Let them try it their way."

So it is with God. If he interferes in our activities, his interference may deprive us of the rightful consequences of our choices and actions. If he did this frequently, we would become careless, always presuming on his rescue. Further, our life could become increasingly chaotic because we could never be certain that actual consequences would follow from our actions.

We don't have to think very deeply to see these "divine" principles at work on our own level. Consider a couple of human examples.

An orchestra has a conductor. Once he steps to the podium it is "his orchestra." He is "god" over the next few pieces of music. Everyone knows their interrelated roles, they each have their particular part of the music, and each is capable (we hope) of performing their part more or less flawlessly. There is no doubt to the performers or audience who is in charge. The conductor has the power and the authority to command the entire orchestra, and if they fail for some reason, he has the power to impose consequences, including dismissal.

Then something goes wrong. The notes from certain horns are played wrong, the percussionist reacts, wobbling into an offbeat, and soon the entire piece is in trouble. One error compounds into numerous errors, frustrations erupt, tempers flare, and soon the conductor at the podium sees that there is no redeeming this gigantic mess. He smacks his baton down hard on the podium, and frowns at everyone, but says nothing. Then he begins the piece over again.

Now, there were a number of other things he could have done. He could have isolated the performer who made the initial mistake, hauled him backstage, and smacked him silly. Or he could have yelled loudly, cussed them all out, embarrassed them roundly, then stomped off the stage. He could have meekly said nothing, and muddled through — and fired the lot of them the next morning. He has that much power. (He actually, humanly speaking, has the power to murder them all that night, but we won't take the example that far.)

Still, although he possesses overreaching power over every member of the orchestra, as its leader and conductor, he has a number options in how to react when they fail, or misbehave. He can intervene strongly, he can do little, or he can simply ignore the whole mess, allow them to play out the piece to its actual end, and let them all join in suffering their own well-deserved embarrassment for a horrible performance and terrible newspaper review. He could suspend the whole performance in an instant, or he can allow each to make their mistakes, commit errors, mess each other up even further, and simply allow them to suffer through.

In other words, by virtue of the very power he possesses, he can choose different courses of action in regard to each musician, and the whole.

There are further things he could try before the next performance. He could provide better instruments that are easier to tune and play. Of course, the musicians will still have to take care of them. He could get larger sheets of music printed so the older members would find it easier to read the music. But then, they must still practice it, and each must *want* to perform well. The conductor could get remedial training for the weaker members.

Still, they will have to work at it, and work hard to follow his direction from the podium.

He has a great deal of power. But he must choose to what extent he will exercise that power.

Consider a different example. Imagine the owner of a very large Chicago hotel. As owner, she is very wealthy and she can provide the General Manager with any tool or resource needed to reach a five-star rating. She can provide extra money for staff training. She can buy the best furniture, the best equipment, and most wonderful bedding and pillows. She can provide extra training for the entire management staff, and advanced training for the front-line staff. She can make sure that the managers coach each staff member daily, especially in being cordial to every guest.

But here's the rub: the G.M. may be a jerk who really doesn't care if the place ever reaches five stars. He may be the kind of person who is really only interested in himself, his personal advancement, the burgeoning size of his paycheck, and the year-end bonus he allocates for himself.

Certain other staff may work very hard every day and do their best to make the place shine, but some staff may be lazy and spend most of their free moments (and some of their work time) out back gabbing over cigarettes. Some may dip into the till when working the front desk; others in the back office might doctor the books to make things looks better than they are in order to weasel a little better bonus for themselves. As time goes on, morale may suffer, the better staff will simply leave, and the G.M. will one day find himself looking for work.

Now, doesn't the owner have ultimate authority and power over the whole operation? Of course. Doesn't she have the final authority to fire anyone she wants? Yes, but will she? What if the labor market is very tight at the moment? What if she doesn't want to flush down the drain all the money she has invested in training her management staff, even though they are failing her?

The fact is, with both the orchestra conductor and the hotel owner, having all the power in the world relative to the particular operation does not mean that he or she will always exercise the most extreme power: to fire an employee, or every last one of them. A good conductor, a good owner, recognizes that he or she is working with human beings, beings who quite often fail, who stray from assigned tasks, or blatantly decide to break the rules. Firing the entire orchestra will not cause it to perform better. The hotel owner can fire the G.M. and every single manager, but that will not ensure that the line staff will suddenly do their jobs better.

The point is simple. In each case there is a balancing act going on, a balance between exercising the full force of one's authority and power versus the wisdom of restraint, exercising less force and trying to improve or redirect those who are responsible to him or her. An action against one employee may backfire with another. There are a great many moving parts to such an organization, as is true in all human organizations — including (especially!) churches.

When God Holds Back

When we apply these insights to the question of evil — evil largely perpetrated, as I have said, by human beings — we don't have to look very hard to recognize that God is in a similar situation. He can exercise immense power and obstruct us, or he can hold back and let us foul things up.

The thought-provoking thing, of course, is that he put himself in this situation. Reflect on that, for it is important as well. In designing the world — not just the outward world but the invisible laws and realities that underlie it — God chose to make creatures who, like himself, have the ability and *the responsibility* to make real decisions. Those choices always have real consequences. Decisions made by one person would invariably affect another (ask Adam and Eve if you get the chance). This is all God's doing.

Now we can grouse about this and debate for hours why God chose to make such creatures in the first place, but that is akin to debating why grass generally looks green instead of chartreuse. It is what it is. The world contains creatures — humans and other spiritual beings we call angels — who quite clearly have the ability to make real choices. We do it every day, nearly every moment.

So there is not much benefit in debating *why* God made such creatures. He has.

While not debating the point, we can to some extent understand the "why," because God has given us obvious clues. We know from his self-revelation recorded in Holy Scripture that God loves the world he made. He especially loves his human children, those who, as Scripture says, he made in his "own likeness." What does that involve? At least this much: it means that like our maker, we are beings who possess a mind and a will. We can make actual decisions. Many choices will be good, many not. But the simple fact is, we are doing it all the time. If we pursue any idea or philosophy that denies this, we quickly descend into silliness.

Here, though, comes the hitch, as I have hinted. Some of our decisions may run *directly contrary* to what God would have us do. Our desire may conflict with his desire for us. He provides direction, and he no doubt uses his power to influence and guide the exercise of our own wills. But because he himself gave us this "freedom" to choose and to act, he cannot at every moment interfere. To do so impedes his own design for our lives. Constant interference would overthrow human nature as we know it. We would cease to be truly human and would be merely well-designed but highly-controlled robots. Simply put, if God in a given instance "willed us" not to act in a certain way, he would be obstructing his own prior will which allows us those choices.

A Related Principle

These truths describe our human reality and our sometimes perplexing relationship with an all-powerful God. But there is something more. In this ability God has given us to make choices lies a further revelation of his own nature. God has shown us throughout the record of Scripture that his essential nature is to be loving. To "love" in any sense means to be in loving *relationships* with others. St. John puts this essence succinctly by saying, "God is love" (1 John 4:8, 16). Now, if we humans are formed in his image, if we reflect essentials of God's own nature, this means that we, too, are designed to be creatures made for deep relationships, creatures who can both receive and express love.

But love is a spiritual thing, and it is fundamentally a matter of choice. As you know if you have ever given or received it, love does not depend entirely, or even essentially, on outward things. It can and does exist as a purely spiritual reality. It is a completely *willing*, voluntary expression of caring, concern, and affection. For if I feel "compelled" to love anyone — God included — I will not be able to love that person at all.

God expresses his love to us in many ways, the first of which is giving us our very life. He invites us to love him in return, which we can do in a variety of ways. Sadly, a great many people — including far too many Christians — seem to believe that they must somehow *earn* God's love in order to enter his kingdom and merit a spot at his table. Behind this idea lies two grand misconceptions. In the first place, these people believe that God's love is something they *need* to earn. In the second and far grander misconception, they believe that they are *able* to earn it. Now, as to the second, if they are even a tiny bit honest, they know we could not merit or earn the staggering breadth of God's love in a thousand lifetimes. As to the first, they fail to see the simplest of truths: if they must earn it, it is not love.

God loves us because he freely wills to. It is an essential expression of his own being and something he wants us to imitate. This circles us back to an earlier point about evil being a "privation" of some good. When we act in an unloving manner toward someone when we could instead show kindness, we are depriving him or her of the care and concern which every person — even a criminal — is entitled to. Our unloving attitude is a manifestation of evil. Refusing to show love when we might is an example of what is traditionally called a "sin of omission," omitting to do some good thing of which we are capable.[3]

Love requires the expending of spiritual energy, shared outwardly from ourselves to others. Love costs us something, always. It always, to some extent, depletes our "well" of love and we must be careful to replenish the well. Love works that way in every human relationship. This is why we feel so refreshed and enlivened when we are loved by someone else. It helps fill the well of our heart so that we hold love to share with others. Picture yourself as a paper tube holding cotton candy. The more we spin in the well of sugars, the more candy will adhere to our own soul, and the more sweetness we possess to share with others.

Love Versus Evil

Now you may be wondering, "What does all this about love have to do with our question about God not stopping evil?" Everything. Please follow this carefully.

I said that love must be willing, *an act of the will* that is entirely voluntary. While the thing we call "love" certainly involves a number of emotions, and often physical expressions, it is not first or foremost an emotion itself.[4] It is fundamentally a spiritual act of the will. I can feel very bitter toward someone at a given moment and yet still love them deeply. I *will* to love that person, to express my affection, my care, my concern, and most generally also my protection, and I can do so regardless of "the feelings" of the moment.

Further, you can draw me toward loving you, but you can't compel me to do so. I either love you willingly, or I don't. If love, then, is an entirely voluntary act of the will, it means that we must actually possess the *ability* to act in a freely chosen way. This reveals something crucial about the essential nature God has given us, for it is a two-edged sword: in giving us this necessary ability to make choices, thereby bestowing on us the *capacity* to freely love, *God has in the very same stroke given us the ability — and freedom — to hate, to be evil toward one another.*

Read that over until it fully sinks in.

I said earlier that evil can be understood as the privation or absence of good. Here is the prime example. It operates at the human level, but it operates more centrally at the level of our relationship with God. God gave you and I the ability to love so that acting in his image, imitating his essence, we could love him in return, and love each other. We must not miss the implication:

this very freedom by which we can love God also contains the ability to hate him, to rebel against him, to dismiss him as unimportant to our life.

If that is not power, I don't know what is.

Here is a great truth about humanity, and human nature. In giving us the ability to make choices and thus the capacity to love, God has also given us the equal ability not only to do evil, but to become evil.

Here we wobble on the brink of a steep, perhaps terrifying precipice, because here we must confront the reality of evil in ourselves. Human wickedness is real; it cannot be ignored, least of all in our own heart. Once we recognize and accept evil as a misuse of human freedom, we see why evil is so damaging to love and our daily relationships. Evil is the very antithesis of God's goodness, and destroys love. To see this is to begin to understand how to overcome evil, and that must always be our goal.

To combat evil, we must understand how it operates, not only why it is present in the world but how it gains its foothold in human lives. Good, evil, love, and hatred are realities of human existence. Life is not a contest, but it does involve a continual battle of these forces. Our seven questions have focused in on evil. Can we combat it? Do we have that power?

We do. In fact, God built this power into his design for creation. And this brings us to another essential fact of human life that we must consider and fully digest. It is a fact so central to the entire record of the Bible that to miss it is to misunderstand everything written there. Fortunately, this "fact" is a treasure hidden in plain sight, a principle that I call "Shared Sovereignty." If we are ever to understand why God permits evil, we must understand this principle, for it is the root from which grows the answers to all seven of our questions.

Endnotes

1. See St. Paul's discussion of this, Romans 1:18-2:6.
2. For why we should pray, and why it works, see Appendix A.
3. "So whoever knows the right thing to do and fails to do it, for him it is sin" (James 4:17).
4. Equating the physical expressions of sex with the essence of love is one of the greatest diseases of our "modern" world.

Four

I have answered the second of our seven questions: God does not always stop evil things from happening because he *chooses* not to. That may have seemed an abrupt, disconcerting answer to many. But it is the truth.

Why God refrains from acting when we wish he would step in can only be answered thoroughly if we understand the biblical principle I just mentioned, the principle of Shared Sovereignty. Once we explore this principle it will make the difficult answer to question two more understandable and less heart-rending. It will also answer our first question, "If God exists and is really good — and loving — why would he allow so much evil in the world?" And it will help answer the third, "If God does not stop a specific evil event, doesn't this lead to the unavoidable conclusion that God is not all-powerful, and is simply too weak to stop tragedies?"

While I cannot offer any cheap or pain free understanding of the nature of evil, I will offer this promise: if you carefully digest these next few pages, it will rescue you from the great modern disease of hurriedly leaping to blame God every time something goes wrong, or when evil seems to triumph.

The Treasure Hidden In Plain Sight

If ever there were a treasure worth finding, the principle I call "Shared Sovereignty" qualifies. Even without further explanation, readers may have an idea what this means. Shared Sovereignty is a fundamental principle of biblical truth that is essential to grasp if we are to understand our relationship with God and his relationship with our world. Most importantly, this principle is crucial in understanding why God sometimes seems to ignore our suffering. We must therefore examine this idea closely, understand it completely, and discern what it means in our actual day-to-day lives.

Simply put, Shared Sovereignty means that the all-sovereign God who made the universe created mankind to share in ruling and caring for this world. The key to understanding Shared Sovereignty is in something I stressed in the previous chapter: God has given us the *ability* to make choices, and thus the *capacity* to love. We have the power to make real decisions that affect not only ourselves but others, as well as the physical world around us. In other words, of his own choice, God has placed tremendous power into our hearts, minds, and hands. He has created us to be "co-rulers" with him of this world.

Did God have to do this? No. He did not have to create the world in the first place.[1] It is not as if he were lonesome. But in choosing to empower humans as he did, God obviously made a very specific decision: he invested certain of his creatures, humankind, with a reflection of his own essence (his "image"), the ability to make real and effective choices. In doing this, God gave us both the capacity to love and the ability to create. We are not just co-rulers, we are co-creators. We are able, within the limits of our God-given power and purview, to make things that did not exist, and to create relationships. (Unlike God, we cannot create out of nothingness; we can only create using the things, and energy, and matter he has put at our disposal.)

This ability to make choices is fundamental to our nature. It was intentional, not an accidental "byproduct" of God's larger creation. God does not act aberrantly or irrationally, or without understanding all consequences of his plan. In creating humankind as he did, he invested us with capabilities far beyond those of the lower animals. Chimpanzees may indeed share a huge percentage of their DNA coding with humans (apparently God utilizes efficient redundancy), but unless you are a first grader you see instantly that monkey antics are just that: antics. When they "seem human" it is because they are mimicking what they see humans do.

Now, it is true that Chimps — as well as many "higher" forms of the lower animals — possess a kind of personality something akin to that of men and women. Indeed, the Old Testament affirms that such animals have a "soul," a form of immaterial personality not unlike humanity, each appropriate to their particular being.[2] A smart dog can learn tricks as easily as a chimp. (A cat can, but doesn't care to.) But neither the dog nor the chimp possesses self-reflective reason. They cannot, as far as we know, reflect intelligently on their existence or ask questions like "Why am I here?" They cannot understand time as we do, or consider what they might do next week or in five years. They can easily learn by trial and error to manage their environment (we do the same) in limited ways, but they would not be able to design a semiconductor or create a computer, let alone understand physics and engineering in a way that would enable them to build a modern skyscraper. And they cannot by self-reflection anticipate their own death. They are also unable to conceive the one who created them to begin with. They may "perform" (imitate) human-like actions but they cannot worship. (Sorry to disappoint those who believe your dog worships *you*.)

In contrast, as I have suggested, God created humankind "in his own image." He invested us not just with reason but with the ability to make actual choices. He also gave us the perception to understand that we have a creator, the one whose image we bear. Doing all this, God invested us with both power and purpose. With power and purpose comes responsibility. We are accountable to our creator for how we exercise the powers he has given us, and we are responsible for whether or not we achieve (or even seek) the purposes for which he made us. Making us thus, in his likeness, God also chose to share his sovereign rule of the creation with us.

Co-rulers?

To suggest that mankind can "co-rule" with God may seem an exaggeration to some; it may seem a sacrilegious insult to others. Surely "God is supreme over all."

He is, yes, and we do well never to forget it. But the principle of Shared Sovereignty is not my idea, nor a new idea. It was not a human idea at all, but God's. The term may be mine but the principle itself comes directly from Holy Scripture.

I referred to this principle as a treasure hidden in plain sight for good reason because we don't have to search far into Scripture to discover it. This seminal principle is so fundamental to everything else we read in the Bible that to miss it will cause us to misconstrue most of what the Bible is telling us — about God and ourselves. Indeed, if we don't understand Shared Sovereignty, we will not be able to correctly understand what we call "sin" or "wrongdoing." If we search with eyes open, however, we find this fundamental principle right in front of us. Where? In the very first chapter of the first book of the Bible.

From The Beginning

The first chapters of the Book of Genesis tell the Hebrew account of God creating the universe, this particular world called earth, and mankind's place in it. I won't cite the entire chapters since many will have already read them, or easily can. I want instead to focus on several key verses which many people routinely read and pass over, not grasping the enormity of what they have just read.

The context of this passage in the first chapter of Genesis is that God has constructed the essentials of the universe and this planet. He has created basic forms of plant and animal life. But he is not done:

> Then God said, "Let us make man in our image, after our likeness. And let them have dominion over the fish of the sea and over the birds of the heavens and over the livestock and over all the earth and over every creeping thing that creeps on the earth." So God created man in his own image, in the image of God he created him; male and female he created them. And God blessed them. And God said to them, "Be fruitful and multiply and fill the earth and subdue it, and have dominion over the fish of the sea and over the birds of the heavens and over every living thing that moves on the earth". . . And

it was so. And God saw everything that he had made, and behold, it was very good. And there was evening and there was morning, the sixth day (Genesis 1:26-31).

"And let them have dominion." Seize that thought and consider the implication. This phrase is said *twice* in these few verses. God says this first to himself, then speaks it *directly* to the men and women he has created. Notice that he is not speaking to an individual, Adam, who does not appear as a described individual until the second chapter. In this first chapter, God is speaking to humankind as a whole, the men and women he has made ("male and female he created them"). Of them together he says, "let *them* have dominion."

Don't miss this, or mistake it. God speaks these words not as a kindly, benevolent gesture but as a *command:* "Be fruitful and multiply and fill the earth and subdue it, and have dominion over the fish of the sea and over the birds of the heavens and over every living thing that moves on the earth . . . And it was so."

God is not simply being courteous to inept, unsophisticated children. He is giving a very specific charge, a direct order: be fruitful, multiply, fill the earth, *subdue it*, and have *dominion.* Over what? Over all things around them and over all other forms of life, plant and animal. If mankind is to have dominion over every form of life, he must share dominion over the material world which supports such life.

In short, mankind is given a job to do. They are to be stewards. They are to be in charge of, and responsible for, a whole range of things they do not *own* but for which they will be answerable. Humans are to co-rule God's world, exercising dominion over the portion of creation which God has put into their care.

This is, in part, why Jesus often used the image of a garden or vineyard in his teaching. The owner places others in charge. If we have any doubt about the seriousness with which God takes our role as stewards, we have only to read two or three of those New Testament parables to find out.

In Plain Sight, But Missed

Over the years I have found that many readers of this passage entirely miss the crucial implication: God made mankind co-rulers with him. The passage cannot be more clear. God, the all-sovereign creator of all that we know, intends that you and I are to share his sovereignty over his world.

Why is this so often missed? I cannot answer for everyone, but I suspect that a large part of the reason is because in our Christian — and now post-Christian — culture, people are so deeply conditioned to think of God as "the one in charge," "the big man upstairs," the one who holds and exercises all power over this world.

As we see from Genesis, though, that is a false view of God's sovereignty because it is *incomplete*. It does not take into account what he himself has revealed through Holy Scripture. If we are to "take God at his word," we must take all of it. We must not neglect this important truth that is stated so clearly (twice) in the first chapter of the first book of the Bible. This very specific revelation of Shared Sovereignty comes early in Scripture for a good reason: it establishes the context and sets the stage *for everything else that is to follow* through the final chapters of the Book of Revelation.

Mankind has a variety of God-given purposes, but one fundamental purpose is to steward the creation in which God has placed us. Man is not a vagrant. He is not on the scene accidentally. He was put here for a purpose. God intends that his creation is to be further created, polished, developed, and refined. Man is his instrument to accomplish all this. What we make, or build, or create, including the finest art, is merely a continuation of God's work in creation. This is not man's choice; it is not something he asked for. It is God's decision and plan.

Further Evidence

That mankind is indeed to be a co-ruler with God is expressed again in the next chapter of Genesis, in the account of God creating the specific individual called Adam. The name in Hebrew, *'Adam* (pronounced *"Hadam"*) can refer to "mankind" in general and involves a word play on *hadamah,* the earth or soil.[3] Thus, *'Adam* is literally the one taken "from the ground" and the account of his creation contains a vital example of what I call Shared Sovereignty:

> ... then the LORD God formed the man of dust from the ground and breathed into his nostrils the breath of life, and the man became a living creature [in Hebrew, *nephesh,* a living "soul"] ... Then the LORD God said, "It is not good that the man should be alone; I will make him a helper fit for him." Now out of the ground the LORD God had formed every beast of the field and every bird of the heavens and brought them to the man to see what he would call them. And whatever the man called every living creature, that was its name. The man gave names to all livestock and to the birds of the heavens and to every beast of the field (Genesis 2:7, 18-20).

The significance of Adam naming the animals is lost on most modern readers. In ancient times, giving a creature (or person) its name was a sign of sovereignty and authority over that creature.[4] In bringing each animal to Adam for him to name, God is directing the man to exercise his role as co-ruler. Indeed, God is assisting Adam in that role.

God makes the animals to be helpers to the man so that he is not isolated ("alone"), but none is a "fit" helper, none are of Adam's "kind." God's intention from the beginning is that mankind should be composed of the complimentary sexes of male and female (Genesis 1:26 again) so that they can "be fruitful and multiply." So, God now creates from man's own flesh his own "kind," a woman. When God shows the woman to the man, Adam recognizes, as we might say, "his other half" and he later names her as well.[5]

The Meaning Of All This

If we are to understand the nature and origin of evil, the implication of these creation accounts must not be missed. God has made us co-rulers. We are charged to be stewards of this world and its creatures, as surely as we must care for ourselves. God is sovereign over all, but he has assigned us to share that sovereignty. This is a part of the weight and dignity of human life. Made in God's "image" (likeness), we are to act as little gods over his world (John 10:34).[6]

If we simply reflect on ourselves, our underlying nature, we see at once that God has enabled us, to a limited extent, to manipulate and in small ways control the world around us. We are able to do this for two reasons: 1) God has given us to the power; and, 2) God has granted us the permission.

Reflect on that. For if God gives us the power to rule but not the *permission*, we become exactly what the Calvinist sadly imagines: a powerful machine that cannot move or operate under its own volition in any direction, even in the smallest of spaces, in any real way. We might imagine we are free to choose and to act but we are merely fooling ourselves (so says the Calvinist) because God ultimately controls our wills; we carry out only what *he* predetermines and causes us to do.

The problem with the Calvinist view, of course, is that our daily experience refutes it. More problematic is the fact that if the Calvinist were right, there can be no such thing as sin — unless God himself is both the author and mover of each one of our specific sins. Sin, rightly understood, is an act of *our* will *against* God. If in the final analysis God ultimately controls our wills, then God intends us to sin. We fall into the absurdity of God directly acting against his own will, and we descend rapidly into irrationality. Whoever such a "god" is, he is not the God of Holy Scripture, but a demon poorly disguised.[7]

No, our moment-by-moment experience verifies that we are not robots. God has given us the power, permission, and responsibility to share his sovereignty over this world. We could spend serious time and spill great amounts of ink examining arguments about "why" he did so, and that might be an entertaining intellectual exercise, but it will carry us no closer to understanding what he expects of us. The obvious fact is, he has given us both the power and permission to co-rule. We could not be effective without the power; we could not act without his permission — for surely his overwhelming power could instantly prevent us from *any* action.

My focus here is not *why* God made us to share his sovereignty, but on understanding what it means for how we should live. If we recognize that we are co-rulers, this has immense implications for the choices we make and the kind of lives we each live day-to-day.

But we must be careful and think clearly about this. To realize that God shares his sovereignty with mankind is *not* to suggest that mankind is thereby a *co-equal* ruler. Mankind's role as co-ruler is always limited. We are still subject to God as the true sovereign, the ultimate king over his creation. By sharing his sovereignty with us, God has not elevated us to deity. We still possess only human purview and human power. We co-rule with God only to the limit of human knowledge and human capabilities, and only within the moral law that God has commanded us to follow. When we fail to do that, when we breach the moral limits he has set, we cease to rule his creation and begin to abuse it.

In other words, mankind is first and last only a "steward." We oversee and govern what is not our own, including our very selves.[8] Creation always remains God's creation, and God's possession. The fact that he entrusts us with its governance does not mean God has stepped away or abandoned us. He is always present, often in the background — but sometimes in the foreground. He is Lord of the manor; we remain servants.

Agents Of His Sovereignty

If we will consider how we function day-to-day, we realize that we *have* been given both the power to act and the permission to act, within our particular little territory of existence, and within obvious limits. We do make decisions and affect the world around us. We can create things and make it better; we can also tear it down and to a limited extent destroy it. We can do good, or we can do evil.

"But wait," someone may object, "I was always told that God is sovereign over *everything*, and no one can stand against his will."

Within the broadest context, as I have already said, both statements are correct. But if we take the scriptural account as true, we must understand the *fullness* of what those statements then mean. God *is* sovereign over all, but his sovereign will includes this reality: he has given each of us a will also, and he has chosen to make us his empowered stewards, investing us with tremendous ability to execute that office. "No one can stand against God's will." True. But once we understand the principle of Shared Sovereignty, we see that it is *his will* that we exercise *our* wills. We are to make choices and exercise God-given power in a loving way to build up and refine his creation rather than defacing or destroying it.

The only real alternative, as I previously suggested, would have been for God to have made us with no effective will, "people" who could not make real, meaningful choices. He did exactly this with the lower animals. But had he made us like them, we would be incapable of giving real love — and likely incapable of receiving it. We would be incapable of caring about anyone else — or anything beyond our next meal. The result? Well-controlled flesh-robots who cannot do wrong, but who — if "who" is still appropriate — cannot love God or each other. Holy Scripture shows us this was not God's plan. He desired creatures who could share his love and give it to others. And as I have said, the power to love requires the ability to choose it.

The fact is, we recognize our role of co-rulers intuitively: we routinely act not only within ourselves but outwardly. We express and implement our thoughts, feelings, and decisions outwardly all the time in actions that affect the people and things around us in an objective way. We do not, as some want to claim, simply "react" to things around us. We think and choose and take decisive actions because we will to do so. This is the very nature of what "human" existence entails.[9]

The Consequence Of Shared Sovereignty

The consequence of Shared Sovereignty, however, is that it opens the door for evil. Indeed, when we look within ourselves, we see the sad reality that evil is "crouching at the door" (Genesis 4:7). Evil is not only real, it has infected our hearts. All but the shallowest thinkers realize that humanity is capable of doing desperately wicked things.

Our first question was, "If God exists and is really good — and loving — why would he allow so much evil in the world?" We now know the answer. God allows evil because he allows us. He made creatures with independent wills who can work against him, who can act in conflict with his own will, and he permits this. And he has entrusted to us tremendous power as his co-rulers. When we turn against his will, evil is the result.

Because this is so, we could fall back and claim, with my friend, that God must therefore be blamed for all evil. Of course, to do that we must overlook a step of reality and a whole class of persons: us, the real authors of evil.[10]

What is worse, evil is not a simple matter. Evil compounds. In fact, we only begin to see the true complexity of life and the ripple effects that our actions have within our environment — and upon others — once we recognize that *every other individual* possesses the same power and the same permission to act as we do. What happens, then, when I decide to do a thing that runs directly in opposition with what my neighbor has determined (with equal insistence) to do? Has either of us lost the power to do it, or lost the permission to carry out our own wishes? No. We have lost neither. The result is what we call conflict or struggle. Our actions clash. In the extreme, this becomes war.

We should not miss an important corollary: the same conflict that can erupt between man and man (or, as is often the case, between man and woman) can arise equally between a man and God. Do not doubt this. If God has given you both the power and the permission to think, to decide, and to act with him as a co-ruler of his world, he knows perfectly well that you may act against his wishes and come into conflict with himself.

Careful reflection, in fact, will reveal that many of our conflicts with each other — man with man, woman with woman — are out-workings of the conflicts we each have with God. Made in his image, with individual personality, the conflicts that develop between our will and God's will may play themselves out in conflicts with other people. This should not surprise us. It is the origin of much evil and should help us understand what is happening when someone says that "evil seems to be running wild." It means that our insistence on doing things our own way has run rampantly against the benevolent will of God and is wreaking havoc on other people.

Here we see the full impact of this hidden treasure called Shared Sovereignty. We discover the origin of so much evil and why God permits it in the first place. He created us to help steward his world: to work it, to care for it, to develop it, to share his sovereign rule over it all. But we often find this role difficult to manage, for in possessing the power to care for God's creation, we also have the power to destroy it.

Endnotes

1. Debates about the "necessity" of God having to do this or that are plentiful in theology but rely on the risky assumption that what may seem to be necessary, as assessed by our human minds, may in fact have nothing whatsoever to do with the inner nature of God-in-himself.
2. Domesticated animals learn to relate to us in a "person-like" manner because they possess their own soul. That does not make them human, nor does it endow them with essential rights or dignity equivalent with humans.
3. In appropriate contexts, "man" is not a "sexist" term. As most high school seniors or college freshman know, English uses some words comprehensively (collective nouns) to include all representatives of a group (in this case, humanity). The pronoun "they" can refer to both men and women. In the same way, in standard usage both past and present, "man" used in this comprehensive sense means mankind, both men and women, girls and boys. It does *not* mean, nor imply, "only men." Such

an interpretation displays an ignorance of our language and its history. Collective words or phrases are common in many languages and it is only in recent years that certain hyper-sensitive individuals have objected to the use of "man" as "paternalistic" or "misogynistic." Interestingly, as I noted, the name "Adam" in Genesis 2 can, in the original Hebrew, refer to "mankind" (*'Adam)* collectively. Thus, when Jesus referred to himself as "the son of man," this phrase would have meant, to his Jewish listeners, "the son of Adam." Jesus thus identifies himself as sharing our common humanity, full human nature, as a descendant of *'Adam.*

4. It is no accident that when someone is baptized into the Christian family they are "formally" given their personal name — and sometimes an additional "baptismal" name. This signifies that the parents are returning the child to God as the child's true Father, who is the one who actually bestows the name.

5. Genesis 3:20. Her name Eve sounds like the Hebrew word for "life giver" and resembles the word for "living." Some modern readers will dislike this fact that Adam names her because it suggests dominion over her as well. But both the Old and New Testaments describe a relationship between husband and wife in which the man must love his wife and is completely responsible for the well-being of his wife and family. Thus, his "dominion" is not one of "power" but of love, care, and responsibility. See prior Endnote 3.

6. It is important to note the fuller context of John 10:

"My Father, who has given them to me, is greater than all, and no one is able to snatch them out of the Father's hand. I and the Father are one." The Jews picked up stones again to stone him. Jesus answered them, "I have shown you many good works from the Father; for which of them are you going to stone me?" The Jews answered him, "It is not for a good work that we are going to stone you but for blasphemy, because you, being a man, make yourself God." Jesus answered them, "Is it not written in your Law, 'I said, you are gods'? If he called them gods to whom the word of God came — and Scripture cannot be broken — do you say of him whom the Father consecrated and sent into the world, 'You are blaspheming,' because I said, 'I am the Son of God'?" (John 10:29-36).

7. For a more thorough examination of Calvinist thought, see Appendix B.

8. "Or do you not know that your body is a temple of the Holy Spirit within you, whom you have from God? You are not your own, for you were bought with a price. So glorify God in your body" (1 Corinthians 6:19-20).

9. Perhaps God could have made us in such a way that we could have interior thoughts and feelings but could not express or transfer those outwardly. If he had made us so, whatever actions we took (if any) would be very different, and vacant, and purposeless. Or, God might have given us the power to act thoughts out, but not the permission. We would then indeed have been merely well controlled flesh-robots who were continually very frustrated.

10. We should at least be honest. Had God not made us with freedom of choice, we would not be capable of even asking these kinds of questions.

Five

As we have seen, Holy Scripture clearly sets out God's plan that we are to be co-rulers with him over his world. He has chosen to share his power with us, and commanded us to care both for this world and for ourselves — our whole spiritual-physical nature.

Understanding the implications of Shared Sovereignty, we can answer our third question: "If God does not stop a specific evil event, doesn't this lead to the unavoidable conclusion that God is not all-powerful, and is simply too weak to stop tragedies?"

The answer is "No" to both parts of the question. God possesses unimaginable power, beyond anything we can comprehend, try as we might. He can do anything he chooses at any "instant" (relative to our timeframe). It is not a question of powerlessness. If God chooses not to interfere with some occurrence of evil, this does not show him to be weak. It shows that he is willing *to restrain* his power for some important reason. That reason in many cases may elude us, but it may be exactly this: *God will sometimes allow evil to occur because we must learn the consequences of what happens when we exercise the power he has given us as co-rulers.*

This may sometimes be a bitter lesson. We may, for example, learn too late — after we have opened our mouth or unleashed our pen — how damaging a few destructive words can be to another soul. It may be that we learn that our craving for some illegal drug, a supposed "victimless crime," helped cause the deaths of innocent children in Mexico at the hands of drug runners who carry our favorite drug across the border. Each such lesson will be painful but necessary, for it reveals the extent of the power God has entrusted to us.

Yes, of course, God could stop all such events. But he could do so only at the expense of making us robots, stripping us of our power to choose. Instead, by allowing a tragic event to occur, God is training us in the concrete realities of the power we have to affect and change the world around us. He is letting us live out the sometimes terrible consequences of what happens to others when we choose to do wrong. These difficult lessons teach us that we must learn to control what God has given us in a godly manner and exercise our power only in careful and loving ways.

Evil At Its Source

I have said that God allows evil because he allows us. But where did evil first enter the human story? If God does not desire evil nor directly intend it, how did evil originate?

The answer — again — can be found in the early pages of Holy Scripture. How far do we need to read this time? Only to the third chapter of Genesis.

A brief review will help us understand how evil came into our world. God created a man and woman and placed them in Eden, a Paradise on earth where all they needed was there before them. There is no mention of cold or inclement weather, so they apparently needed no shelter. They don't need clothing as, so far, they are not ashamed of or uncomfortable with their nakedness. The one thing they most need is food, but food is everywhere for the taking.

God has, however, set one limit — one only. They are free to eat of every plant and fruit tree in the garden (Genesis 1:29) except one. God commands the man not to take the fruit of the tree of the "knowledge of good and evil" (Genesis 2). For eating this fruit would bring them a kind of death:

> When no bush of the field was yet in the land and no small plant of the field had yet sprung up — for the LORD God had not caused it to rain on the land, and there was no man to work the ground, and a mist was going up from the land and was watering the whole face of the ground — then the LORD God formed the man of dust from the

ground and breathed into his nostrils the breath of life, and the man became a living creature. And the LORD God planted a garden in Eden, in the east, and there he put the man whom he had formed ... The LORD God took the man and put him in the garden of Eden to work it and keep it. And the LORD God commanded the man, saying, "You may surely eat of every tree of the garden, but of the tree of the knowledge of good and evil you shall not eat, for in the day that you eat of it you shall surely die" (Genesis 2:5-17).

God gives Adam a simple command: do not eat of this one particular fruit. Why? The answer is simple: it will cause death. We will learn only later in the account that this means *spiritual* death, for when they first eat this fruit, neither Adam nor Eve die physically.[1]

This brings us to the third chapter of Genesis and what is traditionally called "the Fall" of mankind. To understand what happens, we must keep in mind what has already been said:

- The ground is to be "worked" by mankind. God did not create inanimate nature to simply sit fallow: he created it for our use, that it might be worked, developed, enlarged, cared for, and perfected.
- God did not want the man to be alone. He has commanded humankind to "be fruitful and multiply" (Genesis 1) so God creates man's counterpart, the woman, who will make that possible.
- The woman (named Eve only after the Fall) is to be Adam's companion and co-worker to tend the garden and share responsibility for their life, but also his mate, his completing half.
- We know with certainty that the woman, too, is part of God's plan for "Shared Sovereignty" not only from what was said in Genesis 1 ("male and female he created them") but also because of what happens here in Genesis 3.

The Rebellion Begins

Genesis 3 reveals how humankind ran off the rails. The woman, like the man, is free to roam and tend the garden. She is free to a radical extent. Like her husband, she has a will, that is, freedom of choice. We know this because she *chooses* to disobey God:

> Now the serpent was more crafty than any other beast of the field that the Lord God had made. He said to the woman, "Did God actually say, 'You shall not eat of any tree in the garden'?" And the woman said to the serpent, "We may eat of the fruit of the trees in the garden, but God said, 'You shall not eat of the fruit of the tree that is in the midst of the garden, neither shall you touch it, lest you die.'" But the serpent said to the woman, "You will not surely die. For God knows that when you eat of it your eyes will be opened, and you will be like God, knowing good and evil." So when the woman saw that the tree was good for food, and that it was a delight to the eyes, and that the tree was to be desired to make one wise, she took of its fruit and ate, and she also gave some to her husband who was with her, and he ate. Then the eyes of both were opened, and they knew that they were naked. And they sewed fig leaves together and made themselves loincloths (Genesis 3:1-7).

Here is equal-opportunity evil at work. The serpent's actions are evil on two levels. First, he was to be under the dominion of the humans, yet he wants them to fail. Second, he also knows that in urging Eve to disobey God, he is disobeying as well.[2]

Eve's choice is also evil because she understands what she is doing. She acknowledges what God has commanded them, and proceeds to go against it. It is a direct, intentional violation of God's charge to them. The one and only prohibition God has given she now breaks.

Adam's actions are likewise evil. He is the one to whom the command was directly given. And we know he told Eve because she repeats to the serpent what God had commanded.

Almost simultaneously, on several levels and involving several creatures, evil erupts from the rebellious wills of God's creatures. And in considering this eruption of evil, we must recognize two things. God did not cause them to rebel. To the contrary, he has sternly warned them of the consequences. Those consequences are nearly immediate:

> And they heard the sound of the Lord God walking in the garden in the cool of the day, and the man and his wife hid themselves from the presence of the Lord God among the trees of the garden. But the Lord God called to the man and said to him, "Where are you?" And he said, "I heard the sound of you in the garden, and I was afraid, because I was naked, and I hid myself." He said, "Who told you that you were naked? Have you eaten of the tree of which I commanded you not to eat?" The man said, "The woman whom you gave to be with me, she gave me fruit of the tree, and I ate." Then the Lord God said to the woman, "What is this that you have done?" The woman said, "The serpent deceived me, and I ate" (Genesis 3:8-13).

Not only do we see equal-opportunity evil at work but equal-opportunity blame shifting as well. Adam blames Eve. Eve blames the snake. Perhaps the snake turned and looked at the tree.

God will have none of the blame-shifting. All three have willfully rebelled. All receive a punishment. We should take note, because when we choose evil, there will *always* be consequences. God speaks first to the deceiver:

> The Lord God said to the serpent, "Because you have done this, cursed are you above all livestock and above all beasts of the field; on your belly you shall go, and dust you shall eat all the days of your life. I will put enmity between you and the woman, and between your offspring and her offspring; he shall bruise your head, and you shall bruise his heel" (Genesis 3:14-15).

But the woman, though deceived, is not off the hook:

> To the woman he said, "I will surely multiply your pain in childbearing; in pain you shall bring forth children. Your desire shall be contrary to your husband, but he shall rule over you" (Genesis 3:16-17).

Of course, the man is not off any hook either simply because it was his wife who brought him the fruit:

> And to Adam he said, "Because you have listened to the voice of your wife and have eaten of the tree of which I commanded you, 'You shall not eat of it,' cursed is the ground because of you; in pain you shall eat of it all the days of your life; thorns and thistles it shall bring forth for you; and you shall eat the plants of the field. By the sweat of your face you shall eat bread, till you return to the ground, for out of it you were taken; for you are dust, and to dust you shall return" (Genesis 3:17-20).

Because of their willful rebellion, the pristine world God made has now radically changed. The animal world is affected, woman is affected, man is affected, and — significantly — the ground itself is affected. For each there will be long-term consequences of this "first sin."[3]

What fascinates me is what God did next:

> And the Lord God made for Adam and for his wife garments of skins and clothed them (Genesis 3:21).

They have, so to speak, just bitten the one hand that feeds them. Yet God *immediately* shows mercy and kindness. He curses, but then he blesses. And this we will find throughout the remainder of Holy Scripture. Although God disciplines his children when they are wrong, he does not stop loving them, nor does he stop providing for their needs. It is quite ironic. He knows they have become self-conscious about their nakedness. So he makes their clothing. His fatherly love is not cancelled by their rebelliousness, any more than an earthly father will stop loving a rebellious child.

A World Now Broken

Now, before he made humankind, God saw all this coming. What was his plan? He could have simply left the man and woman in their now-broken condition — forever. That is, he could have allowed them to remain in the garden with unfettered access to that *other* tree named in Eden, the tree of immortality. The consequence? They would have endured immortal (undying) life in a broken state of sin.

God did not let that happen, but ask yourself: what if he had? What if he had simply allowed Adam and Eve to eat of that other tree of life and live forever — in corruption, rebellion, and sin — with no way out?

That would have been punishment indeed. So, God eliminates that option. He expels them from the garden and sets an angelic guard to prevent them — prematurely — from getting to the fruit of the tree of life. This was his response plan to man's sin, but it was not to be permanent. There will come a time when God will once again grant mankind access to that other tree, immortality, everlasting life: they will find that "tree of life" in the cross of Jesus Christ.

But at that time, and for their foreseeable future, what God had warned came true: "but of the tree of the knowledge of good and evil you shall not eat, for in the day that you eat of it you shall surely die." Here is the origin of what I have called the more brutal kind of death, spiritual death. Adam and Eve did not drop dead (physically) with the fruit still in their mouth. But their inner spirits, severed from fellowship with God, immediately began to shrivel and die.

I would ask you to mentally file this fact as we go forward, because the reality of *spiritual death* will become prominent again when we reach our fifth question, "Why do we have to die?" The spiritual death that Adam and Eve begin to experience will lead irrevocably to its consequence: eventual physical death. Having humiliated themselves into sin, and having planted the spiritual seed of their own physical destruction, they are now cursed with what may be the most severe penalty of all. That penalty is not just that someday they will die. The true severity is that having brought down this curse on their own heads, they must live from that day on with the *knowledge* that they will one day die. This, I would argue, is the real horror of death: not the momentary event, but the days and weeks and years of anticipating its arrival.

Is this penalty too severe? From our perspective it may certainly seem so. But God sees all history as an instant and, before Adam and Eve sinned, he already had the cure at hand. Before creation, "before the foundation of the world," he had the solution in place. For at a later time very distant from Adam, a second Adam would undergo a unique and history-changing death (1 Corinthians 15; especially verse 22). The spiritual death of mankind brought on by sin would be healed by a physical death that would be offered to overcome it.

Before that distant day arrived, however, history would be riddled with a long succession of new Adams and new Eves falling off the cart. The entire biblical history, in fact, is the story of God's love and provision for mankind and man's continual rebellion against him. And the account doesn't hesitate: it progresses in the very next chapter of Genesis by recording the first murder.

God, therefore, sets in motion an interim plan, a "holding" plan for mankind to learn and suffer the consequences of their own evil in order to prepare for its solution. God's plan moves forward, and his response is swift:

> Then the LORD God said, "Behold, the man has become like one of us in knowing good and evil. Now, lest he reach out his hand and take also of the tree of life and eat, and live forever — " therefore the LORD God sent him out from the garden of Eden to work the ground from which he was taken. He drove out the man, and at the east of the garden of Eden he placed the cherubim and a flaming sword that turned every way to guard the way to the tree of life (Genesis 3:22-24).

Adam will now work the ground in pain, but that pain won't go on forever because God has in place a plan to redeem that pain, to bring a rescue. Here is the first part of our answer to the fourth question: if God allows me to suffer, does it show he doesn't love me? Part of the answer is that God allows us to suffer knowing that it will not go on forever. He has set its limit. There will be an eventual end to all suffering, in his renewed creation. But for each of us individually, there will also be the limit of our own physical death. Why must we die (question five)? In part simply to release us from furthering suffering in the mess that we have all made of this world.

If we break down and begin feeling that all these consequences are simply too much or that they are unjust, I again ask that we consider the alternative. Had God not expelled Adam and Eve from that garden, had he not barred their path to the tree of life, you and I would still have been born, but there would be no physical death. Every one of us would be trapped in sin — forever — with no respite and no escape route. If you want to consider "unjust," consider that.

God chose the alternate path. By barring Adam and Eve from the tree of life, he is sentencing them to physical death. But he is saving them from the torture of eternal sin, unredeemed and unbreakable. Death is certainly a form of suffering; the moments leading up to one's death may be horridly painful. But death itself is not. Death brings the end of pain. That was precisely why God invoked it: it appears at first to be another curse; in the end, it is an act of blessing, a release from the pain.

Indeed, this is the "good news" of the Gospel of Christ. For before the foundation of the world (1 Peter 1:20; John 17:24) the birth and sacrifice of Christ was already set in place. God had planned his counter-attack on evil and his plan to overcome death, both spiritual and physical. The crucifixion and resurrection of Jesus *were* that plan (Ephesians 3:9; Colossians 1:26). God is willing to tolerate evil for an entire age of history but he has always had in place his means to overcome it.

To thoroughly understand why God allows evil, why he tolerates it at all, we must keep the coming of Jesus in our sights, both his first coming and his eventual return. For in the restoration of life inaugurated by Jesus' resurrection we see God's ultimate medicine for sin: the conquest of man's evil by a man, the conquest of death by a death, the restoration of all things by God himself, in the person of his son. This is the key: Jesus is the *ultimate* co-ruler, Son of God but also a son of Adam. Jesus shows us — finally — what Shared Sovereignty means and how we are supposed to carry it out. He shows us what we are to become, and how we should live:

> 1. God has bestowed on us great power and responsibility, to share his sovereignty over creation.
>
> 2. That sharing does not affect nor limit his ultimate power or authority in himself. He remains in eternity — within himself — all-powerful in every instant of what we perceive as "history" moving forward. His power cannot be diminished.
>
> 3. One expression of his almighty nature is his *power to restrain* his power, as odd as this seems to us. He may sometimes choose, in a manner of speaking, to "keep his almighty hands behind his back."
>
> 4. However we misbehave, however much evil we cause, God does not ignore it. He *will* reply; there will be consequences. Those consequences may not be immediate but they will come.

Having said this, we may wish that God would spend less time with his arms behind his back and more time taking a direct hand in human affairs. I cannot doubt that he feels the same. Surely he must often want to slap sense into us.

But we must stay focused on the biblical principle of Shared Sovereignty, for only then will we make sense of God's frequent restraint. He expects us to act. He expects us to confront evil as well. When he chooses not to act, we can be almost certain it is because he is waiting for us to act.

Mankind's role in all this is the central story, the news that we not only cause evil but more importantly have the power to stop it, or at least fight it. That is one message of the Gospel: that in the incarnation of God's son, and by his *willing* death on a cross in ancient Palestine, God and man have acted in concert to break the bondage of human sin. If we keep the life, death, and resurrection of Jesus center focus, the answers to our seven questions will come into clearer focus.

The Appalling Irony

There is one last thing I want to point out before we leave our consideration of the origin of evil. If we look closely at Genesis 3, we see that humankind fell because the serpent tempted Eve to want *to "be like God"* (Genesis 3:5).

Do you see the tragic irony? Though the serpent would be the last of creatures to admit it, the fact is that both the man and the woman *were already like God.* They were both made in God's "own image," and God had given them massive authority — and power — *to co-rule the creation.* They cannot *become* "like God" for they were already god-like.

Not only do readers of Genesis miss this crucial point, Adam and Eve seem to have missed it, too. God had already put *dominion* into their hands, including dominion over all other living creatures on earth — which, by the way, includes the serpent, another feature of this account that often gets missed.

The irony is mindboggling: Eve is tempted to reach for *something she already possesses.* She longs for power that has already been placed squarely into her hands — by God himself. She desires this fruit, the knowledge of good and evil, but she *already possesses* that knowledge. God's word and command are good; to rebel against them will be evil. She knows this, for this is why (at first) she resists the serpent's suggestion.

We must not fail to notice the meaning: her initial resistance is an exercise of her co-sovereignty with God. She already knows right from wrong, good from evil. She has the power to ignore the wiles of this lower creature, for she has dominion over him. In short, she has the ability to say, "No."

Here is the real anguish expressed by this whole event we call "the Fall": Eve already has immense power and authority, yet she wants more. Does that sound familiar?

Evil Becomes A Plague

Like any disease, evil starts small but grows; it does not grow slowly, it mushrooms. The very next chapter, Genesis 4, brings hatred and murder. The biblical account of human wickedness shows how it goes downhill from there.

None of us escapes this tragedy. My view is that each of us early on in life as a boy or girl reenacts the Fall of Adam and Eve. We come into life innocent of evil and wrongdoing, not distinguishing between "good" and "evil." Before long, still a child, we discover that someone has established moral laws to contain our worst instincts. One day we may come to the realization that God is the source of these laws, but here is what we also quickly learn: while these laws may be right and good, they cannot bind us. We say to ourselves, "God says I must not do this — but I think I will just try anyway." The selfish thrill we feel at "breaking the rules" doesn't last. Before long, like Adam and Eve trying to hide in the bushes from the presence of the Lord, we sense our failure and begin to feel shame. We dive off the cliff with willing intent but smash to the ground at the bottom with nothing but regret. There is something inside that tells us we have failed not just God, but ourselves. It is our common story that is, truly, as old as Adam. (St. Paul's personal struggles described in Romans 7 come to mind.[4])

Thus, the very first chapters of the Bible teach us both about our essential gift of Shared Sovereignty and also how we so quickly abused the gift. If we read no further in Scripture (and many don't . . .) but pay attention to what these first chapters say, we would at least understand God's goal: his desire that we co-rule with him. Out of love, the infinite, all-glorious and all-powerful creator placed "dominion" over his creation into the hands of men and women. On a very basic level, that should terrify us. We are tempted to ask, *What was he thinking?*

This much at least: God knew all that was to happen, and he had a perfect plan respond. He allowed great risk in making us, but he knows what he is doing. "Why" he chose this course for creation may boggle our minds. The answer will always remain largely out of our reach, for as A. W. Tozer once said, trying to put the divine mind and plan into a human mind would be like trying to pour the ocean into a teacup.

We are given dominion, but we have our limits. When God allows evil, we must not forget that he also has a broader, overarching plan to overcome the consequences of damage of evil in order to restore and perfect his creation. Our misbehavior will not, in the end, destroy his design; our weakness will be overcome by divine strength, the kind of strength that enabled Jesus to carry that cross to his own crucifixion.

So, although at times we get upset with God, even angry, we must never despair. He is working through the events of our world, drawing our common race toward a goal he has set, orchestrating like a grand conductor the music of history to a glorious conclusion.

As his co-workers and co-rulers, we will continue to make wrong choices, often out of pure self-centeredness. We want to run the world our way, not his. This ancient disease of "self-ism" has grown far worse in modern times. The ever-increasing pace of fun and pleasure and technology is dragging us by the hair into a future we can't predict, let alone control.

Fortunately, God can. In the light of his over-arching knowledge and his time-unimpaired vision, he is drawing history toward a goal he has set. When we recognize this truth, the fuller answers to our first three questions fall into place:

- God does not ignore evil, he despises it.
- He refrains from preventing some things from happening not because he is too weak but out of divine strength.
- A part of the strength is his divine patience (2 Peter 3:8-9).[5]
- He knows that overriding our decisions and actions on a day to day, moment to moment basis would interfere with his overarching plan for each of us, and for his world.

The reality is that we bring the plague of evil on our own heads. God allows this not because he is weak, or thoughtless, or not caring. He permits us to rebel and run afoul of his better will precisely because — ironically — he loves us. He allows us to turn away from him, but he has bestowed on us the power to love him, or turn back.[6]

You and I may not be able to rule much on a given day, depending on our circumstances or position in life, but we do rule one thing: our own selves. If he lets us fail there, we should not be surprised when God permits us to fail on a larger scale. We are not well-controlled flesh-robots programmed by God. God has given us great freedom of choice and movement because he seeks our obedience out of love, not compulsion. He is drawing each of us toward a perfection which only he can see right now. But to reach that perfection is his desire for each of us.[7]

Keeping A Clear Focus
If we can carefully keep the principle of Shared Sovereignty in clear focus, our perception of evil will not only sharpen but we will come to understand it at a deeper level. God designed us to co-rule: to learn, work, and care for each other, to develop not only ourselves but the physical environment around us. It is only when we accept this awesome responsibility that we will stop blaming God for our own wrongs and grow into the stewards he desires us to be.

As long as our selfish wills rebel against God and try to grasp at greater power, evil will be with us. But God did not simply turn humankind loose in his world willy-nilly. From the beginning, he made his presence known among us. He gave us commands and covenantal restrictions for our own good. He patiently desires our ultimate wellbeing. In the end, we are answerable not to ourselves but to him.

The selfishness and brokenness in us must be overcome, the evil we know firsthand. From my experience, I believe we can only overcome these character faults when we ask God's help. At times, the alluring, persuasive power of evil and personal control seems too great to resist — apart from his divine help. In "the Fall" we broke our covenant of love with God. Our rebellion, as a race, has never let up. We don't *want* to be held accountable to anyone but ourselves. In short, we all want a savior, but no one wants a judge.

This attitude of self-centeredness leads directly to the danger of spiritual death. What fallen mankind wants more than anything is simply to be left alone, to be answerable to no one but himself. As C. S. Lewis' mentor George McDonald somewhere wrote, "The one principle of hell is, I am my own." But of course, we are not our own.[8]

We always seem quick to blame God when evil arises. But the truth about evil is most clearly exposed when we look in the mirror. What is true of each of us is true of all. We are powerful creatures; God has made us so. We can reject God's love, and we can try to run our life entirely on our own, come hell or high water. In doing so, we will shrivel and die spiritually.

But that is not God's desire. He can reach past our sin to offer us a saving hand. That is the hand Jesus so often offered the sick, the blind, the deaf when "he raised them up." We are very sick creatures but we need only grasp his hand if we want to change. He is the final cure for evil; he knows it from both sides, divine, and human. God is not to blame; he is the one ready to reach out that hand to change us.

Here is an even greater irony, the irony of the Good News: that hand of incomprehensible power that rescues us was once nailed in absolute helplessness to a cross. His powerlessness has become our hope. God's weakness has become our strength. God has given us the power to refuse sin, to say "No" to evil and "Yes" to him.

For the sake of Christ, then, I am content with weaknesses, insults, hardships, persecutions, and calamities. For when I am weak, then I am strong . — 2 Corinthians 12:10

Endnotes

1. The tree representing the "knowledge of good and evil" must mean something beyond a simple "discerning between" good and evil, for in Eve's resistance to the serpent's temptation we see that she already discerns that difference. So, we should probably understand the "knowledge" given by the fruit of this tree not as mere discernment but a deeper understanding of the *consequences* of good or evil.

2. In later Jewish tradition, reflected in the New Testament, this "serpent" was in fact a demonic angel — Satan — masquerading as a serpent. There are several reasons. First, snakes have never had (as far as we know) volition: they cannot, like angels and humans, make self-conscious decisions. Secondly, we know that Satan is the quintessential deceiver (John 8:44) and sometimes masquerades (disguises himself) in order to deceive others (2 Corinthians 11:14). Third, Satan acts as the tempter. He tried to trip up Jesus himself with lies (Matthew 4, Luke 4). Fourth, since the serpent "deceived Eve" (2 Corinthians 11:3), this suggests he had volition and was therefore not a lower creature but a demonic angel in disguise.

3. This "first sin" should not be confused with the doctrine of "Original Sin" — although they are related. People wrongly speak of "the Original Sin" referring to the initial sin committed by Adam and Eve. The actual meaning of the doctrine of "Original Sin" is that since the Fall, each person has an inherited tendency to fall into sin. I don't doubt the doctrine, but we must remember both Adam and Eve had the capacity to *refuse* evil and choose the good. (This idea is expressed in a rather famous passage, Isaiah 7:14-16, which, by no coincidence, came to be interpreted by Christians as foreshadowing Jesus himself).

4. St. Paul there talks about how his inner will conflicted with his inner desires:

> For we know that the law is spiritual, but I am of the flesh, sold under sin. For I do not understand my own actions. For I do not do what I want, but I do the very thing I hate . . . So now it is no longer I who do it, but sin that dwells within me. For I know that nothing good dwells in me, that is, in my flesh. For I have the desire to do what is right, but not the ability to carry it out. For I do not do the good I want, but the evil I do not want is what I keep on doing . . . For I delight in the law of God, in my inner being, but I see in my members another law waging war against the law of my mind and making me captive to the law of sin that dwells in my members. Wretched man

that I am! Who will deliver me from this body of death? Thanks be to God through Jesus Christ our Lord! So then, I myself serve the law of God with my mind, but with my flesh I serve the law of sin (Romans 7:14-25).

5. "But do not overlook this one fact, beloved, that with the Lord one day is as a thousand years, and a thousand years as one day. The Lord is not slow to fulfill his promise as some count slowness, but is patient toward you, not wishing that any should perish, but that all should reach repentance" (2 Peter 3:8-9).

6. I could go into more depth about our relationship to the God of creation, our very awareness of the existence of "the divine," and his willingness to allow suffering. I refrain from addressing these issues here simply because I consider that the best words that could be written about these topics have already been provided by C. S. Lewis in his small but monumental book, *The Problem of Pain*. It is one of his two seminal books for anyone seeking a primary understanding of Christian faith — the other being *Mere Christianity*. If the reader has not already gorged himself on those two books, I encourage him to devour both until he can stand no more.

7. "You therefore must be perfect, as your heavenly Father is perfect" (Matthew 5:48). See also James 1:4.

8. "You are not your own, for you were bought with a price. So glorify God in your body" (1 Corinthians 6:19-20; see also 7:23).

Six

We have examined evil, suffering, and death, including the ugly reality of spiritual death. We have examined the biblical principle of Shared Sovereignty by which God has made us stewards of his creation. And we have also considered the biblical account of how evil first entered the world. As we consider our next questions, it will be important to keep these realities clearly in mind, including the fact that although God tolerates and allows evil, he made each of us with the ability to say "Yes" or "No" to evil.

Is this freedom terrifying? It can be. The ability to make effective choices that carry real consequences is like continually holding a live grenade from which the pin has been pulled. Missteps and bad choices tend to bring quick consequences. We have the power to do great good — but also the power to cause great evil and destruction.

Certainly, God knows that the freedom of choice he has bestowed on us is often difficult for us to manage, especially when we are younger and less experienced. There were times in my life when I literally trembled at the choices I was being forced to make. Still, I made those choices as best as I could. I am not silly enough to say they were all the right ones.

Shared Power Brings Shared Problems

In sharing his sovereignty with us, God not only shares his ability to make choices, but by the same act, he places on us the responsibility for the consequences of those choices.

We all discover this at some point. Our choices often mess things up, in our own life and the lives of others. But because God has made us responsible for those choices, he will not simply rush in to our rescue when things go haywire. We may want him to, but he is more likely to restrain his hand in order to force us to unsort the mess we created. Part of Shared Sovereignty is the responsibility to correct problems and repair the damage we cause. That is never fun, especially when we have hurt someone close to us. God often allows us to flounder through these messes because in doing so, we learn about love and responsibility at a truly personal level.

All parents face similar dilemmas. Like any good parent, God is not ignorant of our pain, but more often than not, he will leave things in our hands that we wish he would take off of them so that we will shoulder our proper responsibilities.

Indeed, I believe this is why God allows certain evils to continue for a time: he will not simply jump to our rescue, because he expects us, as his co-rulers, to act first. As I have suggested, he may — to use *very* figurative language — place his hands behind his divine back like a wise father and wait to see what *we* will do about the problem. To our frequent vexation, he may keep his arms back there for a long time. It may seem he is ignoring our pain or problem; in reality he is teaching us how to deal with the evils we so often cause ourselves.

When we grasp this, we find the further truth of the answer I gave to our third question: If God does not prevent a specific evil event, does that lead to the conclusion that he is simply too weak or powerless to stop that tragedy? Again, no: if God sometimes stays his hand when he might otherwise act to prevent some terrible evil, it may be because he has charged us — as his co-sovereigns — with *the responsibility to act first.* Most evil is created by humans. Why should it not be our responsibility to end it or allay it?

Like the answer to our second question, we may not like this truth. I often don't. I would much rather God jump in to rescue me from every little pain or problem I stumble into. I especially want him to extricate me from the more massive problems I create. But if he does not, it is not because he is weak or uncaring. It is because

I have not only the ability but the responsibility to address the problem first.

As I have already suggested, we do not really want to live in a world where God jumps into the fray at every moment. He would not then be God, but a house-servant. The fact is, we would grow tired of that world very quickly. It would be daily uncertainty and hourly insanity. As C. S. Lewis points out in his book *The Problem of Pain,* if God begins to intervene every time the least bit of trouble or evil rears its head, our world would become very unstable and thoroughly unpredictable.[1] Our freedom of choice — that power he himself gave us — would become a mere vapor, useless and meaningless against the constant interference of God.

We cannot have it both ways. We can't complain that God does not intervene at every moment to stop evil yet still want to maintain the freedom he has given us. In our weakness, we may want God to shield us from the effects of evil — even (perhaps especially) when we ourselves cause it — but God has entrusted stewardship of his world to us. We cannot blame him for not stepping in and overruling us at every turn. After all, is it not true that what most of us want is to be in charge of our own life as far as possible? I think most of us would say we do. God knows our hearts. So, as we discover, he generally honors our freedom and choices, even when they are bad and cause harm. As with my illustrations of the orchestra conductor and the hotel owner, having ultimate power over a situation does not force one to use that fullest power at any moment.[2]

When confronted with any evil, we will always wonder why God is permitting it. We must not, however, leap to the unreasoned conclusion that permitting it means he approves it. God hates evil. I cannot say it often enough. But he also loves us, and respects our choices and actions unless his own ultimate goal for our life requires him in an extreme circumstance to intervene.

How and when he will do so will always be opaque to us. We should always, of course, pray for his help, but we should never demand that he insulate us from the damage caused by our own decisions. He is not, in fact, our house-servant.

If we keep this clear, we will be more reconciled to the answer to our first question: "If God is truly good and loving, why would he allow so much evil in the world?" The answer was, because he allows us. As his co-rulers, he allows us to carry out that role even when we do so wrongly, and cause evil as a result. Although God loves us deeply and is himself entirely good, he allows evil to exist as a direct result of *our* misuse of the power he has bestowed on us.

Yes, he could prevent all evil by overruling our wills and obstructing our actions. But if he did that constantly, to prevent every instance of evil, we would have to circle back and ask, "Was it not pointless, then, for him to give us freedom of choice to begin with?"

Are We Really Free?

Now, some Christians will argue that since our "freedom" to think and to choose is deeply tainted by sin, we are not truly "free" at all, and so we cannot avoid evil entirely. I will agree with the fact that we are stained by sin, that our wills are in some sense broken — or at least twisted — from birth. That is what the doctrine of Original Sin is meant to express. But if we take the stand that because of this "stain" we simply cannot avoid evil, we are fundamentally denying that we have actual freedom of choice. The danger, of course, is that we then drift toward the false worldview of Calvinism, believing that human freedom of choice is merely an illusion, and that we are utterly powerless to say "No" to evil.[3]

Were we to accept the faulty view that the human will is so badly damaged that it cannot be trusted at all, we would be forced to this obvious question: would not God then take back the gift? If no good can come from mankind either choosing or acting, why would God continue to allow us any freedom of choice at all?

It is plain that he would not. God would not allow us to keep exercising our freedom unless we are still capable of some good, and of some right choices. The fact that God does not strip us of our freedom altogether tells me that God knows we are still capable of right choice and right action, however badly we may exercise those gifts at times. Most importantly, we are still capable of love. Were he to strip us of our freedom, as I previously explained, he would strip us of our ability to give and receive genuine love.

To more fully understand all this, it is helpful to distinguish clearly between what God *intends* and what God *allows.* In theology this distinction is referred to as the difference between God's "manifest will" — what he himself directly wills and intends — as opposed to his "permissive will," what he allows to happen that may be in opposition or contradiction of his own will. It is not a difficult idea. As I said previously, that very fact that God has made creatures with independent wills means that he freely chose to allow us independent action. That we can choose and act at all is only the case because God *permits* us. We must not be foolish enough to imagine that everything you and I choose will automatically be in concert with God's own manifest will. Were that true, we would have to accuse God as the author or propagator of all sin — indeed, all evil. Such thinking runs contrary to our day-to-day, moment-by-moment experience of reality.

But as I suggested in Chapter Five, the fact that God permitted the Fall of Adam and Eve — and the fall of every one of us since — does not mean he "stands idly by" and ignores sin and evil. To the contrary, his perfect plan to deal with evil was laid in stone before evil made its first appearance. This is in part the message of the Gospel of Christ. From "before the foundation of the world" (1 Peter 1:20; John 17:24) the mission of Christ was in place: God had his counterattack on evil set before evil erupted. The crucifixion and resurrection were always part of that plan (Ephesians 3:9; Colossians 1:26). God will tolerate evil, and has. But we must never blame him as its *cause.* All evil is contrary to his own will (James 1:13).

Remember, God chose to share his sovereignty with us. The fact that most evil erupts from within the heart of man is a result of us abusing that co-sovereignty. The irony, of course, is that the consequences of evil — generated within our hearts — almost always comes back directly onto our own heads. Maybe that is why we are always on the lookout for a scapegoat, seeking to shift blame to God, or someone else.

Why?

If God knew how we would abuse our power of choice, some may ask, "Why did he give it?" In part, as I have explained, because it is requisite if we are to have the capacity to love. But grasping the broader "why" of this gift may be plainer if we approach that question from a different angle. What would have been the alternative? Could God have made us differently? Did he have other choices?

The short answer is, God's power is without limit so he always has choices. But the least consideration makes it plain that the only *functional* alternative to giving humans the ability to make choices was to have made us without that gift.

What would that have been like? Like nothing human. God could have made us in such a way that we would simply *perform* his will as puppets; we would then have done so without fail. He could also have put warm, fuzzy feelings inside us so that when we thought of him we would sense something akin to affection. Such feelings, though, would not be actual "love." They would be merely a preprogrammed response instilled by God. He could even, perhaps, have built into us an irresistible longing to be near him, but that also would not have been true affection. It would only have been like putting a piece of metal near a magnet.

In any such case, whatever we would have been, we would not have been human in the sense we mean.

Since this was all God's own design, creating us to reflect his own image and nature, we share in the volitional aspect of his being: we have an independent will. If God is anything, he is the *supreme* will, the supreme "decision maker." We reflect his nature in several ways, but this volitional reflection of God's essence is central to what we understand "human" to mean. God made us so that within the limits of our realm and reach, we can carry out our own will, although we can never fundamentally obstruct God from carrying out his own.

In other words, we need not worry that by sharing his sovereignty with us that God has somehow lost power, or lost his grip of the overall course of history. He remains the first and true sovereign.

Some may be curious about this, wondering if God is less powerful now than before he created mankind. Is it not the case that by *sharing* power, he has *lost* power? Not in the least. Every person who holds any authority has, as part of that authority, the ability to delegate authority, along with its attendant power and responsibilities, to someone else. In doing so, the one who delegates loses nothing. He *retains* his full and original authority in himself.

Consider a simple example. When I went into law enforcement (as a younger and more foolish man), I was sworn in as an officer by my police chief. By swearing me in, the chief was giving me the power to share his own police authority which, in our particular case, was vested in him by city and state statute.

When he swore me in, however, he lost nothing. His own power was actually enhanced and broadened by sharing it with me. That his power was not diminished was evident in the fact that he could have fired me ("swear me out") any time he chose. (He swore me out a couple of times, but not in that sense.) I simply shared his authority. Anything that I could do as an officer, he could still do. Anything he could not do as an officer of the law, I could not do either. (Granted, he had higher authority that he did *not* delegate, or we would have both been chief.)

In other words, I shared in the "sovereignty" of the police chief as his delegate, both his authority and his power. When I acted in any official capacity, I acted only as his delegate, both of us acting as officer-delegates of the law itself.

It is similar in our relationship with God. By him sharing his sovereignty, delegating power to us creatures, God loses nothing of his power, let alone his sovereign authority. In one sense, his authority is enhanced in terms of its effectiveness by being broadened amongst us as empowered delegates.

But God remains sovereign. He is king, and there is no challenger, contrary to those foolish people who speak as if Satan were somehow God's equal. God has chosen to share his sovereign power with us, and with his angels. Satan, remember is an angel, a creature; he has never possessed any power except as it was delegated to him by God.

Be careful here. Some will ask, why then did God allow Satan any power at all? There is a simple answer: why does God allow *you* any power at all? Like us, Satan rebelled. God allowed Satan's fall in the same way (though not in the same moment) as he allowed man to fall. The only difference is that some people will turn and repent. As far as we know from Scripture and its record of Satan's behavior, the Deceiver has no intention of ever turning.

So, God *shares* his sovereignty, but *remains* sovereign. He does not give anything up in the sharing. He does not lose sovereign authority to any degree. He allows us to *co*-rule, but he still rules. And he can *overrule* us at any moment he chooses.

Delegates Of The King

Once we fully comprehend the principle of Shared Sovereignty, we understand more easily why God chooses sometimes *not* to act when we think he should. This central principle, revealed in the first chapter of Holy Scripture, is expressed in countless ways, overtly or less overtly, throughout the entire Bible. A clear example leaps out at us from the hymnbook of ancient Judaism, the Psalms:

> The heavens are the Lord's heavens, but the earth he has given to the children of man (Psalm 115:15-16).

Psalm 8 expresses the same idea in more detail, beginning by emphasizing God's own sovereignty:

> O Lord, our Lord, how majestic is your name in all the earth! You have set your glory above the heavens.
>
> Out of the mouth of babies and infants, you have established strength because of your foes, to still the enemy and the avenger (Psalm 8:1-2).

Then the writer beautifully expresses how God has shared his power and sovereignty with mankind:

> When I look at your heavens, the work of your fingers, the moon and the stars, which you have set in place,
>
> what is man that you are mindful of him, and the son of man that you care for him?
>
> Yet you have made him a little lower than the heavenly beings and crowned him with glory and honor.
>
> *You have given him dominion over the works of your hands; you have put all things under his feet,*
>
> all sheep and oxen, and also the beasts of the field, the birds of the heavens, and the fish of the sea, whatever passes along the paths of the seas.
>
> O Lord, our Lord, how majestic is your name in all the earth! (Psalm 8:3-9; *emphasis* added).

We hear in these verses the ringing echo of the first chapter of Genesis, but the message repeats over and over as Scripture describes the generations-long relationship between God and his people.

I have argued that most of the time, God does not interrupt our affairs; he is content to tolerate our evils and misbehavior so that we learn better ways in the process. But this is not to say he never intervenes. He can, and he does. He has done so many times. The incarnation of his son Jesus is the chief of all examples. When God does not stop a particular tragedy, it does not mean he is weak, nor does it mean he does not care about us. Indeed, if the incarnation of Jesus teaches us anything, it shows us the depth of God's love and the depths to which he will reach to pull us back from our own destruction.

If we see this, we understand why God did not intervene to stop the greatest tragedy of all history: the execution of his innocent son on the cross. Evil? Yes. But God permitted it. Indeed, Scripture tells us that even this most horrid of man-inspired evils was accounted for by God before the beginning of creation: God has made the death of Christ to be the medicine that will ultimately heal mankind. Thus, the New Testament, too, affirms the rule of Shared Sovereignty, by revealing how God used it to accomplish his purposes in the incarnation:

> For it was not to angels that God subjected the world to come, of which we are speaking. It has been testified somewhere, "What is man, that you are mindful of him, or the son of man, that you care for him? You made him for a little while lower than the angels; you have crowned him with glory and honor, putting everything in subjection under his feet." Now in putting everything in subjection to him, he left nothing outside his control. At present, we do not yet see everything in subjection to him. But we see him who for a little while was made lower than the angels, namely Jesus, crowned with glory and honor because of the suffering of death, so that by the grace of God he might taste death for everyone (Hebrew 2:5-9; emphasis added).

The Letter to the Hebrews expresses how Jesus, "the son of man" (literally, "son of Adam") fulfills the role of *co-sovereign* most supremely through his suffering and death. As the first Adam abused his power, so Christ now sets the world back to a right relationship with God by sharing his power in perfect subjection to the love of the Father. This is the mystery of the Gospel: the perfect powerlessness of Christ on the cross manifests most perfectly the role of co-sovereign that God originally entrusted to Adam. Jesus, as Son of God and son of Adam — the one through whom this world was created — now takes up that role of Shared Sovereignty in human life in his birth, death, and resurrection.

To accomplish our redemption, Jesus shows us the perfect *shared* role of son and king, the "image of God" made perfect through suffering, and restored into glory.

No Ignoring Evil

Here, then, is the greater mystery: God not only hates evil, he turns it against itself in such a way that ultimately it can serve his own purposes. The evil of the cruel torture and death of Jesus is turned back against those who perpetrated it. Their evil intention, as with God's intervention into the life of Joseph in the Old Testament, is made to work for God's purpose and glory as the means by which Christ will rescue us from sin and the permanent destruction in death.[4]

Indeed, Holy Scripture assures us that far from ignoring evil, God is constantly addressing dealing with it, albeit it in ways that may not be visible to our sight nor conscious to our experience. Not only does God not ignore evil, he actively restrains it. Let's take a short rabbit trail and examine how.

Endnotes

1. C. S. Lewis, *The Problem of Pain,* Chapter 2.
2. I once had a seminary friend argue that in order not to diminish God's perfect omnipotence (his almighty power), God *must* exercise his full power at all points and in all moments. The argument sounds good until we recognize that if this were true, you and I would be unable to tie our own shoes — for it would be God doing the tying.
3. Appendix B addresses Calvinism in greater detail.
4. Joseph's brothers sold him into slavery, but that evil led eventually to Joseph becoming Pharaoh's righthand-man over the kingdom of Egypt. When a great famine struck, Joseph's brothers ended up at his feet begging for food. Joseph expressed God's wisdom in it all: "As for you, you meant evil against me, but God meant it for good, to bring it about that many people should be kept alive, as they are today" (Genesis 50:20).

Seven

We have looked at the origin of evil in the "Fall" of mankind — we should more properly call it the "Rebellion" of mankind — and have seen how God's decision to give us freedom of choice and share his sovereignty over creation led to evil erupting in the world.[1]

Was evil, then, a necessary component of God's creation? Was it unavoidable? Theologians and philosophers have debated that question for centuries. I hold it was not, for two simple reasons.

First, evil cannot be said to be necessary in the sense of being "utterly unavoidable" because each of us retains the ability — always — to say "No" and choose the good.

Second, I am reluctant to use the word "necessary" in any context when speaking of God or of God's work, since he is the ultimate "will" in all things. His choices are not only boundless but infinite. Whatever he does, including his work in creation, is in the most basic sense a "choice." So, creating us in his image with an operative, effective will did not limit God's own choices in any way. He retains the power to intervene in our affairs if he chooses. But even when God refrains from some action, that, too, is a choice, not a limit.

I have admitted that in creating humankind and empowering us as his co-sovereigns, while not making evil *necessary*, did make it *possible*. Blame him for that if you choose. But never forget the alternative: you would then be a mere robot, you would have no genuine thoughts or feelings, and no actual ability of independent, personal action. You would be nothing more than a high-class machine made of flesh; all your actions would be those of a semi-brainless puppet.

That is not the world God desired, nor the creatures he desired who could love him and each other. Our freedom has long been corrupted by wrongdoing; still, we retain both the ability and the responsibility to make right choices.

Understanding this, and before we move on to our fourth question, I want to consider a question that may be lurking in some minds as we considered evil: is evil simply "running loose" in the world, utterly unrestrained?

The Lurking Question

We may be tempted to jump to this conclusion when we hear the daily news. Evil does seem to run wild. When some terrible tragedy happens, we jump to the conclusion that God must be completely ignoring evil. But is that true?

How *does* God respond to evil? If we reflect half a moment, we will realize that since God is all-knowing, he knew evil would enter the picture through mankind's sin. Did he simply ignore this potential? No. From the beginning, he took steps to head off the full damage that evil might do.

God's most basic response — his prior plan to restrain evil — was that in addition to giving us freedom of choice he implanted in us something else that directly reflects his image: an innate sense of moral right. As I have already suggested, we each have a sense of this even as children. This inborn "moral code" is not merely a feature of religious thought. Even the modern humanist-atheist bears the mark of this moral conscience within, and expresses it frequently.[2]

While it took time for specific systems of moral law to develop, including the Mosaic Law embedded in the Jewish Old Testament, it seems clear that even before that — from the beginning, in fact — mankind possessed this sense of right and wrong. As I mentioned in Chapter Five, we recognize this embedded law acting in the heart of Eve when at first she resisted the serpent's ruse. That resistance was evidence of her inborn sense of right and wrong, good versus evil. Her first reaction was to *abide* by God's command rather than break it.

This seemingly inborn desire to obey God reflects a universal moral sensibility. Yes, this sense gets warped and sometimes crushed by social pressures, but it does not entirely disappear except in the most damaged sociopaths. Each of us, even in our fallen, sinful state, retains the ability to distinguish right (following God's word) over wrong (disobeying it).

This sense of moral law runs deep. We find it across cultures and across time, even in those who tend to reject the idea of a God who is loving and intimately involved in the affairs of mankind. We become aware of this moral sense early on in life. It is no doubt reinforced by our parents and society through codified law and behavioral norms. But I know from my own experience, as you likely do from yours, that as a child I came to sense that certain things were right and wrong apart from specific things my parents, or church, or school taught me. I had an inner sense of right and wrong even regarding issues that had never come up in my life before. With few exceptions, I think this is true of most of us. I believe God uses this inner moral sense to restrain how far evil may tempt or distract us, and how far it may interfere with our happiness and peace. It is also through this innate morality, I believe, that God helps us recognize evil and act on our own to restrain it.

Our inner "code" is a built-in moral armor that God has provided to shield us from temptation. There is, however, a backside to this blessing: because we have this sense of God's rightful will and moral law, we have less of an excuse when we break it. Indeed, we have to strip off our moral armor in order to wield the sword of evil.

God Stays Involved

God may restrain evil in other ways, although we will not always know how he is doing so. But because his entire self-revelation through the record of Scripture assures us that he loves us deeply and desires our perfection and good, we can be confident that he is working (often behind the scenes) to protect us from the full damage of evil, and limit our suffering. We are quick to blame God when he allows evil; we are less quick to look for how he may be engaging evil in a direct way to interfere with it and limit its effects on us.

With a little reflection, though, we can see instances where God's providential hand played a role in restraining evil. September 11th, 2001, comes to mind. Ask the question that most of us failed to ask that terrible day: with all the death and tragedy, *how much more* might have happened? Did God intervene in ways we likely missed?

Consider just one example, United Airlines Flight 93. Had not those brave souls on that aircraft acted swiftly and courageously, how many more people might have died in New York or Washington when the terrorists aboard struck their intended target? Hundreds? Thousands? We can't know exactly but we can be certain the actions of several passengers — which cost them their lives — saved others.

Where did their unimaginable courage come from, attacking the terrorists who had taken their plane, knowing it meant almost certain death? Who inspired that courage?

We know from recordings that some were praying on Flight 93. I believe that through their prayerful cries, God took a direct hand in what happened next and gave them that courage. In those terrifying moments, the brave men and women on board were no less co-rulers with God than at any other moment. Faced with evil in the flesh, they made a choice: a choice to confront those evil monstrosities head on, come what may. In that sense, the passengers acted on God's behalf, engaging evil with force and preventing the worst that might have occurred except for their bravery.

So, even on such a day when evil seemed literally out of control and gaining the upper hand, God and some of his co-rulers were at work to disrupt it. I have said that God generally does not overrun the freedom of choice he has given us. But I firmly believe he can and does set limits on how evil may run its course. Often, as with Flight 93, he may do that by working through us — you and me — as his instruments of good.

I believe, in fact, that any time God allows any evil, he sets its limit. The nature of evil is that it feeds on itself; it mushrooms if left unchecked. It will consume all around it, then consume itself. It is the proverbial serpent swallowing its own tail. But because we see only the immediate effects evil has on us, we generally cannot know what God has done to limit the damage. Only he knows where the line was drawn, and what greater evil he prevented.

When we worry, then, that evil is running unrestrained, we need to recall that the God who created everything is able to control the damage evil may cause.

God's Power Over Evil

We should also consider that God does not act randomly. He is the consummate planner. If he permits evil, he has some purpose in allowing it. (I will not hazard to say "some greater purpose" because we do not know the length of God's measuring stick in these matters.)

If we fail to remember this, we would make him out to be a bumbling idiot who did not understand the consequences of his actions, nor ours. Such a god would be no God, certainly not divine, and certainly not worthy of our worship. Unless God has a purpose in allowing a specific evil, we would be forced to assume, as our third question implies, that God is weak or thoughtless. Were that true, we would be justified in believing that he doesn't really care about us after all (question five).

When we dig into Holy Scripture, though, we find examples of what I have just argued: God does account for every evil, and he does set a limit on evil. An excellent example is recorded in the Gospel of Mark, in the account of demons who had infested a man. The demons see Jesus approaching and instantly recognize him as the "Son of the Most High God." More interestingly, they beg for mercy:

> They came to the other side of the sea, to the country of the Gerasenes. And when Jesus had stepped out of the boat, immediately

there met him out of the tombs a man with an unclean spirit. He lived among the tombs. And no one could bind him anymore, not even with a chain, for he had often been bound with shackles and chains, but he wrenched the chains apart, and he broke the shackles in pieces. No one had the strength to subdue him. Night and day among the tombs and on the mountains he was always crying out and cutting himself with stones. And when he saw Jesus from afar, he ran and fell down before him. And crying out with a loud voice, he said, "What have you to do with me, Jesus, Son of the Most High God? I adjure you by God, do not torment me." For he was saying to him, "Come out of the man, you unclean spirit!" And Jesus asked him, "What is your name?" He replied, "My name is Legion, for we are many." And he begged him earnestly not to send them out of the country. Now a great herd of pigs was feeding there on the hillside, and they begged him, saying, "Send us to the pigs; let us enter them." So he gave them permission. And the unclean spirits came out and entered the pigs; and the herd, numbering about two thousand, rushed down the steep bank into the sea and drowned in the sea. The herdsmen fled and told it in the city and in the country (Mark 5:1-14).

"So he gave them permission." Notice that. The demons need a place to go. Jesus allows them to go into the pigs.[3]

I share this example because it demonstrates Jesus' power as God: no one had the strength to restrain or subdue this man — he could literally shatter chains — but *with a simple word* Jesus set the man completely free. The event also shows how good can come out of evil: the man's horrid suffering is quickly ended and he is restored to his right mind.

The account also shows us something further which may seem peculiar, until we recall something I said previously: God does not wish to destroy any creature he has made. Notice what Jesus did: he expels the demons but does not destroy them. These demons are wicked, fallen angels who like us have a personal will; like us, they rebelled. Cast out of God's immediate presence ("heaven"), they roam the world of man, disrupting lives.

As Jesus comes on the scene, they immediately know him.[4] They beg for mercy. He does not destroy them, but he sets a limit to control them: they can no longer torment this poor man. They have begged not to be driven from that place. But Jesus ignores that plea and does exactly that. He dispatches them into the chaos of the sea, an appropriate place, biblically speaking, for the forces of chaos.

Jesus has spared the man but sacrificed the pigs. One man is apparently worth a great deal more than 2,000 pigs (see Luke 12:7). The death of the infested animals is horrid, but less horrid than the suffering this poor man had endured, tearing off shackles, screaming wildly, cutting himself with stones. The power of the voice of God's son restores him. Far from ignoring this evil, God contains it and drives it away.

This is the point we must seize: God permits evil, but he never ignores it. If we are tempted to think God lets evil flourish unrestrained, we must remember that he still holds it on a leash. We just can't see the leash.

If we reflect on this incident and many others in the Gospels when Jesus heals and forgives people, we learn that even though God tolerates evil, he always sets its limit. We may not understand his reasons, but we must credit his love for us enough to know that those reasons are worthy.[5]

Again, we may balk at this truth; we may find it uncomfortable. That is because we are sharing sovereignty with a sovereign God whose knowledge is beyond what we can grasp. His ways will always stretch our minds past their limits. But the essential quality of "faith" is trust.

Endnotes

1. As I have hinted, God gave the same ability of choice to the spiritual beings we call angels, who were likewise created to share God's rule over limited aspects of his creation. One, whom the Bible identifies as Satan (literally, "the Adversary") used that freedom in rebellion against God apparently as long as mankind has, and perhaps before. A thorough discussion of the relationships between God, mankind, and the angels

would consume an entire volume so I have chosen to steer away from the topic. My focus here is on humanity, our roles, and our responsibilities. For more about the subject of demonic powers, see Appendix C.

2. Indeed, one of the most common objections to God from the modern atheist is the accusation that God himself must be immoral for allowing evil at all.

3. There are a number of explanations for why Jesus sacrificed the poor pigs, but they would not satisfy most readers today. It is a detail of the event we can simply take at face value.

4. I have always been fascinated by the fact that the demons always know Jesus instantly, even though his own people — indeed, for a long time, his closest disciples — fail to recognize who he is.

5. I chose this account for another reason. At the end of the incident, we find this fascinating detail:

> As he [Jesus] was getting into the boat, the man who had been possessed with demons begged him that he might be with him. And *he did not permit him* but said to him, "Go home to your friends and tell them how much the Lord has done for you, and how he has had mercy on you." And he went away and began to proclaim in the Decapolis how much Jesus had done for him, and everyone marveled (Mark 5:18-20).

"And he did not permit him." Jesus remains in charge, to fulfill his own purposes. He has miraculously healed the poor fellow from impossible suffering and bondage. Now he will use that healing for a further good: this man, formerly feared, will tell others about God's power to save and set free.

Eight

We have answered our first three questions, and it may help to review those answers before we move on.

1. Our first question asked, "If God exists and is really good — and loving — why would he allow so much evil in the world?" The concise answer is, because he allows *us* to exist. God made us with the ability to make actual choices, and we have both the power and the permission to carry those choices into action. Further, as we learn from Genesis, God delegated limited power to us as his "co-rulers" through what I have called Shared Sovereignty. "Evil" is the name we give to thoughts, feelings, choices, or actions to run contrary to the will of God.

With our ability to make actual and meaningful choices comes the capacity to love but also the capacity to hate. It is from within us, out of our heart, that evil is generated.[1] Evil does not originate in the external world but from within, because it fundamentally results from the misuse of our wills. When we choose to conform our will to God's, we are doing the good. When we choose to go against God's will, or to intentionally try to frustrate his will, we are doing evil. Evil grows out of putting ourselves in first place and God in second — or third, or last.

In giving us the nature he did, God allowed the possibility (but not the necessity) for evil to be generated. And although God retains the power to obstruct our actions, to do so also obstructs a major component of his own creation: the integrity and inherent value of the co-ruling wills of his human creatures.

2. Our second question wondered, "Why doesn't God intervene to stop a specific evil event?" The answer: because he chooses not to. This answer is directly related to the answer to

question one (although I addressed them in reverse order). Because God chose to share his sovereignty with us and placed the wellbeing of our world into our hands, he generally does not interfere with our decisions or the course of actions we set in motion. In a given circumstance this may be a bitter pill to swallow, but it is a pill of our own manufacture. The evil we face is mainly of our own creation, either personally or caused by our fellow man. God allows this because he allows us to experience the consequences of our selfish, rebellious choices.

Some object that "It is not fair" for any of us to suffer because of the decisions of someone else. I have addressed the fairness question. Beyond that, the reality of societal life cannot fail to be complex and interactive. What one person does must invariably affect others. That is the nature of human community. We could isolate ourselves as solitary monks in a desert, but such escapism will not save us if someone pushes a button that launches a thousand nuclear missiles and annihilates us all.

In short, we can throw angry stones at God but we would better direct them at ourselves. Our actions have consequences for everyone within reach of those consequences. If I rob a convenience store, my action will affect many more than just the clerk on duty. It will (eventually) affect me, all those close to me, those who depend on me for support or care; it will affect the clerk; it will affect his family who will forever fret about his safety at work. It may affect countless police, investigators, judges, appellate judges, and their families. And, of course, it may make it harder for that store owner to hire clerks and thus make his own living.

So, when God allows a specific evil event that seems unfair, we must remember these complexities. I choose to credit his greater sovereignty and superior knowledge enough to believe that he has our eventual, greater good still in focus.

By this juncture, readers hopefully understand that Shared Sovereignty means God must continually carry on a balancing act between what he knows and desires for us and what he has given into our power to govern among ourselves. When evil seems to prevail, we should trust that his love has not left us. (This truth leads us toward question four.)

3. Our third question asked, "If God does not stop a specific evil event, doesn't this lead to the unavoidable conclusion that God is not all-powerful, and is simply too weak to stop tragedies?" The answer: not at all. God's essential, unlimited power, an aspect of his very nature, is in no way altered or diminished simply because, 1) he vests limited power in some of his creatures, or because, 2) he stays his hand in a given instance and does not intervene in the human drama. Neither action implies that he cannot instantly unstay his hand. He retains supreme power that cannot shrink or weaken. The one who made the entire cosmos has complete power over it. He can over-power us at any moment, though generally he chooses not to.[2]

We may certainly question why God chooses not to act in a particular situation, but this should not cause us to question his ability or power to act.

The Fourth Question

We come then to our fourth question: "If God allows something terrible to happen to me personally, doesn't that show he really doesn't love me or never cared about me in the first place?"

The initial answer has three parts, and they germinate in the soil of the first three answers we just reviewed.

1. God allows me to suffer because he allows me to exist. Like it or not, I am part of a common humanity, and thus part of the cause of evil. Unless I am utterly sinless (most unlikely), I have contributed to evil in the world. It is therefore possible — and at times obvious — that some suffering that falls on my head was generated in part by my own decisions or actions.

2. God could intervene to rescue me from suffering in every instance, but generally he chooses not to. Like everyone else, if I am to mature as a person, I need to experience the consequences, and perhaps the pain, of my own decisions. When I suffer because of the actions of someone else, it forces me to understand how the human community is inextricably interwoven.

3. God has not lost his power to help me, but in choosing to let me live out those consequences, whether caused by myself or someone else, he lets me suffer. When he allows me to suffer, however, he will always set its limit.

Allowing me or anyone else to suffer is one consequence of our share in his sovereignty. If God rescues us from every consequence of evil, he would in fact be stripping us of our privilege, freedom, and responsibility as his co-sovereigns. Thus, though it seems paradoxical, in allowing us to suffer God is expressing his love for us as his co-rulers, respecting what he has vested in us. It is our fault evil is present, not his.

To get to the core of this fourth question, however, we need to recognize that it is a deeply personal question: "Why does God allow *me* to suffer?" I have given an overview answer. To arrive at the deeper answer, we must reflect more fully on the nature of personal suffering.

When Something Happens To Me

Suffering is common to all of us but always difficult to fathom. Its very nature disrupts our enjoyment of life. It is not only difficult to understand *why* we suffer, it is complicated to understand exactly what suffering is.

Most simply put, suffering occurs whenever we experience — and sometimes endure — pain. The pain may be spiritual, emotional, physical, or a combination. Physical pain is a fact of life, but pain is just as real, and as deeply felt, when it is spiritual or emotional.

Some examples will help. I jam my foot against the foot of the bed and cry out. I am feeling physical pain first of all. If (as is likely) I have jammed this same foot against this same bed foot in the past, I may also be suffering a small degree of emotional pain, wondering how I can be so careless or stupid as to keep running into the darned thing. There may even be the tiniest degree of spiritual pain: God, why did you let me do that (again)? Granted, this is spiritual pain of a very low grade, but it may be hiding there.

Emotional pain comes when someone we care about is hurt, or when they hurt us. Our spouse gets angry at us and in a moment of irritation says, "Why don't you jump off a cliff?" They do not mean it, but it may sound like they do. While it is unlikely that they really want us to carry out such a radical response to a simple flare of anger, the feeling expressed is real and the hurt we feel in reaction is real, too. If only briefly, we suffer emotional pain.

If we are mature spiritually, such an antagonism can also cause spiritual pain. We may wonder if the spiritual bond that was established between us in marriage has begun to fray. We will almost certainly be asking God quietly why the other person is acting this way. We may wonder why God has allowed this breakdown and the painful feelings it stirs in both of us.

On a larger scale, a catastrophic event can cause all three types of pain at once. A tornado strikes our city. We may be physically injured, perhaps gravely, perhaps permanently. Our emotions swelter: we feel a complete loss of control and safety. We will likely experience spiritual pain, too, demanding of God, "Why did you have to let this happen?" The core question again is, "Why did you let this happen to *me*?"

Physical, emotional, and spiritual pain often compound like a loan shark's interest and can crush us if we are not strong. Catastrophes do crush people, in all these ways. The death of a child, for example, not infrequently leads to a breakdown of the larger family. The death of a parent sometimes unleashes pent up anger from a child, feelings that were suppressed as long as the parent was alive. And, of course, once the parent is gone, the child cannot process those feelings in a productive way because the person concerned is no longer around to work things out. Thus, the emotional pain may just extend indefinitely.

Suffering comes in all these different forms and it always feels like an attack, an assault on our well-being, our safety, or our security. We naturally want to preserve those things. We want to be well and to "feel good"; we want to always feel safe, not threatened by others or our environment; and we want to feel secure, that is, we want to know we are in control of our life and can manage whatever comes.

Our first reaction to any suffering is almost always to try to protect ourselves, to insulate ourselves from the cause of the suffering (if we know it) so that it doesn't get worse. If it is emotional pain, we may "wall off" the person that has caused us this hurt. Husbands and wives do this quite often, to a greater or lesser degree. We will also defend ourselves. Sometimes that defense takes the form of a counterattack — and engenders more suffering all around.

Perhaps the worst kind of pains are those that are self-inflicted. They are the worst because, 1) we have no one else to blame for what we are suffering, and, 2) we often don't know exactly why or how we hurt ourselves so badly. A person suffering from chronic depression, for example, often loses sight of the original experience or feelings that led toward depression to begin with. And it is not uncommon for a person suffering severe emotional pain to hurt themselves further. That might be a suicide attempt, or something like cutting themselves, inflicting physical pain as a distraction or compensation for what seems unbearable and unending emotional pain.

Enduring The Pain

Whatever its origin or cause, and whether self-inflicted or caused by others, every kind of pain is unpleasant. Except with chronic illness, physical pains tend to come and go. Emotional and spiritual pains tend to mount, to compound, and to bore deeper into our soul over time, causing longer term damage (leading, sometimes, to spiritual death.)

Please notice something here. Every one of these examples — and most others we could dredge up — have nothing to do directly with God or our relationship with him. Some people may claim an event like a tornado is the exception. But, as I will address shortly, even "natural catastrophes" cannot be laid directly at God's feet either. (See the section Natural Evil in the next chapter.)

Why *does* God allow things to happen that cause us to suffer? The simple answer is because he allows evil in general. Suffering is just one result of evil. But we must be clear and careful in our thinking. To say that God "allows things to happen that cause us to suffer" is not the same as saying God "causes us to suffer." There is a chasm of difference between those two statements. We must keep clear the distinction between God's "manifest" will versus his "permissive" will. We can learn his manifest will through Scripture or from communal experience over generations. We often learn his "permissive" will from events as they unfold and affect us personally.

God's manifest will is demonstrated when he directly causes certain things to happen. For example, he causes creation to exist, and to continue. This act of "causing" is operative at every instant, or creation would cease to exist in that instant. Further, God indirectly causes things to occur that are the outworking of physical and spiritual laws that he sets in place in the world.[3]

We also see God's manifest will in the creation of each new human person (Psalm 139) although he accomplishes that (normally) utilizing the genetic and biological processes of a man and woman to create that new person.

In addition, God is continually "causing" the physical creation to progress toward a goal he has set, although, again, he generally does this according to those routine "laws" established in the beginning of creation, and often using us as his creative instruments or agents. Consider the simple analogy of a computer where the hardware is the cosmic "machine" and God's governing but invisible spiritual laws act as the divine "software" controlling the hidden operation of all things. The basic "operating system" and essential programs can run much of the time with little input from the designer (or operator).

God's manifest will is also demonstrated in those times when he does intervene into our world or affairs. Having made all the governing "laws" he is competent to supersede or expand them for his own purpose. When he does, he knows it will disrupt the normal course of things. Sometimes such intervention is glaring and obvious, and will be called "a miracle." But it is quite likely that God frequently intervenes — subtly "tweaking the system" — in ways we never detect. With little trouble, he can do something "under the radar" of human awareness. Or, he may influence our thoughts is such a way that it affects a choice we will make, and prevent us from doing something stupid. He might redirect our attention to help us see a better course, or wave a spiritual "flag" to warn us of danger.[4] Thus, while God allows us to suffer, he may warn us ahead of time, or help direct our course through it. Indeed, his "commandments" are intended to do just that.

We know of instances, not just in Scripture but ever since, when God does overrule his "normal" natural laws in a miraculous way to accomplish some purpose or particular good. Such an event is also a "sign" of God's presence and purpose among us.[5] An obvious instance is when a person who is otherwise beyond the reach of medicine or human care is healed of disease or infirmity. I have already given examples. And of course, God may intervene directly in response to prayer. (See Appendix A on why prayer works.) In one sense, God answering prayer is not miraculous, because it happens all the time. It is, as a matter of simple fact, an example of a "normal" *spiritual* law operating.

In each of these examples, God enacts his "manifest" will by direct action. The obviously miraculous instances are infrequent (at least to the extent we can perceive such things) because, as I have said, God generally refrains from interfering in our activities out of respect for the co-sovereign role he has given us. When he does intervene to disrupt the usual course of events, it will be for good reason. What that reason may be, he alone will know. It may be because he can foresee damage from our actions that we *don't* see.

Still, as we must admit, God does not always intervene when we wish. We act, and our actions bring "live" consequences. Those consequences may cause ourselves or someone else to suffer. Respecting our co-sovereign rule, God sometimes permits great suffering, and that suffering may be incredibly hard to bear. We will wonder why he stops some things but allows so many others.

When we swirl in that sea of dilemma, we must always remember that death is not the worst thing that can happen, and we must hold onto the fact that virtually everything that brings suffering is directly caused by human beings, not by anything God has done.

"Why does God allow *me* to suffer?" In part because God knows the value of what we learn from the experience. Suffering hurts, but the outcome is not always bad. It is when we burn our hand on the stove for the first time as a child that we learn to respect fire and heat. As we age, we "get burned" in many worse ways. Each time we learn a valuable lesson. And each time we suffer from evil, we learn to hate evil and to steer as far away from it as possible.

We must remember another key point as well. God knows our suffering is limited. It will end. In each case, he knows exactly how, and when. For us to realize this won't make our suffering less difficult to endure but it may help us see a light we do not yet see. It may help us seek a broader vision of things, from God's point of view, that shows us how our suffering might serve some good. Soldiers in wartime, confronted with the constant possibility of injury or death, face this terrible truth daily.

"But suffering often seems so unjust," some may say. I don't disagree. But then I must ask, would it be more just if God in every instance came rushing in to rescue me from the consequences of my actions or the actions of someone else? Where and when would we have him draw the lines? How would we split the hair of God's rescue versus leaving us our freedom, suffering what sometimes comes with it? How would we create that measuring stick? And how would we ever judge its accuracy — or *its* fairness?

You see the problem. If God performed a thousand daily miracles, disrupting the world to save us from every consequence of evil, we would be thrown into chaos. Our lives would become not only unpredictable but unmanageable. What we know as the freedom of our choices would not vanish, but those choices would become ineffective.

God Does Take A Hand

God allows our suffering but he does not simply ignore it. We do well to remember a key revelation of Holy Scripture: God does not witness our suffering as a cold, impartial bystander. He learned the intensity of human suffering personally, the hard way. He learned from the terrible pain for both mother and child in the birth of Jesus. He learned it more potently from our savior's unjust arrest, flogging, and brutal crucifixion. Pain may be a mystery to us, but not to God. By making himself one of his human creatures, taking our full nature into himself — the ones he made in his very image — he learned of suffering in its depths. You and I know nothing of suffering that God does not share. That is the wondrous news of the gospel: pain and suffering are not a secondhand experience for our God. Since the incarnation, suffering is, so to speak, in God's blood stream.

So, in every case of evil or suffering, God continues his balancing act between his love for us and our freedom. Like any loving parent, he does not enjoy it when we suffer. But he respects our need to learn, experience, and grow. In my own case, I can assure you, the best lessons came through the hardest times.

If we are tempted to challenge God with "Is that just?" we challenge him standing on the thinnest of ice. Ask: are humans just? All that we mean by justice, after all, is derived from him, who is Justice in person. Our limited understanding of justice is often warped. Do we imagine that God is less just than we? My heart is marred and corrupted; it is the heart of a self-centered sinner who mostly wants his own way. How many lightyears beyond my own must God's comprehension of justice be? Human justice is dry and cold. God's justice is tempered continually by his love and mercy for the weakness of his human children. If, then, he permits me to suffer, I must begin from the certainty that not only his love but his wisdom allows it. And he knows I will survive it.

As with the answers to some of our other questions, this answer may leave a bad taste in our mouth. Remember, our taste buds have been soured by sin for a very long time. We want the easiest road through life; God wants the best. The best road may sometimes find us barefoot on sharp rock. This does not mean God has ceased to love us, or guide us. If he generally "lets us be" in our freedom and its consequences, we should recall that he did not rescue his son from the cross. If Jesus' suffering was worth it, our suffering is, too.

Come back to square one and ask: do I cherish the freedom God has given me? With that comes the ever-present possibility of evil; with evil comes suffering. Do I really want God to overrun my life and my will? Am I applying to become one of those flesh-robots? Or am I prepared to endure the cost of that freedom?

Truth, And Consequences

Why God allows us to suffer in a specific instance will often be opaque to us. His purpose may be profound yet elude us. Or it may be perfectly plain: it's our own darned fault.

Consider a simple, fictional example. Let us say a young man has had a breakup with his girlfriend of eight months. He is angry. He begins to tell his friends — and some of hers — that she is a compulsive thief and that is why he broke up with her. It's a lie, but one he hopes will hurt her.

The girlfriend is a teller at the local bank. The boyfriend's angry rumor reaches her boss. One afternoon her cash drawer comes up a bit short, due to an honest error on her part. But her boss, having heard of her "problem" and afraid it will be a pattern, fires her on the spot.

She has two small children at home. He parents disowned her when the first was born out of wedlock, not to mention the second. Her own bank account looks like a creek bed in late August. Within a month, unable to find another job, she and her children are evicted.

Her former boyfriend learns all this and begins to feel guilty. But it's too late. The breakup was already painful; now, due to his lie, everything has spun out of control. He can't bring himself to go tell her that he was the source of the lie, the cause of her latest problems. Yet his guilt is real and he has trouble sleeping. Two of his friends know the truth, and break off their long friendship with him. The young woman's parents remain unbending and won't take her in. She is now spending her nights with two young children in her car, and it's December.

There is suffering all around and it will go on for some time.

Now ask: in all of this, what did God do? Then ask, what would we have him do? Should he have shielded this young woman from her own actions? From her boyfriend's actions? At what point? Did their complicated problems begin with their splitting up, or long before? Who caused the suffering for these two young people, their immediate friends, the young woman's children, and her parents?

The answer is obvious. The two young people fueled their own suffering. God did not cause any of it. He merely allowed the consequences of their decisions to follow them.[6]

Though fictional, this kind of thing, sadly, happens all too often. Our culture has come to a point where we encourage weak, insecure living relationships and then try to ignore the problems that result. As we see from this example, emotional and spiritual suffering can mushroom out of one bad choice, then compound into physical suffering (hungry and cold children). A young man makes one very bad choice, and someone he once loved suffers terribly.

The truth is, many profound evils can grow out of seemingly "small" things. A popular quip says, "Don't sweat the small stuff." I say, sweat them. Pay attention to those small things. Life is made up of exactly these little details, and how we handle them says a great deal about our character (Luke 16:10).[7]

"But God should have prevented all their suffering," someone may respond. Again I must ask, what would we have God do? Could not this young couple have prevented all the problems? Why didn't their friends or family intervene to ease the suffering? When we are tempted to point a finger God, we may want to stand close to a mirror.

This illustration highlights an important realization: when God allows me to suffer it may simply be because he knows I had *the knowledge, the wisdom, and the ability to avoid it.*

I will give just one personal example. I have been extremely drunk only twice in my life. The first time I was sixteen. God let me endure the physical results of that drunkenness — which were not pretty — because I needed to learn an important lesson about myself: never get that drunk again. The second time, I was in my mid-thirties. I had long forgotten my lesson. God allowed me to suffer miserably again, except that it was much worse. My older system could not recoup as easily from that much alcohol. I passed out on a couch at a friend's apartment. Late the next morning, I stumbled home and crawled into my bed. I would have been happy to die there.

Could God have spared me this latest suffering? Yes. But for what reason? So that I could get even drunker the next time? Look at this from God's point of view: the hellish night and hangover I suffered was a small price to pay. I have never overindulged like that since.

It is easy to make God our scapegoat when he allows evil, and even more tempting when he allows me to suffer personally. Yes, I have succumbed to that temptation a few times. With very few exceptions, though, most of what I have suffered in life has been my own fault, the direct result of my own choices.

While neither of these examples of "suffering" (the young couple, or my drinking) are catastrophic, it remains true that nearly all suffering in this world results *from human actions.* Sometimes it is from outright wickedness. As I was first writing this chapter, a thirteen-year-old girl in Wisconsin was rescued from a twenty-one-year-old kidnapper who had held her captive for three months. First, however, he had murdered her parents — in front of her, in their own home — to abduct her.

This man (if I can be forgiven for using the word) kept the murder weapon at hand the whole time he held her captive, continually threatening the poor child. The horrors she certainly endured should never be put into print, though I'm sure some odious Hollywood mogul will want to make it a movie.

The pure evil and wickedness of the kidnapper's actions defies what most of us can even imagine. This is one example why I believe there is — and must be — hell. (More when we come to question six.) Why God allowed this tragedy to happen, like so many others, is also beyond what we can grasp. I cannot know the source or cause of the evil in that kidnapper's heart. God knows. I can't know the severity of the harm and emotional damage that was done to the poor girl, or how it could ever be healed. But God knows. So before I start blaming God, I bring my mind back to the pathetic excuse for a human who actually did these unspeakable things, and I am grateful that he will ultimately face a just God. We should not doubt that both God's love and his justice will endure beyond every evil that evil men can brew up.

Better Choices

As unlikeable as it may be, we are our own worst enemies. God respects the freedom he has given us, even when we hurt ourselves or someone else because of it. He honors that freedom because he loves us and has invested his trust in us.

Now, that may seem backward. Aren't we supposed to trust him? Yes, but because of Shared Sovereignty it works both ways. As we are each drawn toward the perfection God wants for us, we will go through periods of pain and suffering. Remember, they have a limit; they will have an end. Suffering is not the worst that can happen to us, nor is physical death. God's goal for each of us extends beyond both. If we seek his plan and learn his will, the suffering we endure can take on a different color and character. Whether it is minor or severe, we will learn how to face it.

Thus, the answer to our fourth question brings us directly back to the principle of Shared Sovereignty. God has placed great power into our hands. That power, too often misused, causes suffering. God holds back his hand in the normal course of events so that we might inhabit a predictable and stable world, but also so that we will learn how evil injures, and how to curb it in our own soul.

For God, this is not a short-term or one-time project. He is preparing us for everlasting life in fellowship with himself. What he allows, he allows with a purpose. And I believe that the more we grow to be like him, the better we will understand.

There remains, however, a broader aspect of suffering, the suffering that results from "natural disasters." That is where we now turn.

Endnotes

1. Jesus taught very clearly that the problem of evil and sin is not (as some Greek philosophers taught) a consequence of our outward bodily nature, but comes from our inward spiritual nature. Our bodily needs and appetites do not beget evil. Evil generates from what comes out of our hearts: "Are you also still without understanding? Do you not see that whatever goes into the mouth passes into the stomach and is expelled? But what comes out of the mouth proceeds from the heart, and this defiles a person. For out of the heart come evil thoughts, murder, adultery, sexual immorality, theft, false witness, slander. These are what defile a person. But to eat with unwashed hands does not defile anyone" (Matthew 15:16-20; see also Mark 7:14-23).

2. We ourselves know, if we have ever wielded any level of actual power, that we can restrain our own power. As a law enforcement officer, I always carried a weapon. If my life was threatened, as it was a number of times, I could have killed the threatening person to protect myself, or someone else. I didn't, in any of those cases, because I was able to restrain the full power vested in me by lawful authority — the power and authority to take a life — and was able to resolve the threat short of taking that life. God, who is much more powerful than a sidearm, is perfectly capable of exercising the same kind of restraint, as he chooses.

3. All science is thus theological in a sense, since it is fundamentally the study of God's creative work and the ordering principles that underlie creation.

4. I have had this experience many times: I just happen to "notice" something which is unremarkable yet grabs my attention for no seeming reason, and that awareness influences what I was doing, or was going to do. I suspect many people have had this type of experience.

5. In John's Gospel, Jesus' great miracles are called "signs"; they are intended to educate us about his purpose or his ways. (See, for example, John 2:11.)

6. Their damaged relationship could continue rippling out, damaging even more relationships. Maybe the young woman's retired grandmother will alter her life to care for the kids so that mom can try to find work and a home. Her grandmotherly love may strain her relationship with her own husband, since she will be tied to the house more and unable to enjoy recreation with him. If the young man or woman blames God for the consequence of their own bad choices, it may cause them spiritual suffering that could last for years.

7. "One who is faithful in a very little is also faithful in much, and one who is dishonest in a very little is also dishonest in much" (Luke 16:10).

Nine

In our consideration of why God allows suffering, we cannot neglect the often-widespread suffering that results from what is usually called "natural evil" in theology. This is a difficult area because many people seem to harbor an unspoken assumption that God should routinely intervene to head off any natural disaster.

That is why these events are often called "an act of God" in public discussion. Many people seem to feel that because God does not prevent it, the event was therefore directly caused by him. And since such disasters often result in large loss of life, a common reaction is that they seem "so unnecessary." Yet in the next breath — from the other side of their mouth — the same people may insist that nature is merely following the "set laws" God put in place, so these catastrophes are unavoidable. The lawmaker, of course, must automatically be at fault.

We end with conflicted thoughts about why such events happen at all and where blame falls. As I have with our other questions, let us consider what Holy Scripture has to say.

"Natural" Evil

I have argued that God is not the direct cause or source of evil. But we know God *allows* evil; he may even utilize evil against itself, drawing on its horror to prevent similar acts. He can also obstruct evil by redirecting or mitigating the effects that evil will have on us.

I have said that evil is directly caused by wills — human or angelic — that are in rebellion against God. If so, what about those events in nature that answer to no person and seem to arise on their own? If no human has caused them, and if God does not cause them, where do they come from? What is their real origin? "Who, if anyone, is responsible?" we ask, meaning of course, "Who can we blame?"

The answer is not far out of reach. But we should begin by admitting a fact that is the polar opposite of our concern: the very laws of nature that seem to *cause* catastrophic events actually, in the normal course of things, continually prevent them. The world runs along very well most of the time, along the patterns that God designed into creation. Nature normally provides us a very stable environment. Most of the time we are reasonably safe and healthy and able to function without worry. Admittedly, tornados and earthquakes happen, but they are not happening every three minutes.[1]

Still, they do happen. Stable though it is, the natural world is not entirely safe. "Natural" disasters occur and we can rarely predict them with any accuracy. Further, they tend to be of such a magnitude that we cannot prevent them.

Why didn't God make this world a place that is always stable and entirely safe? When he first made the world, he called it all "good" (Genesis 1). Surely, hurricanes, tornados, and earthquakes are not "good" in God's book, are they? No, they are not.

So our problem, our "theological dilemma," is to understand how something so *unnatural* can happen in the world of nature. What has gone wrong?

It should be no surprise if I answer, "mankind."

The Operation Of Nature

The reader may also not be surprised if I say next that hurricanes, tornados, and earthquakes are not directly caused by God. That is, none of them are "acts of God" (contrary to your insurance agent) in a direct causative sense. Obviously, I must explain.

First, we need to understand what we mean by "the natural order" and discern how natural "law" and natural events interplay in the current state of things. God's world in creation was indeed good, but because he allowed for the *possibility* of evil coming into play, the world was not from its inception "perfect." Things could go wrong, and did. Sin entered the picture quickly and defaced the crown of God's creation, the creatures made in his image, humankind.

We see from Scripture that human events began to go off the rails almost from the beginning. What we generally fail to recognize, though, is that mankind's rebellion against God had profound affects not only on our moral nature, but on Mother Nature. This truth, like others recorded in the biblical account of our origins, is often missed.

What, if anything, does Genesis have to say about "natural evil"? What it says, quite clearly, is that evil in nature is a product of evil in the chief stewards of nature: you and me.

The Deadly Effects Of Our Sin

I have discussed how the outward, physical world is governed by inward, spiritual laws. God's real but invisible spiritual laws operate like the computer "software" for the world he made. Spiritual laws govern the material world. But mankind is unique in creation: we are a hybrid, both matter and spirit, and we operate continually — whether conscious of it or not — in both the physical and spiritual realms. When we run afoul of God's spiritual laws as we often do (daily, it seems), the result is sin. Every sin is a turning against God, a revolt against his laws.

In Chapter Five we looked at "the Fall" of man in Genesis 3. I want to return to it briefly to highlight something which likely passed the reader by with little notice. It is a simple but profound statement of "what went wrong" at the beginning, what damaged the natural order. God chastised the serpent, you recall, who will forever be at odds with mankind. God chastised Eve. He then chastised her husband:

> Because you have listened to the voice of your wife and have eaten of the tree of which I commanded you, "You shall not eat of it," cursed is the ground because of you; in pain you shall eat of it all the days of your life; thorns and thistles it shall bring forth for you; and you shall eat the plants of the field. By the sweat of your face you

shall eat bread, till you return to the ground, for out of it you were taken; for you are dust, and to dust you shall return (Genesis 3:17-19).

Perhaps this time the one phrase leapt out: ". . . cursed is the ground because of you." What is this saying? It means that *moral evil* has infected *the natural order*. Before this, the man and woman roamed the garden at leisure. All they needed was there for the taking, with a pleasant climate (no clothing or shelter was needed) and food aplenty. But now the very ground they walk on has become cursed, polluted. The earth will no longer yield its increase with ease. Man will now sweat out his existence, pulling food with painful labor from the soil; the woman will now bear her children in great pain. Both pains are a result of sin: their sin has warped not just their relationship with God, and not just their relationship with each other, it has warped the entire natural order. Instead of just pleasant fruit trees, the damaged earth will now bring forth thorns and thistles as well.[2] Worst of all, the blessed earth from which Adam was taken will now take him back in death, his final pain of this present life.

Consider the overall picture we are given in Genesis so far, not just this single passage. We are left with several broad impressions which I believe the writer did not want us to miss:

1. God created a pristine world and called everything *he* had made "good." I don't think that statement would be there if the writer believed that the subsequent natural disasters were inherent in that original design.

2. Into this good creation God places mankind as co-ruler and co-creator, his steward in charge of working and protecting the creation. Man's charge is to "work the ground" and develop the world to reach the goal for which God has destined it. (Ultimately, the entire creation will reach its God-designed perfection, although not in the present period of history.)

3. Into this pristine picture mankind (Adam and Eve) brings sin. Their sin is fundamentally a rebellion against God, a refusal to abide by a limit God has set. They overreach. In exercising their God-given power, they cross a line from which there is no return. We can say the serpent tricked Eve, we can argue that perhaps Adam was not clear enough in passing on to her God's prohibition about that tree (the prohibition being given before Eve was made). But deflect as we may, the simple truth is that Adam and Eve have been given freedom of choice, and they have chosen wrongly.

4. What is the result? Their entire personal nature is altered. When before they were naked but felt no embarrassment, sin now corrupts both their vision and their self-image. They feel shame toward the physical nature God has given them. This shame may seem very human to us now, but it was of their making, not God's. The deeper result? Suddenly, their spiritual nature is at odds with their physical nature. Sin will bleed into their bones; their "flesh" will war against their "spirit."[3]

5. The damage of sin does not just affect their interior lives. Mankind was "taken from the ground," that is, God draws our physical body from the elements of the earth itself. Being dust, and being barred from the tree that gives immortality, Adam is now condemned to return to the earth in decay.

6. But the dry rot of sin goes deeper yet. Man's brokenness is only the tip of the iceberg. The earth itself now becomes a curse to him throughout his life. The natural order is corrupted; it is no longer "natural" but spoiled, suffering the effects of man's sin. The earth itself deteriorates; disruptive disasters in nature begin to occur.

In short, man's moral evil, generated in the will of man, now infects the natural order over which he was placed in charge. He, its master, is now corrupted; his "servant," the natural order, suffers corruption as well. If we refer again to the computer metaphor, this means God's original software has become corrupted. Once the software is corrupted, the entire machine becomes erratic, running all right much of the time but frequently doing completely unpredictable things. In a similar way, "natural laws" laid down by the original "programmer" — God — will still operate fine most of the time, but there will be continual glitches: sporadic errors and changes will happen and foul up the whole enterprise. The system is no longer reliable in the way it was designed to be.

This analogy is apt because, as I noted, God's natural laws in fact do still operate effectively most of the time. They generally *prevent* what we call natural catastrophes. But not always. Serious problems occur in the overall system; disasters result.

To us, the disasters seem unfathomable and unfair. But in a different respect, they are entirely "predictable" as a result of a fouled system. We can't know when they will happen, but we can be sure they *will*.

Put simply, the "natural" order no longer operates as it was designed. We are forced to contend with the disruptions. They are not God's direct doing; they occur because man, living under physical laws, keeps breaching God's spiritual laws. The conflict keeps damaging the system of creation. And this brokenness that affects the physical world around us also affects our own bodies.[4]

"Un-natural" Disasters

We, the stewards of nature, have shattered God's design for the natural order, so we should call natural disasters "*un*natural" disasters. Scripture is very pointed here: the sin of mankind, like Abel's blood, has bled down into the soil and the earth that we were intended to steward, and the earth cries out to its maker in protest:

> Then the LORD said to Cain, "Where is Abel your brother?" He said, "I do not know; am I my brother's keeper?" And the LORD said, "What have you done? The voice of your brother's blood is crying to me from the ground. And now you are cursed from the ground, which has opened its mouth to receive your brother's blood from your hand.

When you work the ground, it shall no longer yield to you its strength. You shall be a fugitive and a wanderer on the earth" (Genesis 4:9-12).

Painful, ugly, but clear. As Adam was warned, the good earth will now serve back thorns and thistles. "Natural disasters" are examples of these "thorns" that our sin has planted into the earth, the painful writhing of a world broken by man's sin and murderous immorality.

Let me take one short sidetrack. I do not mean to discount the role or importance of certain angels in creating this mess. The Bible is quite clear that angels — other rational, spiritual beings created by God — were also given specific roles for governance and stewardship over parts of the larger cosmos. Some of them, Scripture shows, rebelled like man. One, the "prince of the power of the air"[5] sometimes called Satan (the name means "Adversary") was an "archangel" whose principal duty was to be a liaison between heaven and earth, between the spiritual realm of God and the material realm of mankind.[6] While not ignoring the role of these wicked angels reported in Scripture, I have focused here on man's rebellion because it was our sin, according to the Genesis accounts, that *directly corrupted* the natural order of the earth. Satan may have tempted Eve, but it was she and Adam who disobeyed. Their disobedience brought the curse that fouled the natural world.

A Pill Hard To Swallow

Some readers may find this worldview difficult to digest. Why? Because it shows us "in living color" the downside of what I have called Shared Sovereignty. The deep power entrusted to us as God's stewards can backfire — and has. When we assess natural evil, we must, if we are true to Scripture, take mankind's role and responsibility into account. God did not break the natural laws he set in place, we did.

How exactly our moral evil bores down into the broader inner workings of the natural order is beyond my competence to understand. But I can see that there is the connection because I see similar connections play out in my daily life. When I make bad moral choices — like those instances of getting wasted-drunk — I recognize how my moral choices bore down into my body and produced very direct damage. Only consistently better moral choices on my part created the time and space for my body to heal. We have all had similar experiences on the individual "micro" level. We should not doubt, then, that our sinful moral choices on a broader scale can wreak similar havoc at the "macro" level, damaging the "body" of the created world.

Once we grasp this fundamental connection between our moral action in the spiritual realm and our life actions in the physical realm, we will see these connections playing out. The twin towers did not collapse on September 11, 2001, because God made faulty natural laws. They were brought down by immoral men who made intentionally evil decisions, seeking to wreak pain and havoc on our citizens — out of irrational hatred. In a similar way, the hurricane of 2019 that took many lives in the Bahamas was not a result of God making faulty natural laws: it is another instance of the long-brewing infection of evil in nature playing itself out, Abel's blood crying out from the soil.[7]

God will, of course, remain a convenient scapegoat for those who cannot, or will not, see this. But like so much else we have discussed, the cause of "natural evil" is close at hand: as close as our *own* hand, and connected to our corrupted hearts in a way we would prefer not to see. The stable order God first created has been altered — by us. With sin, we have thrown a large wrench into the machine. (Picture hitting that computer with a sledge hammer.) Sin stole from us our ability to master our own spiritual nature, but that is only stage one. Our spiritual degradation plays out into the natural order at a second stage, where spiritual and physical laws conflict and a damaged physical world is the result.

In short, there is more to this world than meets the eye. When the steward misbehaves, the soil beneath his feet suffers.[8]

"*Un*natural disasters" do not happen because God directly wills them but, like all evil, he allows them. The massive damage and death caused by such events disturbs us because — though we try not to — we get caught in the trap of believing that "death is the worst possible thing that can happen." Even though we know this is not true, and that death is not final, we feel it is when so many souls are caught in the meat grinder.

We do better to pray for the people lost in a catastrophe, because where they each are spiritually — dead, or alive — is much more significant to their future life than is the timing or manner of their deaths. Do I long for the pain of being swept away in a violent tornado? No. But I also know it will make no final difference to God, or myself. What I think of him today — and, more importantly, what *he* thinks of *me* — is what I will choose to be concerned with.

Good, But Not Yet Perfect

Because of sin, we do not yet live in a perfected world. We have broken the machine, and the longer humankind "progresses," the more damage we seem to invent. The solution will not come from our hands but from God's. He has shown his plan in the coming of Christ. In the resurrection of Jesus, God has shown us the new creation that he is preparing for us all — all, that is, who will receive it on God's terms. That horizon may seem very far off, but it draws nearer each day:

> You, however, are not in the flesh but in the Spirit, if in fact the Spirit of God dwells in you . . . If the Spirit of him who raised Jesus from the dead dwells in you, he who raised Christ Jesus from the dead will also give life to your mortal bodies through his Spirit who dwells in you . . . The Spirit himself bears witness with our spirit that we are children of God, and if children, then heirs — heirs of God and fellow heirs with Christ, *provided we suffer* with him in order that we may also be glorified with him. For I consider that the sufferings of this present time are not worth comparing with the glory that is to be revealed to us. For the creation waits with eager longing for the revealing of the sons of God. For the creation was subjected to futility, not willingly, but because of him who subjected it, *in hope that the creation itself will be set free from its bondage to corruption*

and obtain the freedom of the glory of the children of God. For we know that the whole creation has been groaning together in the pains of childbirth until now. And not only the creation, but we ourselves, who have the firstfruits of the Spirit, groan inwardly as we wait eagerly for adoption as sons, the redemption of our bodies. For in this hope we were saved (Romans 8:9-25, *emphasis* added).

St. Paul's vision of what awaits us is deep, and powerful.[9] This present world, cursed by mankind's sin, is caught "in bondage and decay." Our present physical bodies must suffer the same fate (our fifth question). But when God "cursed" the ground because of Adam, he did not subject it in perpetual doom but "in hope" (8:20). Why? Because *"the creation itself will be set free* from its bondage to corruption and obtain the freedom of the glory of the children of God" (8:21). This is God's redemptive plan, his plan laid in place "before the foundation of the world." Because humankind is tied so deeply to the earth, and the earth to him, God's plan requires not just the saving of mankind but the redemption and restoration of *the entire created order.* Man's sin brought injury and destruction to the natural world. Man's redeemed freedom, freed from his sin, will mean freedom for the earth as well.

Look at Paul's words closely: "For we know that the whole creation has been groaning together in the pains of childbirth until now. And not only the creation, but we ourselves, who have the firstfruits of the Spirit, groan inwardly as we wait eagerly for adoption as sons, *the redemption of our bodies"* (8:22-24). Paul here expresses the fruition of what the Old Testament prophet Isaiah foresaw in his vision of ultimate hope — not just for man, but for the world. Isaiah heard God speak this promise:

> For behold, I create new heavens and a new earth, and the former things shall not be remembered or come into mind. But be glad and rejoice forever in that which I create; for behold, I create Jerusalem to be a joy, and her people to be a gladness. I will rejoice in Jerusalem and be glad in my people; no more shall be heard in it the sound of weeping and the cry of distress (Isaiah 65:17-19).

Suffering and death are erased not just from life but from memory. Isaiah affirms this vision in his final chapter:

> For as the new heavens and the new earth that I make shall remain before me, says the Lord, so shall your offspring and your name remain. From new moon to new moon, and from Sabbath to Sabbath, all flesh shall come to worship before me, declares the Lord (Isaiah 66:22-23).

This new creation is not merely some "fixed up" version of our present world. The new heavens and new earth are *wholly* new, creation not only *restored* but *perfected*. It is the very same vision St. John described in the closing chapters of Revelation:

> Then I saw a new heaven and a new earth, for the first heaven and the first earth had passed away, and the sea was no more. And I saw the holy city, new Jerusalem, coming down out of heaven from God, prepared as a bride adorned for her husband. And I heard a loud voice from the throne saying, "Behold, the dwelling place of God is with man. He will dwell with them, and they will be his people, and God himself will be with them as their God. He will wipe away every tear from their eyes, and death shall be no more, neither shall there be mourning, nor crying, nor pain anymore, for the former things have passed away." And he who was seated on the throne said, "Behold, I am making all things new" (Revelation 21:1-5).

This regenerated creation does not just restore the original, it supersedes it. No weakness or corruption remains: the original creation is perfected, as God planned from the beginning. Man has not overcome man's sin; God in union with man has: in one perfect human life, in the one sacrifice of the cross, God has overcome the damage of mankind's long reign of sin. The reign of God begins in the risen Jesus Christ, for we now see him enthroned with his Father. "The throne of God and of the lamb," we discover, is now a single, *shared* throne (Revelation 22). God's plan of Shared Sovereignty has come to its perfect fruition.

Take careful note of this, for you see here in sharpened focus the principle I have stressed throughout the book. As God first shared his sovereignty with Adam, the "son of God" (Luke 3:38), he now shares it with the new "son of Adam," Jesus, the *man* into whose hands all judgment and reconciliation have been placed. This is not a change of course or some last-minute plan from God. God's son who became flesh as the new Adam was involved from the beginning (John 1:1-4) to guide us from our self-inflicted destruction into the freshness of his kingdom.

Here we see unveiled the definitive purpose of Shared Sovereignty, mined from Holy Scripture. I have often said that unless a person correctly understands the first three chapters of Genesis and the last three chapters of the Book of Revelation, he will misunderstand everything that happens in between. The opposite is also true: once we come to truly understand those first three chapters of Genesis and the last three of Revelation, everything in between takes on new and clearer meaning. We discover not only God's plan for creation, but *who we are,* and our part in that plan. Just as God does not want us to languish forever in the consequences of our sins — if we are willing to take the lifeline he hands us in Christ — so he will not let the creation suffer forever under the corruption of our moral error.

The common, glorious vision seen by Isaiah, Paul, and John shows us God's goal: the ultimate family reunion of himself with his children — for eternity. The world is restored. Pain and disease are gone. *Un*natural disasters cease. This is the true "act of God": the unending incarnation of his son Jesus that restores us into perfected fellowship with the one in whose image we were made. That completed likeness is revealed fully in Jesus:

> He is the image of the invisible God, the firstborn of all creation. For by him all things were created, in heaven and on earth, visible and invisible, whether thrones or dominions or rulers or authorities — all things were created through him and for him. And he is before all things, and in him all things hold together. And he is the head of the body, the church. He is the beginning, the firstborn from the dead,

that in everything he might be preeminent. For in him all the fullness of God was pleased to dwell, and through him to reconcile to himself all things, whether on earth or in heaven, making peace by the blood of his cross (Colossians 1:15-20).

Endnotes

1. A further kind of catastrophe is widespread illness of the kind known as an epidemic. I will address physical defect and disease in the next chapter.
2. It is no accident that just before Jesus was placed on the new "tree of life" a reed was put in his hand, and a crown of thorns placed on his head.
3. This being "at odds" within themselves was feverishly developed by later Greek philosophers who viewed the physical body as inherently evil and unredeemable. By contrast, the Christian view is that since our physical body was made by God himself, it is essentially good by design and will be fully redeemed along with our broken spirits at the resurrection. As noted in Chapter Five, St. Paul knew well this "inner war" that tears at our soul (Romans 7:14-25).
4. Here we find at least a partial answer to the dilemma of animal pain. It is doubtful that even the "higher" animals can be said to suffer pain as punishment, since they are incapable of what we consider moral wrong. But if, as I show in this chapter, the entire physical order from top to bottom has been corrupted by human sin — as if the basic software and operating system of the computer has been damaged — then every creature within that system will suffer some effect. When it comes to suffering, the animals are in the same position as a human who suffers unjustly because of the evil actions of some other person. Both are innocent. When someone causes widespread evil, all will feel the pain. Man's sin has brought widespread evil into the whole system. Animals are caught up in the damage; they, too, suffer the torments of a corrupted creation.
5. St. Paul writes how Satan, this angelic "prince of the power of the air" partly influences human behavior toward sin:

> And you were dead in the trespasses and sins in which you once walked, following the course of this world, following the prince of the power of the air, the spirit that is now at work in the sons of

disobedience — among whom we all once lived in the passions of our flesh, carrying out the desires of the body and the mind, and were by nature children of wrath, like the rest of mankind (Ephesians 2:1-3).
6. Thus, we hear of Satan "patrolling the earth" in Job 1-2.
7. Some present-day climatologists argue that man's physical actions are causing damage to our world climate and thus to our ecosystems. To what extent human activity causes what damage is a matter of scientific debate. What Scripture tells us is that there is no doubt whatsoever that mankind's *spiritual* actions and disposition have been causing severe damage to our environment since man first sinned.
8. There is a great deal "more than meets the eye" when we consider the complexity of the natural order. Beneath, behind, or "inside" the outward appearance of the world, unseen "rules" and forces are constantly at work. An analogy would be how present-day science presumes there are measurable but 'un-seeable' causes behind the behavior of certain physical matter. Energy and matter, as presently understood, are seemingly indivisible: energy can transform into perceptible matter — and vice-versa. It should not seem odd, then, that physical forces (matter or energy) can be influenced by un-seeable spiritual forces that are beyond the perception of our instruments. Holy Scripture tells us that the entire material universe came into being as a result of a spiritual command: God, who is pure spirit, "spoke" (very figurative language) and the universe was brought into being (Genesis 1:1). The Psalmist agreed: "By the word of the Lord the heavens were made, and by the breath of his mouth all their host . . . For he spoke, and it came to be; he commanded, and it stood firm" (Psalm 33:6-9). These spiritual forces have traditionally been called "metaphysical" for the simple reason that they cannot be observed or measured as physical entities or properties in the normal scientific sense. But often, even in the present state of physics, we "observe" the existence of certain physical particles *only* by their effect on matter or energy fields around them. We can thus "know" they exist but we cannot "see" them directly. We are also now told that there is a great volume of "dark matter" in the universe, but it, too, can only be quantified or measured by mathematical speculation.

Once we reach this depth in scientific study, we are not far from the un-seeable spiritual realities at work behind whatever we can observe. This insight is really not new. Theologians have known, over the centuries, that spiritual realities and laws can only be known by the *effect* they have in the visible world. (See Paul's argument as to why all men know of God, Romans 1:19-20). Spiritual realities interact with the physical order but are not themselves physical. How this interaction works, at least at our present level of scientific understanding, remains a mystery. Perhaps it always will; or perhaps, at some point, God will reveal this. But we know spiritual forces operate. Otherwise, why pray? (See Appendix A). We pray in the spirit, God replies by spiritual means, but the outcome — we hope — will include something outward and effective in the physical world. Many readers will have experience of this truth.

9. Some biblical commentators consider Paul's Letter to the Romans to be his *magnum opus*. If so, the 8th chapter is the *magnum* of the overall *opus*. I describe this chapter as the "hinge pin" of Romans on which both ends pivot, and on which much of Paul's whole theology rests. It is, on a different level, the hinge pin of the entire Bible, for it ties together the Old and New Testaments dealing with creation, its degradation by man's sin, God's act of redemption in Christ, and how that plan incorporates and affects us today.

Ten

We have looked at evil manifested as pain and suffering, including the suffering that results from natural disasters. Our consideration of suffering will be incomplete, however, as will be our answer to question four, until we consider two causes of suffering that affect many of us personally: physical or mental defects that occur all-too-often among us, and the various diseases that continually harm mankind.

What is the origin of defect and disease in the human community? Why do they happen at all, and is God is to blame? The answer emerges directly out of our discussion in the previous chapter, because defect and disease are two narrower but specific examples of natural evil. From a biblical standpoint, both are destructive results of human sin and its direct effect on the natural order.

In the previous chapter, I discussed how Scripture describes the corrupting effect of sin on the natural world. Nature has been marred by our sin. As stewards of God's creation, our spiritual rebellion has sunken into the soil; the earth is stained with our blood and hatred. Our violation of God's spiritual laws disrupted the physical laws of nature so that the spiritual and physical realms are now doing battle.

This conflict between God's design and our corrupt stewardship has deeply affects the natural order, damaging the processes God set in place. Genesis 3 and 4 describe how the earth became cursed because of our sin. We should therefore not be surprised that the curse has also infected ourselves as part of that natural order. The damaging effects of sin have corrupted not only the larger natural order but our own physical organism, not just individually but as the whole human race.

Let us first consider physical and mental defects in mankind. These range from obvious physical deformities and faulty organ function to mental and emotional defects which often grow progressively worse.[1] Present day medicine suggests that some physical deformity is caused by improper cell development in the womb, but we cannot always explain in a given case what triggers the error. It might be a genetic miscue or might result from some environmental influence. We know, for example, that certain deformities can be triggered by drugs ingested by the mother, as in the tragic Thalidomide cases that harmed over 10,000 infants with serious deformities. Many did not live.

Similarly, science is divided over whether, and to what extent, mental illness and emotional defects are rooted in biological causes. Some believe that all disease, whether physical or mental, is rooted solely in the organism. And there is little doubt that some mental defects may be at least in part physical in nature and can be effectively treated with medication. In other cases, physical defects in the brain or nervous system directly cause mental illness or breakdown. But there is no universal agreement here. Others in the "nurture" camp argue persuasively that most emotional or mental distress is directly caused by the person's environment, upbringing, and present circumstances.

Besides such inborn or developed defects, humanity suffers from a wide variety of physical diseases. Looking at the Genesis creation narratives, it seems that no such "brokenness" was present in the world at first. Like physical defects, I believe all physical disease came into the natural order as a result of moral evil and sin which, to follow my analogy, corrupted the divine software (spiritual laws). The nature and extent of disease changes over time but disease affects humankind across time and cultures. No one is fully immune.

Then there is the complexity of a middle ground, where arguments are made that certain mental and emotional problems are themselves a form of "disease." Alcoholism, in recent years, has been characterized by some as a purely physical disease while others argue that it is a complex problem equally rooted in social and learned behavior.

The whole area of addiction, indeed, is embroiled in this debate. Arguments have mushroomed over the causes and cures of various addictions and whether addictive feelings and behaviors result solely from biological causes or whether they are entirely "learned" behavior. In the area of sexuality, for example, there has been (as most readers will know) a major shift in recent years among physicians, social scientists, and mental health professionals about whether sexual "identity" and personal sexual "preferences" are biological, whether either (or both) are conditioned by environment and prior behavior, or whether certain identities are merely "chosen." Thus, we find ourselves caught in a period of rather biting, even paradoxical, controversy: some pansexual activists argue that homosexual "preference" is inborn and absolutely "cannot be changed," yet the same individuals will argue — in the next breath — that "gender identity" is entirely fluid, can be "chosen" on a given day, and can be changed just as rapidly. Those pushing these two wagons down the social freeway apparently don't recognize the obvious (and brilliantly glaring) contradiction.

The debates continue and flourish. Whatever the facts are — scientific, declared, or presumed — we cannot fail to recognize the plain fact that there are defects and problems in the human race that continue to manifest themselves in personal, social, and sexual patterns in society, and that for some individuals, those problems become overwhelming.

If we are to fully understand these problems, however, the most important thing to recognize is that defects and disease are not just physical or mental, they are *spiritual* as well. Just as the larger natural order is governed by underlying spiritual laws, so are our minds and bodies. The human person is a unified, *whole* being; our spiritual nature cannot be subdivided from our physical, mental, or emotional functioning. Indeed, the biblical view of humankind is that our "soul," from the Hebrew word *"nephesh"* used in Genesis 2:7 (the making of Adam), refers not just to the spiritual aspect of man but to the entire human person, body and spirit as a whole person. We don't possess a soul; we *are* a soul.[2] So, whatever is going on in us spiritually at any point will affect our physical organism and mental condition, and vice-versa.

Indeed, based on the perspective revealed in Genesis, I would argue that *all* physical and mental disorders are ultimately rooted in the conflict that human moral evil has engendered between the physical and spiritual laws that govern our world. That is part of St. Paul's point in Romans 8: the entire created order in presently slogged down by the detrimental effects of human sin and is anxiously waiting for the redemption of humankind that will reset the process and overcome the worldwide damage. Paul's phrase, "the revealing of the sons of God" refers to the time when redeemed mankind will place itself back under the ruling sovereignty of God and become (at last) right stewards of this world. Then, and only then, will the natural order be healed (see Revelation 21:4).

This re-creation began in the resurrection of Christ but it is not complete. Each of us is still broken from birth. Moral evil and natural chaos erupt within us at an early age. (Just ask the parents of a toddler.) This is what the traditional doctrine of "Original Sin" speaks to. We are born with an innate tendency toward sin and selfishness, an inherent "bent" that leads us — from toddler land onward — to rebel against God and his spiritual laws. When we bend or break those laws, we bend or break something in the natural order.[3]

A Caution

Although, then, human defects or disease are forms of natural evil and can be broadly tied to the ongoing damage caused to the natural order by man's sin, that does not mean that every disease or birth defect is *directly caused* by some specific sin, either of that individual or his immediate parents. That assumption was common among the Jews in the Old Testament period, and we find hints of it in the New Testament as well. Paul, for example, says that some Christians were suffering illness, even dying, as a direct result of not properly and reverentially receiving Holy Communion (the Eucharistic bread and wine), not "discerning" that it is the Body and Blood of Christ.[4] St. James also implies that unconfessed sin may play a part in someone's illness.[5]

But we must make a careful differentiation here. Sin can and does affect our physical organism, but not every sin will cause a direct, immediate illness or sudden defect (like an emotional breakdown). To the contrary, it is true that sometimes the illness or defect comes about from some other cause. A good New Testament example is in the Gospel of John:

> As he [Jesus] passed by, he saw a man blind from birth. And his disciples asked him, "Rabbi, who sinned, this man or his parents, that he was born blind?" Jesus answered, "It was not that this man sinned, or his parents, but that the works of God might be displayed in him" (John 9:1-3).

The cause of any particular disease may elude us. The good news is that God can heal or help us overcome any of them.

Now, while we should not jump to conclude that every physical or mental defect or illness is directly caused by some *actual* sin, it might be. If my mother, for example, polluted her body by abusing potent drugs during her pregnancy, her sin may indeed cause a birth defect in me. But let's say she was also a prostitute. Will her sin of corrupting her heart through prostituting her body cause me to be born with some physical defect? We should not conclude that — even if a defect appeared. While it is true that "the iniquity of the fathers" is sometimes visited on their children to the third or fourth generation (Exodus 34:7), it is also clear that God holds each of us accountable for our own sins, not someone else's.[6]

Reality — and common sense — tell us that we are born into a defective, malfunctioning world. Physical or mental defects are just particulars of the overall brokenness of that world. That brokenness, as we have seen, has a direct cause: not just Adam and Eve's sin, not just Cain's, but our own.

Knowing this, we should be able to recognize that our own life and misbehavior contribute to the moral morass of history, a mess which has only gotten messier since Eden. Yes, our *personal* sinfulness continues to damage the natural order. Each time we sin, a little fresh curse is thrown upon the world. We cannot see this, but it is real. At times that curse may directly hurt our own mental and physical health. We tend to focus on the large, terrible plagues mankind has suffered, but the original plague on the entire universe is sin.[7]

Just as God permits evil in the first place, he will permit its consequence to play out in individual lives. A personal example. I was once desperately ill at home for several days and was finally hospitalized in severe pain. The doctor said if I had delayed getting to the hospital even another 24 hours, I would not have lived. At not a few moments during those days, I would have welcomed death. The pain was beyond anything I thought I could bear. But I can tell you with certainty what I came to realize through those days: my utter dependence on God. I came quickly to terms with my frailty and actual mortality. (Tests eventually showed that I had a severe salmonella infection of a kind often fatal.)

While we all anticipate our death to some extent, not everyone comes this close, even once. My experience here may be somewhat unusual. Between that severe illness and several incidents when I was a police officer, it is truly a miracle that I am alive today. (Add to this the fact that I started smoking when I was 12 and did not stop until I was 36.) So I have learned to be very grateful for each day. As someone has said, "Any day I wake up looking at this side of the grass, it's a good day."

Evil, pain, and suffering are very real. Our question has been, "If God allows me personally to suffer, doesn't it mean he never really loved me or cared about me?" This I can answer not only from Scripture but from personal experience: No. As bad as our personal suffering sometimes is, as hard as it is to weather those storms, God is simply allowing us like the rest of humanity to experience the pain we have all brought into creation. St. Paul also knew firsthand about pain and suffering, yet wrote this to one of his churches:

> No temptation has overtaken you that is not common to man. God is faithful, and he will not let you be tempted beyond your ability, but with the temptation he will also provide the way of escape, that you may be able to endure it (1 Corinthians 10:13).

The same can be said about suffering, for in a very real sense, all temptation involves a form of suffering. God will allow us to suffer, but not beyond what we can endure. Part of enduring the pain, in my case, was throwing my life and future fully into his hands. I trusted God to preserve my life or let it end in "natural" (unnatural) death. That trust enabled me to endure those days of excruciating pain and sickness.

God is never ignorant of our suffering (Exodus 3:7; Nehemiah 9:27). Our suffering can and does build character and endurance (Romans 5:3), and our suffering, in particular as a result of our faith, is in a real sense a sharing in the suffering that Christ endured on our behalf (2 Corinthians 1:5). This "participation" in the suffering of Jesus, for the Christian, is real and is part of what Paul meant when he said his own suffering for the church was in some mysterious way "filling up" the universal suffering of Christ himself (Colossian 1:24). Christ's suffering did not begin at his arrest and crucifixion; it began in Eden.

So, we should never minimize suffering, and we should never minimize its redemptive value. It can help rescue us from ourselves. Christ's crucifixion, after all, was a self-surrender and sacrifice that required of him terrible suffering. The pains he endured can free us from the pains of spiritual death that threaten to destroy our lives into eternity. In Jesus, God understands our pain in a personal way we rarely give him credit for.

Paul expressed this as well in that magnificent 8th chapter of Romans:

> ... we know that for those who love God all things work together for good, for those who are called according to his purpose ... What then shall we say to these things? If God is for us, who can be against us? He who did not spare his own Son but gave him up for us all, how will he not also with him graciously give us all things? Who shall bring any charge against God's elect? It is God who justifies. Who is to condemn? Christ Jesus is the one who died — more than that, who was raised — who is at the right hand of God, who indeed is interceding for us. Who shall separate us from the love of Christ? Shall tribulation, or distress, or persecution, or famine, or nakedness, or danger, or sword? As it is written, "For your sake we are being killed all the day long; we are regarded as sheep to be slaughtered." No, in all these things we are more than conquerors through him who loved us. For I am sure that neither death nor life, nor angels nor rulers, nor things present nor things to come, nor powers, nor height nor depth, nor anything else in all creation, will be able to separate us from the love of God in Christ Jesus our Lord (Romans 8:26-39).

What a magnificent "telephoto view" of life and suffering, and what a deep insight into the redeeming value of what often seems like pointless suffering. How often do we feel like sheep to be slaughtered? This was no pleasant metaphor. In Paul's day, Christians were actually *being* slaughtered. After years of arrests, interrogations, floggings, and imprisonments because of his faith, Paul would finally fall victim to the headman's ax. Today western culture seems content with the carnage of ridicule and contemptuous laughter toward Christians, but the resulting pain is still felt. And in some parts of the world Christians are being killed for their faith to this day.

Remember Paul's overarching point. God knows our weakness and our suffering. In the resurrection of Christ, he has given us a foreshadowing of the restored creation that will come. Nothing in this life, not even the worst suffering, need derail us from pursuing holiness and pursuing the gifts God has for us. Though born in sin the first time, we have in Jesus the means to be reborn into a kind and quality of life that will redeem our days here and bring us joy into eternity (John 3).

The Answer

When God lets me suffer, does it mean he does not care about me or love me? To the contrary, he is teaching me reality: the sad reality of sin and its consequences. And he is showing me the doorway to something different:

> Through him we have also obtained access by faith into this grace in which we stand, and we rejoice in hope of the glory of God. Not only that, but we rejoice in our sufferings, knowing that suffering produces endurance, and endurance produces character, and character produces hope, and hope does not put us to shame, because God's love has been poured into our hearts through the Holy Spirit who has been given to us. For while we were still weak, at the right time Christ died for the ungodly. For one will scarcely die for a righteous person — though perhaps for a good person one would dare even to die — *but God shows his love for us in that while we were still sinners, Christ died for us* (Romans 5:2-8; *emphasis* added).

What About "Good People"?

A final question about suffering should be addressed here because it is so commonly asked. "Why do bad things happen to good people?" Some seem to think that Christians in particular, trusting deeply in the love of God, ought to be immune from suffering.

The fact is, the New Testament tells us quite the opposite. We find many passages that speak of the suffering we will face precisely *because* of our faith. The quotation just given from Romans 8 is only one example. In the opening chapters of Revelation, John records Jesus' promise to his churches that they are about to go through tremendous tribulation and suffering. Some will die. The Lord calls them to remain faithful despite this. The chapters of Revelation that follow contain instances where large portions of mankind suffer catastrophe, Christians alongside of nonbelievers.

The truth is, Christians suffer right along with everyone else. Catastrophe is indiscriminate and no respecter of persons. We need not just look at the past. Many Christians died in the Twin

Towers and the Pentagon on September 11th, 2001. Several were on board Flight 93. God did not insulate them because of their relationship with him.

"Bad things happen" to people we may personally think are "good." None of us, of course, are as good (or innocent) as we wish to pretend and as we hope others believe of us to be. A fairly easy case can be made that many of us — based solely on personal sins committed so far — deserve hell, not heaven. No, God does not insulate Christians from suffering. (This is one reason why the popular "Rapture" mythology is so insidious.[8]) What he *does* promise is that he will be present with us through our suffering (Revelation 2:9-11). Suffering is a given of Christian life because it was the essence of Jesus' life given for us:

> "You are those who have stayed with me in my trials, and I assign to you, as my Father assigned to me, a kingdom, that you may eat and drink at my table in my kingdom and sit on thrones judging the twelve tribes of Israel" (Luke 22:28-30).

Notice Jesus' promise, to share his ultimate sovereignty in the coming kingdom. Many of these disciples faced their own trials and suffering after his resurrection precisely because of their testimony to the resurrection and the divinity of Jesus. St. James (son of Zebedee) we know was executed by King Herod:

> About that time Herod the king laid violent hands on some who belonged to the church. He killed James the brother of John with the sword, and when he saw that it pleased the Jews, he proceeded to arrest Peter also. This was during the days of Unleavened Bread (Acts 12:1-3).

We know from early histories of the church that both Peter and Paul died by execution in Rome in the mid-60s AD. Suffering and death do not bypass Christians, nor should we expect them to. God promises us resurrection life beyond the grave; he does not promise that we will escape the grave.

Now if this is the case for Christians, in whom God has planted the seeds of his new creation (2 Corinthians 5:17), it will also be the case for others who may live outwardly "good" lives. Those we may think — by our personal value judgments — are relatively good people may be seething with sin on the inside. Even if not, they are not without sin completely, for we are all guilty at some level. We are in the meat grinder we call human society; we all suffer the consequences of rampant sin and hatefulness around us. None are immune. The damaged natural order will catch our own arm into the machine just as quickly as some wicked fellow who we think really deserves it.

Bad things happen to good people because bad things happen to all people. Common sense and common sympathy demonstrate that daily.

God Still Loves Us

As long as we continue to burden and damage the world by our sin, suffering will continue. But God does not leave us helpless. He has created, in this present world, a spiritual "kingdom" which we enter by his invitation, but only by our own choice. Greater news: all are invited. God "desires all people to be saved and to come to the knowledge of the truth" (1 Timothy 2:4), but he compels no one. If we seek his lordship, we do it voluntarily. There are no conscripts in his army.

But entering his kingdom will not suddenly insulate us from pain. Indeed, we have his promise that we will face new ones. The deepest of those pains will be spiritual not physical, for once entered under his lordship, he will ask us to give up those things that harm us — and almost invariably harm those around us. It is a very simple proposition: he calls us to obedience, to reverse the pattern set by Adam and Eve's rebellion.

We are not very good at this. It will always be a struggle, probably daily. Because God loves us, he will not compel us to obey. But he has given us powerful reasons to obey, and spiritual strength to do it. He gives us new purpose. But it means we must peel out of our selfish snake skins.

We often bring suffering down on our own heads. And God may at times influence events in such a way to bring us to our knees. It may be that he wants us to surrender more fully to him, or to surrender some particular idol or sin from our life. God's "nudge" to do so may involve suffering, some serious pain or illness, or loss. But as the Christian thinker Jim Elliot once said, "He is no fool who gives up what he cannot keep to gain what he cannot lose." God may lead us into a time of suffering because it will help strip off our selfish pride, and melt down the golden idol we have made of our self. Like what Jesus endured, it may be suffering with a steep price, but a glorious purchase.

Every bit of suffering seems brutal at the time. But God, who is all-knowing, is not oblivious to your pain. That he allows it does not mean he does not love you. He did not love Jesus less on the cross. Suffering means he loves you enough to teach you sacrifice, the kind of complete self-giving that he knows from rude experience.

Endnotes

1. I could list page after page of examples. Many readers have probably experienced the occurrence of some serious birth defect within their immediate or extended family, or at least among the families of friends. Sad to say, birth defects are still common, despite various medical attempts to eradicate them or reduce their frequency. The other sad reality is that while having now fully "mapped" the human genome, we still do not fully understand why a particular defect occurs in a particular individual or group. Less do we understand what seems to be the random occurrence of a specific defect. It has been proven that certain defects are the direct results of drugs (including alcohol, illicit drugs and prescription drugs) which the mother ingested while pregnant. But other defects just seem to pop up out of nowhere, where there is no family history of it in an earlier generation.

2. Thus, for example, in times past when a newspaper would report "1100 Souls Lost In Disaster," they meant the loss of those persons. No one imagined only their "spirits" were lost.

3. Many people completely misunderstand the doctrine of Original Sin. They will speak of "the original sin," referring to the "first sin" of Adam and Eve. One is related to the other, but "the first sin" is not the same as Original Sin. Original Sin simply means that we are all stained by sin "from our origin," that is, from our human parentage and human history. We thus carry the taint of sin before we individually commit any actual sin. Paul writes that "as in Adam all die, so also in Christ shall all be made alive" (1 Corinthians 15:22). We all die not because Adam sinned, but because we all sin. We thus *participate* in the sin of Adam (Romans 3:23). I am not due punishment for what Adam did; I deserve punishment for what I have done.

When the psalmist complained that he "was brought forth in iniquity, and in sin did my mother conceive me" (Psalm 51:5), he was not suggesting that the sexual act leading to his conception was sinful. It was, after all, God himself who commanded us to "be fruitful and multiply" in that exact way. And the Psalms say that God himself "knitted me together" in the womb (Psalm 139:13). There is nothing wrong or sinful with our reproductive process. The psalmist's point is that we are all born with a "sin nature" and delivered into a sin-tainted world. From conception on, we develop with that damaged spiritual-physical nature now inherent in the human race. In this sense, we all suffer from one common birth defect: it is called sin.

Thus, for example, in the context of the aforementioned debates about "sexual orientation" or "sexual preferences," when a person says he cannot help a certain behavior or orientation because "I was born this way," he is partly correct; yet in the same breath he indicts himself. For we all carry the defect of sin. In some, that may manifest itself in a certain emotional propensity, say to anger, or to a certain set of behaviors such as compulsively ridiculing others. Any seemingly "uncontrollable" addiction grows out of this inherent tendency toward sin which violates God's design and purpose for each of us. Still, as I have said throughout, we each also have a will and the ability to make *right* choices. That is, what *we do* with a penchant toward a particular sin is still a matter of choice. A person born with a predilection toward anger may be more prone to commit murder. That cannot justify the murder once he commits it. A man who claims he must live out homosexual behavior "because I was born that way" is essentially saying he has no longer has any effective will, and must bow to whatever debased desire comes along.

4. 1 Corinthians 11:27-32.

5. James 5:13-16.

6. The notable exception is when a "watchman," a prophet of God, fails to warn others of the danger and consequences of their sins: "If a righteous person turns from his righteousness and commits injustice, and I lay a stumbling block before him, he shall die. Because you have not warned him, he shall die *for his sin*, and his righteous deeds that he has done shall not be remembered, but his blood I will require *at your hand*" (Ezekiel 3:20). That is why not many should risk taking on the role of prophet or preacher.

7. One of the truths partially seen in pantheistic religions is that "everything is interconnected." If I assault or stab someone to death, the spiritual effects may impact someone a thousand miles away, or in a succeeding generation. Here, the Christian will agree. The difference is that the pantheist believes everything is merely happening either by random chance or as a result of an unbreakable "chain" of cause and effect (impacted perhaps by the "payback" effect of "karma"); while the Christian believes that history is not random and that God is taking a hand in the outcome of things, to heal and to restore. The pantheist sees all events from inside of time. The Christian trusts the God who sees all events from outside of both time and space. It is that omnipotent Lord whose laws we are breaking, so we should not be surprised that the effects of our misconduct may be very broad across the "natural" order.

8. One (just one) of my principle objections to the modern "secret rapture" mythology is that it tries to do exactly that: it would have Christian "true believers" believe that they are so much superior to others that God will not let them undergo any serious suffering or "tribulation." This false assumption entirely contradicts those opening chapters of the Revelation to St. John. Rapturists want you to believe that Jesus will swoop down from heaven to rescue these "best" souls from the catastrophic struggles that will come upon the rest of the world (those "left behind"). This is completely contrary to many passages in the New Testament, and Jesus' own words. It is also an insult to the countless generations who have remained faithful yet died for their Christian faith — and to those still dying today.

Eleven

"I never asked to be born!" Many an angry child has yelled this at his parents. Many angry adults have yelled it at God. Although it arises out of anger or frustration, there is actually a profound truth concealed here. As a matter of simple fact, none of us asked to be born; we had no part in the decision. I have said God has no conscripts in his Church, but the reality is, we are *all* conscripts into this present humanity.

As odd as it may seem, this realization is the first step in answering our fifth question: "Why do we have to die?"

We recognize that we have great freedom of choice, but we had no choice in being here to begin with. If God indeed wants only volunteers in his new kingdom, those who don't wish to be part of it must have the opportunity to choose. Has God provided for that?

Ask first, *why are we* here? I believe God created us for a simple purpose: to choose life with him, and enjoy that life everlastingly in a perfect, willing communion with himself, sharing in his divine love and joy. But this is difficult in a world consuming itself with sin. If we are to be put right again with God, he must provide the way into that life, but also a way out for those who refuse it.

So, before sin ever entered the picture, God launched his plan to draw us back to himself in a way that would challenge each of us with the reality of our sinfulness and give us the means of forgiveness. His plan was to offer life as a gift, as an actual choice, but not compel anyone to submit to him — because to compel anyone would be to violate his nature as love. In Scripture, this gift is called the gift of eternal life, life in and with God (Romans 6:23).[1]

We are all in the broadest sense "children of God" made in his image. But not all are willing participants in his ongoing plan of creation. To enter God's kingdom means first to submit to his lordship, but we must enter of our own will.

How? The 3rd chapter of John's Gospel speaks of this choice. There Jesus says we can only enter through him: if we wish to come into his kingdom, we must first be "born again" by entrusting our life to him. The original Greek wording here in John means "born over again" or to be "born from above." It means taking up an entirely new and fresh start in life, what Paul refers to as becoming "a new creation" in Christ (2 Corinthians 5:17).

This "new birth" Jesus speaks of seems, at first thought, to be impossible. His listener, Nicodemus, certainly did not understand him. But if we listen carefully to Jesus' words in that chapter, we can recognize what he means: we must make a choice to enter God's kingdom. We have to *want* it. And to enter means a completely new start. We must leave behind anything of this present life that would dog us and hold us back. How many times did Jesus ask would-be followers to "let go" of their past and all that held them back in order to follow him?

What dogs us and drags us down most? Not just sin but our whole fallen nature. I have said we are a complex whole, body and spirit, a complete "soul." But that whole working organism is sick: it is infected with a serious disease called sin. And there is a deep conflict in us over sin. We both love and hate our sins. We hate them because they damage us and those around us; yet we love them because they reflect our self-centered desires and, in some sense, feed our vanity. We do not *want* to be rid of them — at least not all. Most of us, I think, fundamentally like who we are, even though we dislike some things about ourselves. Jesus knows all this so he says quite bluntly, "You must be born all over again." That means from scratch. That means surrender of whatever enslaves us. Many people just won't do this.

Here again we face a choice, a mammoth choice: to exercise our Shared Sovereignty with God at its most intimate level and decide if we truly wish to live, or simply want to be left to ourselves. Jesus asks each of us to make *that choice.* It has everlasting consequences. Fully-blessed life through eternity, or spiritual death. "Choose this day whom you will serve" (Joshua 24:15), the true God, or the false god you call your "self."

All right, you say, I choose life. So, again, *why* do I have to die? And we still have those related questions: didn't Jesus promise us eternal life, and didn't he supposedly overcome death? Why is death still necessary?

We can answer these questions together since they are interconnected. But we must tread lightly and think deeply: tread lightly because death is so serious a matter to each of us; think deeply, because if we don't, we will not fathom the truth about the nature of physical death. And as with so many things in this present life, there is more to death than meets the eye.

A Short Story

Let me begin with an allegory, a brief story that will shed light on the real question. The story is not long — except for the outcome.

A young husband and wife, newlyweds, are honeymooning in the Caribbean. They go off alone snorkeling one morning to a small island just off the coast from their resort. They swim into a previously unexplored cove and discover — entirely by accident — the Fountain of Youth. They are flabbergasted but elated, and in moments they have drunk their fill from the spring gushing from a small rock near the shore.

They suddenly feel like gods, feeling a surge of power. Their skin softens but becomes instantly more resilient. Their hair becomes thick and wavy. They see each other with renewed sight and look at each other in an even more longing way. Full of new life and heady with newfound vitality, they decide to explore this island further. They swim into a low cave-like opening in the cove at the base of a cliff. They snorkel down under a deep rock overhang through a long underwater tunnel and emerge inside a gigantic hidden cavern. They are amazed that they were able to hold their breath for over 18 minutes as they swam through the 200-foot-long tunnel. Their new youth is showing.

They step from the water onto the rocky shore inside the cavern. They have one light between them which the husband pans around to get their bearings. The cavern is huge, covering many acres of underground sea and the vault of the ceiling rises at least 70 feet over their heads.

But just as they begin to explore, they feel an earthquake. Out near the passage entrance, a volcanic fissure has opened up in the most-untimely way and pumps their underwater entrance full of lava. The quake stops just as abruptly, the lava flow is shut off. But their underwater access tunnel is now lava quickly cooling into solid rock. The stunned couple stand holding each other just inches out of the water — water which had nearly boiled from the lava flow, but is now also cooling back to normal.

They begin to fret and worry. Soon the battery in their light grows weak. In their short time here, they have discovered only two things helpful in the cavern. The walls are covered with what appears to be a fast-growing, lichen-like substance, and there are a number of pools of fresh water around the edges of the cave, fed by ground water dripping down from overhead.

They taste the mossy substance. It is tasteless except for a slight bitterness. They drink from the fresh water pools. It's not nearly as fabulous as what they had received from the fountain not a half-hour ago, but drinkable. It can keep them alive.

The young couple takes in their situation. They see no way out. The entrance is impossibly and permanently blocked. Though the cavern is huge, they can see no other passage out. While their flashlight lasts, they hurriedly search for an alternate underwater passage. They find only one. Panicking, they dive in and begin swimming — only to discover the tunnel dead ends only 50 feet from where they jumped in. They swim back.

They are trapped.

As their battery-powered light dies, they discover there are several tiny vents in the roof of the cave through which they can just make out a glimmer of light. The vents are also letting in a tiny amount of fresh air. But the vents are no wider than a pencil thickness and offer no escape. They are so far overhead the two could never reach them anyway.

They have only their swim suits and snorkel gear. They brought nothing else in. They stand staring at each other, as the dread of their situation sinks in. Barring some sort of miracle, they are here to stay. There is no way out. They have nothing to survive on except the tasteless lichen. And they have, really, nothing to do. They have no tools and can't make anything interesting or useful. They are truly stuck.

This goes on and on for weeks which turn into months. Desperation and anxiety deepen. Will there be no end? No. They fight bouts of panic, then depression. They get angry with each other. The wife says, "I wish I could just die!"

Of course, she can't. She and he, having drunk from that fountain, are now immortal. In complete desperation one morning, the husband picks up a sharp rock and gashes his arm. There is a cut and two seconds of blood, but suddenly the wound closes itself and in moments is fully healed.

More desperate yet, the wife takes a larger rock and smashes it down on her leg, hoping to damage herself beyond help. Her lower leg breaks. But apart from a sharp, brief pain, the attempt fails. Not only can she not die, she can't even sustain any long-term injury. Her bone straightens itself; the pain is gone in seconds, and the bone is fully restored.

What are they to do? They are mentally and emotionally numbed from what has become the endless, meaningless daily routine. They would gladly die — if only they could.

Now, imagine you are God. You are full of pity for this young couple. What do you do? They have become immortal (the word simply means "undying.") Would you somehow destroy them? The most merciful solution, some might suggest, would have been prevention. God could have stopped them from drinking from that fountain. But he didn't. It was their choice. So, now what?

"Now what?" is the reason I tell the story: it can help us understand what the Bible shows was the origin and *reason* for God's sentence of physical death for the human race. It will help answer our question, "Why must I die?"

Like so many other amazing truths, that answer, too, is right there in the opening pages of Genesis. We have already looked at the Fall and Adam and Eve and the subsequent curses imposed on the serpent, on Eve, and on Adam. Adam was told, "By the sweat of your face you shall eat bread, till you return to the ground, for out of it you were taken; for you are dust, and to dust you shall return" (Genesis 3:19). But in telling Adam that he must now eventually return to the dust, God is only foreshadowing what he does next:

> Then the LORD God said, "Behold, the man has become like one of us in knowing good and evil. Now, lest he reach out his hand and take also of the tree of life and eat, and live forever — " therefore the LORD God sent him out from the garden of Eden to work the ground from which he was taken. He drove out the man, and at the east of the garden of Eden he placed the cherubim and a flaming sword that turned every way to guard the way *to the tree of life* (Genesis 3:22-24).

Notice carefully what God's concern was: "lest he reach out his hand and take also of the tree of life and eat, and live forever — "

Think now of our fictional couple in the cavern. When God looks in on them, what he sees is what he would have seen if he had left Adam and Eve in Eden, if he had not barred their way to the tree of life. For that tree — from which, remember, they had *permission* to eat — would have given them *immortality*. If they had eaten from it, they would become like our two newlyweds, young gods trapped forever: trapped in this case not in a cave but in a beautiful garden, but trapped nonetheless in a state of unbreakable sin.

Here was God's dilemma. He had given them the ability to eat from the tree of the knowledge of good and evil, but not the permission. Now he must withdraw both the permission and the ability to eat from this other tree, the fruit of which would have been their "Fountain of Youth." It would have made them like the young couple in my story: undying, and un-killable.

So, God responds. They have broken trust with him and damaged the natural order. Their innocence is lost. Ironically, they are not in mortal danger but in *immortal* danger. If they now eat from the tree of life, they will be trapped just as surely as those young newlyweds in their cave. Adam and Eve have fallen into a deep valley of sin and brokenness, a valley from which they can never climb out on their own. Sin will bore in. Their children will likewise be affected, as we see in the very next chapter of Genesis.

God knows that they will not be able to free themselves from sin. He knows he must save them from their predicament becoming permanent, so he acts. By barring their way to the tree of life, he effectively places them under a sentence of death, as he had foretold Adam ("to dust you shall return"). They died spiritually when they violated God's command; now, over time, they will die physically.[2] While this may seem cruel at first sight, we have to stare the alternative in the face: to leave them for all eternity in a state of unredeemed and unbreakable sin would have been *the cruelest thing God could have done*. As we know, sin self-propagates and evil mushrooms. We know full well from the events of history that evil only grows worse over time. Wickedness invents new means of human cruelty toward each other.

God's sentence of death for Adam, Eve, and all their progeny was his remedy to prevent brokenness from becoming an unsolvable, permanent condition for humanity, enslaved in unending sin. That would have been a far worse sentence than physical death. Just pause for a moment and imagine if every human who has ever lived remained alive at this moment, suffering the evils of the present world. Imagine, in that case, what a true "world war" would look like. Imagine the hatred and brutality affecting countless more souls and what the consequences could become.

God's judgment was right. We may not like it, but we can see why death is necessary. We know ourselves. If we are ever to be truly free of this broken world, and our own broken life, it means a complete letting go of this present world. Death will be that door. All of us will walk through it.

Painful Truth

Like the answers to some of our other questions, we find a distressing truth here. "Why must we die?" Not because Adam sinned, or Eve, but because we too sin. We find ourselves, in that respect, in exactly the same position that Adam and Eve were in after they disobeyed God. Not only do we sin, we have tried to make ourselves our own God. We think we know all, and know best. In many ways, if our actual behavior is any clue, we really think we can manage our lives perfectly well without God.

Does this ring true?

"All right," some may say, "but go on. Jesus' death supposedly saved us from the power of death, did it not? Isn't this the good news of the gospel?"

Yes, exactly. Jesus saves us from the *power* of death because from Adam to Jesus, death reigned *as a permanent condition.* We hear of accounts in the Old Testament where a few souls were resuscitated shortly after death. But no one dead for a hundred years returned. The Old Testament contains passages that speak of the horror and permanence of death.

When we go to the New Testament, we find that Jesus does not promise we will not undergo physical death. Rather, he saves us from *the power of its permanence.*

Go back to where we began this chapter. We never asked to be born. To enter willingly into God's kingdom, we must be born again. We must want to enter that life in a permanent and right relationship with God. But as long as we drag this present broken, dying physical organism along with us we will never be truly free to do that, because — if we are honest — our body is *the one very thing* that we absolutely do *not* want to give up!

We all feel this. Even a soldier in the battlefield confronted with certain death still hesitates, still resists. He will try, as far as he can, to protect himself. Yes, at a point he may surrender his safety and sacrifice his life, to further the battle or perhaps save a friend. But he didn't greet that day thinking, "Lord, I hope I die and get to give up this body today."

Jesus' incarnation and resurrection open the way for us to enter everlasting life, but he never said we will not go through physical death on the way there. To the contrary, he warned his disciples about what they would face, what they would suffer for his name:

> "But before all this they will lay their hands on you and persecute you, delivering you up to the synagogues and prisons, and you will be brought before kings and governors for my name's sake. This will be your opportunity to bear witness. Settle it therefore in your minds not to meditate beforehand how to answer, for I will give you a mouth and wisdom, which none of your adversaries will be able to withstand or contradict. You will be delivered up even by parents and brothers and relatives and friends, and *some of you they will put to death*. You will be hated by all for my name's sake. *But not a hair of your head will perish*. By your endurance you will gain your lives" (Luke 21:12-19).

At first this passage seems contradictory, but take a closer look: ". . . and some of you they will put to death . . . But not a hair of your head will perish." That is the key, and that is his promise: we will all go through death, but we will not *perish* in death. As horrid as it is, we will survive it.

To understand why Jesus says this, we must know that through much of the Old Testament period of Judaism, the Jews did not believe in a resurrection of the dead. They believed death was the end of each person, that it was final and permanent. The spirits of the dead went to "Sheol," the place of the dead, and no one came back. Belief in the possibility of a future resurrection did not develop among the Jews until much later. By the time Jesus was born, hope for a resurrection was still a view held by only a minority of Jews, mainly those of the strict Pharisee party, who interpreted certain Old Testament Scriptures as a promise of personal resurrection.[3]

Even after his own resurrection, however, Jesus warned his disciples that they would still undergo physical death. Speaking to one of the early churches through his disciple John, he warns:

> "Behold, the devil is about to throw some of you into prison, that you may be tested, and for ten days you will have tribulation. Be faithful unto death, and I will give you the crown of life. He who has an ear, let him hear what the Spirit says to the churches. The one who conquers will not be hurt by the second death" (Revelation 2:10-11).

Scripture is clear: Jesus does not exempt his disciples from physical death; he pledges that if they face it and remain faithful, he will be there at that gate to greet them:

> "He who has an ear, let him hear what the Spirit says to the churches. To the one who conquers I will grant to eat of the tree of life, which is in the paradise of God" (Revelation 2:7).

Finally, after centuries and countless generations, "the tree of life" that gives immortality reappears. We first heard of it in Eden — that second tree from which Adam and Eve were barred after the Fall. Here, in Revelation, it becomes prominent in the capital city of the resurrection world, the new Jerusalem. The gate of physical death is the gate back into that city, a reversal of the gate through which Adam and Eve were expelled from Eden. The new Jerusalem, indeed, is a kind of restored Eden, a garden become a garden-like city, glorified and perfected. Those who are "faithful unto death" get to enter:

> "The one who conquers, I will make him a pillar in the temple of my God. Never shall he go out of it, and I will write on him the name of my God, and the name of the city of my God, the new Jerusalem, which comes down from my God out of heaven, and my own new name" (Revelation 3:12; see also Revelation 21:2).

Digesting It All

Part of our fifth question was this: if Jesus promised us "eternal life" and himself overcame death, why must we still die? This particular question grows out of a misunderstanding of two phrases frequently used in the New Testament: "eternal life" and "everlasting life." These two phrases refer to different aspects or "states" of our new life in Christ and are often mixed up, but they are not simply interchangeable. If we clarify what each term means, it will help answer this question, and it will help us understand some of the perplexing things Jesus said about death, like this:

> Jesus said to her, "Your brother will rise again." Martha said to him, "I know that he will rise again in the resurrection on the last day." Jesus said to her, "I am the resurrection and the life. Whoever believes in me, though he die, yet shall he live, and everyone who lives and believes in me shall never die" (John 11:23-25).

What does he mean, "though he die, yet shall he live"? And how can he then add that "everyone who lives and believes in me shall never die"? The answer to the seeming contradiction lies in something recorded earlier in John's gospel:

> "For I have come down from heaven, not to do my own will but the will of him who sent me. And this is the will of him who sent me, that I should lose nothing of all that he has given me, but raise it up on the last day. For this is the will of my Father, that everyone who *looks on the Son and believes in him should have eternal life*, and I will raise him up on the last day" (John 6:38-40; *emphasis* added).

There is the distinction we must grasp: one who believes in Jesus gains "eternal life" *now;* when Jesus raises him on the last day that new kind of life becomes "everlasting life." In other words, "eternal" life does *not* begin at death, or at resurrection. It begins the moment we are "born-over-again" by faith in Christ and baptized into his body, the Church.[4] Eternal life extends to, and through, the grave. Thus, Jesus says that even though we die, we still live. Physical death cannot interrupt eternal life. It cannot destroy the spiritual life in the Father that we share through Christ, for that life flows from God. We cannot be separated from Christ (John 6, Romans 8) because we have been grafted into Christ, the vine that gives true life (John 15:1, 5). It seems paradoxical, but even as we continue to live in our fallen flesh, we already possess "eternal life," and we have already been released from the sinful corruption of this present world (Romans 8:9; Colossians 1:13-14; Ephesians 2:4-6). Jesus confirms this further in the passage from John 6:

> "Truly, truly, I say to you, whoever believes *has eternal life.* I am the bread of life. Your fathers ate the manna in the wilderness, and they died. This is the bread that comes down from heaven, so that one may eat of it and not die. I am the living bread that came down from heaven. If anyone eats of this bread, he will live forever. And the bread that I will give for the life of the world is my flesh" (John 6:47-51; *emphasis added*).

This is a deep and somewhat difficult passage, no doubt referring in part to the Eucharistic bread of Holy Communion. (It was so difficult that some of Jesus' disciple walked away for good when they heard it.) But it confirms the point: as soon as we place ourselves into the hands of Christ by faith, eternal life begins. Recall what Jesus said to Nicodemus, in what is perhaps the best-known verse of the New Testament: "For God so loved the world, that he gave his only Son, that whoever believes in him should not perish but have eternal life" (John 3:16).

". . . should not perish." That is the promise of the Gospel. We will die, we will *not* perish. God holds us in life, even in death (Romans 8:38). This is what the New Testament means by "heaven": it is not the "eternal home" of saved humanity, for earth is the home God has given us. Heaven is that place where God holds our personal spirit in "eternal life" even when we die, until the resurrection of the dead. Once we are resurrected — and we don't know when that will be, nor how long after our death — we will be raised to "everlasting life" in a redeemed body like Christ's own (Romans 8; 1 Corinthians 15; 1 John 3).

Put a little differently: "everlasting life" refers to the ultimate continuation of the "eternal life" that begins at our baptism (John 3:5). "Eternal life" speaks of the nature and quality of our new life in Christ, sharing in the divine life of the eternal God; "everlasting life" speaks of its duration.

Thus, Jesus' seeming paradox makes perfect sense: we *have* eternal life now, but will still die; yet even though we die — physically — we will not perish but will live a full and everlasting life in the resurrection.

Absorbing The Truth

This hard truth will make deeper sense when we remember that Jesus himself was not exempt from death. Certainly, he possessed in himself eternal life, being himself life's true source (John 1), yet he underwent death to redeem our suffering. He was born among us to take up into the godhead all that is human, and that had to include the awful reality of physical death. Are we silly enough to imagine that he was anxious and happy to face death, to surrender his own body? Not when we witness the terrible anguish he suffered that night before his crucifixion in a different garden, Gethsemane.[5]

Is God being cruel by requiring us to go through physical death? No. He alone knows what surgery we need to cut away the spiritual cancer that has corrupted us down to our heart and bones. Our present physical bodies — as I discover more and more each day — begin to die almost as soon as we are born; as we age, they deteriorate beyond repair. All this, like decay in nature, is the product of our sin. But our body is part and parcel of what Scripture means by our "soul," the whole person God made us each to be. Our body is broken but it too can be reborn, quite literally, in a resurrection body (1 Corinthians 15:35-49).

It will be good to recall here what I said early on: physical death is not the worst thing that can happen to us; the much more painful and consequential death is *spiritual death*. God can save us from both. He can implant in us eternal life now, and he can also save us from the grave because Jesus has broken the power of its *permanence*.

So, we need not fear the coffin or the tomb. These are not permanent. God uses them to convey us beyond this present world's corruption to something greater, a restored physical nature no longer subject to pain, or decay, or death.

As if rescuing our young newlyweds from the doom of their cave, God sent Adam and Eve out of Eden. Death was a punishment, yes, no doubt. But it was also their means of rescue. It was the most loving thing God could have done without stripping them of their wills, without overthrowing their role as his co-rulers of this world. We are all outside of Eden, to learn how to exercise our co-sovereign authority instead of abusing it.

Was God's solution too severe? It may seem so. But the fact is, death is our only escape from an eternity of bondage and suffering under sin. Long before sin, and long before invoking this death sentence, God was at work, his rescue plan was already in place:

> . . . you were ransomed from the futile ways inherited from your forefathers, not with perishable things such as silver or gold, but with the precious blood of Christ, like that of a lamb without blemish or spot. He was foreknown *before the foundation of the world* but was made manifest in the last times for the sake of you (1 Peter 1:18-20).

Before the very founding of creation, God set out his plan to save us from evil and from ourselves. As we grow, he trains us to become better stewards of this present creation, broken as it is. He allows us to suffer, but that suffering has its limit: our death. It will free us from the corruption of self that binds us so that we can become worthy stewards for that age and creation that is yet to come.

"Why must I die?" Because I am sinful; sin has grown down into my bones. As Paul described so powerfully in Romans 7, sin has taken such root that our very wills, "free" though they are, have become badly corrupted — the weakened freedom of a bent, broken branch.[6] Now ask: what if, like our fictional newlyweds, I could *not* die? I would be trapped in this deep cavern of sin with no escape — forever.

When we see death in this light, we can see that it is an act of mercy from God. I want to become perfect, but I am not. Far from it. Death is a step in our transformation, a transition to our eventual healing, the healing of our *whole* human nature, spirit *and body*. The resurrection promises something entirely new: a spirit set free and a physical body that will obey our will and not fight it, that will relish in God's love and not abandon it.

It is a scary path, but a path every one of us must walk. Death is like a bitter dose of cod liver oil, but is medicine that will set us free from the trap we have built around ourselves, the trap of sin. The cave in my story was a barely-survivable existence with no joy, no hope, no future. That is exactly what our present life would be if there was no way out. Death is the escape hatch God has placed in our hand-hewn cave.

Is it frightening? Absolutely. Who wants to be ripped in half, our spirit shorn from our body? Personally, I wish there was some other way. But I am a coward. We want a hypodermic needle; God treats us with an axe.[7]

But then I remember spiritual death — going on into infinity — and I realize how much more frightening that looks, a slow, unending kind of death of blind isolation.

What, then, should the Christian attitude toward death be? We should not seek it but neither should we fear it. Christ has gone before. He knows what death is. He has broken its power and permanence. Death is still evil, but Christ has sanctified it for the rest of us. By his crucifixion, Christ has crucified death. And so, with a robust, trusting faith it is possible for us to have a holy death, the final genuine surrender of a life that was his all along, on loan as it were.

Christ stared into death's horrid face and cried out in anguish from the cross, "My God, my God, why have you forsaken me!"

Yet this was not an ultimate despair. As death came near, the anguish passed, for his final words were, "Father, into your hands I commit my spirit."[8] Let us be ready to do the same. For his cross is the Tree of Life.

Endnotes

1. "For the wages of sin is death, but the free gift of God is eternal life in Christ Jesus our Lord" (Romans 6:23). See also John 4:10, Ephesians 2:8.
2. Death is a one-time event but the result of a long process. Our physical organism, impacted by sin, dies slowly over many years. Anyone living into older age discovers this. We reach physical maturity, our body thrives for a time, but soon suffers deterioration of one kind and another.
3. The other major party in Jesus' time, the Sadducees, rejected any notion of a resurrection from the dead, which is why they and the Pharisees were often at each other's throats. In the New Testament, however, resurrection is not seen just as a reward for the righteous. All are to be raised from death for a purpose: the good and the wicked are resurrected to face God. We will all be judged for the kind of stewards we have been. Those saved in Christ are judged but not condemned because they have accepted the gift of eternal life in Jesus. They are already forgiven, and free: "Truly, truly, I say to you, whoever hears my word and believes him who sent me has eternal life. He does not come into judgment, but has passed from death to life" (John 5:24; see also Romans 8:1). Those not in Christ are judged by how they lived, and many will find themselves condemned by their own actions.
4. When Jesus speaks of being "born over again" in John (3:3), he adds that "unless one is born of water and the Spirit, he cannot enter the kingdom of God" (3:5). Since the early generations of the Church, this has been understood as a reference to Christian Baptism through which the person is incorporated into the Body of Christ by water and receives the gift of the Holy Spirit.
5. Going a little farther, he fell with his face to the ground and prayed, "My Father, if it is possible, may this cup be taken from me. Yet not as I will, but as you will" (Matthew 26:39).

6. "So I find it to be a law that when I want to do right, evil lies close at hand. For I delight in the law of God, in my inner being, but I see in my members another law waging war against the law of my mind and making me captive to the law of sin that dwells in my members. Wretched man that I am! Who will deliver me from this body of death? Thanks be to God through Jesus Christ our Lord! So then, I myself serve the law of God with my mind, but with my flesh I serve the law of sin" (Roman 7:21-25). "The body of this death" was his fallen flesh, warring against his redeemed spirit, sabotaging his will; our new body in the resurrection will not have that weakness.

7. Death is a tearing apart of the whole human person. But the resurrection is God's divine restoration. Like some grand magician, God saws us in two but then puts us back together again, healed, free of a corrupted heart.

8. As Jesus hung dying, these two sentences reveal that he was solemnly singing from the ancient Jewish hymnbook: the first sentence being from Psalm 22:1; the second from Psalm 31:5. See Mark 15:34, Matthew 27:46, and Luke 23:46.

"The doors of hell are locked on the inside." — C. S. Lewis

Twelve

We have reached our sixth question, the most serious question for God so far, for it is a direct accusation: "How could a loving God condemn anyone to an eternal hell?"

This question is so hotly debated, I suspect, in part because each of us knows someone — or more than one — whom we fear might end up there. If any of us were God, we imagine, we would have made a better plan, where no person ends up in a place of sorrow or torment. So if we want an honest perspective, we must look beyond our bias and go deeper to ask, 1) is that even possible, and, 2) is that desirable?

We must also contend with a wider bias, for in our present culture there are a good many people who are genuinely anti-God. Some identify themselves as atheists but are, more precisely, "anti-theists." It is not that they are fully persuaded there is no God; they just don't like how he governs the universe. If we read or listen to them, we find not dispassionate disbelief but passionate anger. For anyone with both feet planted firmly against God, the very idea of hell is an abomination. It appears so terribly unfair: a permanent condemnation and imprisonment for someone's "temporary" sins or misdeeds.

The issue, though, is more complex. It is not just anti-theists who condemn the idea of hell with virulent seriousness. There is a whole cadre of self-professed Christians today who also reject the idea of hell, feeling that it somehow diminishes God's love.[1]

My goal is not to minimize their objections. I simply want to make clear what the biblical view of "hell" actually is and clear up a number of falsehoods and misconceptions. There is a great deal of wrongheaded speculation about hell among Christians and non-Christians alike. If we are to discuss the topic intelligently to answer our question, we must first know what the Bible actually teaches. Paradoxically, when we understand the biblical view of hell, we find that far from diminishing God's love, it is *precisely because of God's love* that hell exists.

What Do You Mean By "Hell"?

First, ask yourself what "hell" means to you. Jot some notes down. It may give you a headache, but try. Then inquire of several your contemporaries (as I frequently have) and ask them to describe hell. You will get a wide variety of answers. Most will not agree with your own ideas. Invariably, the picture they will draw will end up including various medieval images: hell, they imagine, is where wicked people go immediately — and forever — at death. It is seen as a place of unrelenting pain overseen by a red-suited, horned devil harvesting tormented souls with a pitchfork. Interestingly, though, these "souls" also seem to have bodies because they are suffering *physical* torments. There is always some form of fire.

This caricature reveals the problem: there is a great deal more fiction than fact floating around about what the Bible says about hell. There is a simple reason: few people actually read the Bible anymore. So when someone says, "I object to the whole idea of hell," we cannot be certain to what he is objecting. Moreover, we cannot understand "hell" without also having a correct understanding of what the Bible says of "heaven." So my goal is simply to clarify some basics, what the Bible says — and does *not* say — about heaven and hell.[2]

In the popular imagination, there are two "places" where someone goes when they die. Some will say they are not really "places" but merely "states of existence," whatever that may mean. One place is "heaven," a permanent place (so it is imagined) of eternal peace and joy; the other is hell, a permanent place of pain and torment. The "soul" of a dead person goes immediately to one place or the other at the instant of death and remains there forever. They have reached their "eternal destiny": they will exist (so the popular myth goes) in this "spiritual," disembodied state forever. These disembodied souls in heaven won't mind because they are happy; those in hell are not.

The problem is, the Bible does not teach this. What it *does* say may surprise you.

During most of the Old Testament period, as I mentioned previously, the Jews believed the departed spirit of a person simply went to the grave, the place called Sheol. The Greeks called it Hades or the underworld. There, whatever was left of the dead person languished forever in a shadowy, disembodied, and largely impersonal kind of existence. The dead were dead; no one returned. There was no "heaven" or "hell," just Sheol. Everyone, the good, the bad, the ugly, the indifferent, ended in Sheol, side-by-side as it were forever.

By the later Old Testament period, however, as the Jewish understanding of God and creation deepened, some Jews came to see that even in death, God's love and justice must prevail. It would be unjust for the spirit of a righteous person to suffer eternity alongside the wicked of their own and previous generations. Some came to believe that God would carry the righteous dead to a "Paradise," a place of peace and rest, while the wicked still went to Sheol, that place of sorrow and loss. Paradise was sometimes pictured on the side of a high mountain, separated from Sheol (*Hades*) by a great chasm (Luke 16:22-26). But like Sheol, Paradise was not "human" life but a kind of vague shadow life, a place of the dead.

For many generations, this was the entire picture of "the afterlife" among the Jews. Death was a state of permanent disembodiment, a spiritual languishing from which there would be no return.

Later prophets of the Old Testament period, however, began to speak of a coming time of restoration, the "time of the messiah" when the righteous dead would be raised back to life and a new age of history would begin, the "kingdom age" when the reign of God would finally be established over all the earth.

With the coming of Jesus, this *hope* for a future resurrection suddenly became *reality,* for in the resurrection of Jesus himself, God revealed his broader plan for mankind. The dead would be raised, but not just the righteous. All the dead would one day be raised for a specific purpose: God would pronounce judgment on each person based on the life each had led. Following this "final judgment" there would be a new separation of the righteous from the wicked. But we must carefully understand the biblical timeline: this final separation does *not* happen at each person's death; it happens only at the final return of Christ to bring about the restoration of all things (Matthew 25:31-46).

With the incarnation of Jesus, the plan for God's final judgment is revealed. Because Jesus has come and lived among us, God has entrusted the judgment of all people to Christ, the God-Man:

> "For the Father judges no one, but has given all judgment to the Son, that all may honor the Son, just as they honor the Father. Whoever does not honor the Son does not honor the Father who sent him. Truly, truly, I say to you, whoever hears my word and believes him who sent me has eternal life. *He does not come into judgment, but has passed from death to life.* Truly, truly, I say to you, an hour is coming, and is now here, when the dead will hear the voice of the Son of God, and those who hear will live. For as the Father has life in himself, so he has granted the Son also to have life in himself. And he has given him authority to execute judgment, because he is the Son of Man. Do not marvel at this, for an hour is coming when all who are in the tombs will hear his voice and come out, those who have done good to the resurrection of life, and those who have done evil to the resurrection of judgment" (John 5:22-28, *emphasis* added; see also Roman 8:1).

Thus, at the resurrection the disembodied spirits of *all the dead* — those in both Sheol or Paradise — are restored in a very real body. But for those who long ago "passed from death to life" through Jesus, their destiny is already settled. In Christ, they have already been forgiven and set free from the eternal consequence of their personal sins.

For those who have rejected God in life, however, there is now the reality of his just judgment. God does not "condemn" them, for they have determined their destiny themselves. God merely "pronounces sentence" on the existence they have chosen: an existence outside his love and presence. It is what they chose in this life. It is what he grants. This is their final hell, "the second death" (Revelation 20:14, 21:8). As those who are in Christ will enjoy everlasting life, those who have chosen separation from God will experience an everlasting hell. Remember what I previously said: once created, each of us is eternal. God does not destroy what he creates. He separates the wicked to their destiny; he does not destroy them.

St. John in Revelation described this final separation, the second death, as "the lake of fire," and this is one source of "the fires of hell" imagery (Revelation 20:13-15). But make no mistake: this fire is no normal, earthly "fire," and no one drowns in this "lake." This fire is the continual consuming fire of God's judgment against wickedness, his eternal rejection of evil. Like the bush Moses saw (Exodus 3), this fire burns yet never consumes or destroys (Revelation 20:10).

This final isolation for the wicked is not the Sheol (*Hades*) where they went immediately at death. That was a temporary state, until the resurrection. This final hell, "the *second* death," will be permanent. They will exist there in a permanent separation from the God they despise. We must be very clear, though: this destiny is not something God arbitrarily chose for them. It is the result of their own choices and actions: in life, they scorned God and his ways, they separated themselves from him. God merely executes their self-imposed sentence.[3]

In short, their "assignment" to hell in this final sense is in no way unjust because it reflects their own actions and choice. Their torment is that of having lost their soul inside themselves. These prison walls were built with their own hands. There is no escape for a very simple reason: they *desire* no escape.

So, there is no question of God unfairly "condemning" someone to hell. They have condemned themselves. They sought a life apart from God. In truth, this final hell is not a place to which God "sends" them. It is the place they have fled to, the refuge of one running from God, a hoped-for hiding place willfully chosen. "I do not need God. I do not want God in my life!" In affirming his final "sentence," God merely answers, "So be it."

Does that sound cruel? What then would you have God do? Dishonor that person's own choice? God's love means that he respects our choices. Even this one. He has given us such power, to close and bolt the door that would bring us into his presence at our death.

"But shouldn't God have mercy?" some will still ask. God is always merciful. But be clear: mercy that compels is not true mercy, but demand; it is not love, but forced compliance. The sweetness of mercy would become brutality, violence against one's will.

So, God has made provision for those who reject him and chose wickedness. Those who wish an eternity apart from him get it. That is hell. It may be frightening that God would honor our freedom to that final extent. But it is, after all, his own gift.

We must also ask this difficult but candid question: why would someone who has spent a lifetime rejecting the very idea and person of God suddenly — at the instant of death — change his mind? That is not human nature. If a person goes through his entire life thinking and behaving in opposition to God, why in the end would he suddenly be struck with remorse and want a never-ending life in God's presence? Personalities don't form or operate that way. If someone has done his best for years to deny and avoid God, why would we think this man would suddenly hope to be commanded into God's presence at death? Such thinking is foolishness.

We are who we are, we become the person of our own choices. The old song by "The Moody Blues" said it well: "Just what you want to be, you will be in the end." God knows this better than we.

Still, our visceral reaction to hell is triggered not just because we may know someone else who might end there. Our real anxiety is that we all know *one person* who deserves hell without question: our self. Our true aversion is personal. We know ourselves too well not to imagine we might merit hell. And so we recoil. We will argue with ourselves: surely my sins have never been quite *that* bad. Surely, we hope, God's mercy is greater than our moral corruption. But can we assume either to be true? If we are demanding God be "fair" with us, are we being fair with him?

No Hell

John Lennon asked us to imagine a universe with no heaven. I would ask you to imagine one with no hell. When our heart rebels against the idea of hell, we must be willing to ask, "What is the alternative?" What of those whose lives and actions have shown them to be truly corrupt and thoroughly wicked? Consider butchers like Josef Stalin, Adolph Hitler, or Osama bin Laden. Should they end in hell? Most of us will say, "Of course." There is the bind. We each think we are not suitable for hell; yet we are quite certain *some* people are.

If there were no hell, what then? What of the Hitlers, the Stalins, the bin Ladens? If there is no place of "just dessert" to punish their unrepentant wickedness, it means we must all spend eternity with them, holding hands, singing "Kum Ba Yah" around some eternal campfire.

Does that alternative speak of a more just God? No. It would be pure injustice. If there were no hell, we would be forced to conclude that those nineteen skyjackers from September 11, 2001, who trained and honed their hatred and skill in destruction — as well as those who funded and supported them — all deserve a place in God's kingdom alongside the thousands of innocent souls they murdered.

If we are troubled by the idea of hell, we should be more deeply troubled by this alternative. Because if there is no hell (Lennon and Lenin would both be pleased), then we are proposing what "universalists" have suggested: if there is no hell, everyone spends eternity in fellowship with every moral monster of history.[4]

Is that what we would require from a "more just" God? I hear people complain that hell is immoral and unjust, but the complainers offer no other plan. They accept the reality of evil, but they have no idea what should become of those who viciously perpetrate evil on their fellow man. Such objectors have found the appalling problem, but they seek no solution. Their idea of justice seems to be that God should just "love everyone equally." My question is, *do they themselves?* Do they really love Hitler and bin Laden? Is "Hitler in heaven" an authentic demonstration of divine love, or even their own?

Consequences

Affirming both the reality and necessity of hell is nothing extraordinary. It merely argues for what we all know is right: that all of us should equally have to face the consequences of our actions. If, as I have argued from the beginning, we are co-rulers with God, we must be accountable for how we wield the awesome power he has given us. To shortchange or obstruct God's fair justice would be to attack the very human dignity we might seem to be defending.

If we want to do away with hell, what we are really asking is that God make malice and evil free, evil that has no final consequence. That is not justice, but evasion. We would be asking God to suffer our evil actions, including the murder of his own son, but require no culpability. If so, we are not seeking a God who is more just but one who simply condones evil.

God's justice forbids this, but so does his love. Here rings one bell of the Christian Gospel: there is a cost to our evil, a price to be paid for the murder of God's own son, and Abel, and all the other murders and evils perpetrated by mankind. The companion bell is this: the price was paid by Christ himself, who freely chose death over our sin. His sacrifice reveals God's cure for evil: love prevails, love reimburses our hatred.

If we want a God who does away with hell, we seek a God who does not exist, a God who runs outside his own rules. Those who deny hell want their freedom at no cost, refusing any consequence for their actions, and also refusing what Christ did personally for them. In other words, they are busy building their own throne in hell.

God made us co-sovereigns over his world. We are responsible for our conduct, and its consequences. Scripture is clear: God does not judge us arbitrarily but based on what we do with the freedom and power he has given us. God does not "condemn" someone to hell. It is a place some choose — and deserve — by their own actions:

> And I saw the dead, great and small, standing before the throne, and books were opened. Also another book was opened, which is the book of life. And the dead were judged by what was written in the books, by what they had done. And the sea gave up the dead in it, Death and Hades gave up the dead in them, and all were judged by what they had done (Revelation 20:12-14; see also Revelation 2:23).

"All were judged by what they had done." That is the clear and consistent message of the Bible, not only the New Testament, but throughout the Old. Hell and heaven are not places to which we are arbitrarily "predestined" by God.[5] God is not a monster. He determines where our spirit goes at death, but that determination is based on what we each have done in this life. As his co-rulers in creation, he has placed into our own hands power over our personal destiny. For good or ill, God respects the choices we make and who we become. And he holds us to *the just consequences* those choices deserve.

Knowing this, we come to see why the gift of forgiveness and new life in Christ is so essential, for it is the one way back to God, the one path of forgiveness, redemption, and restored freedom (John 14:5-10). God knows us. He allows us to commit evil, he allows us to stray, but he has given us the way to return. As we have seen, he does not desire the death or destruction of the children he has made. He made us for himself, and will do everything short of stripping us of our wills to bring us back. All will be judged by what we have done. Thankfully, accepting Christ as Lord is one of those choices. As badly as we deserve hell, God makes provision so that we can reach him instead.

This "good news" of the Gospel is the only medicine that will ever assuage our distaste for hell. For it shows us the paradox so hard to see: hell is necessary precisely *because* of God's love. God desires that all should return to him, that all should become obedient to him, that all should be saved (1 Timothy 2:4). But if someone rejects life in relationship with him, God honors that choice *precisely because* he still loves the person. God will "send" them to their self-chosen and well-deserved hell just as the shepherd in the parable separates sheep and goats into separate pens (Matthew 25). But God did not make them goats.

There is a profound irony here which many find difficult to understand: God still loves those who end in hell. There will not be any point in their existence when he stops loving them. But they will never be able to see or experience his love. It is God's very love that refuses to force them through the gates of his kingdom. They end instead behind the gates of hell. And as Lewis insightfully said, "The doors of hell are locked on the *inside*."[6] The goal of those inside is not to keep anyone in. It is to keep God out.

Living Hell

Lastly, we must not neglect this fact: just as eternal life does not begin at death, neither does hell. Hell is not a place where someone arrives suddenly, or unexpectedly. It is like a reptilian skin that grows over a person; in time, they grow into it. It is a process, sometimes of years. It is willful. Hell begins when someone begins to purposely pull away from God and flourishes in selfishness as they sink deeper into isolation and sin. It is a spiritual and moral morass that culminates first in that other death: spiritual death. Thus, hell begins here, not in the afterlife. This earthly hell does not result from some arbitrary or unfounded judgment by God. Quite the contrary. Like a backpack he carries everywhere, a person builds his mini-hell over years of sweat and labor. The pack becomes heavier and heavier. Finally, he reaches the place he wants to be: apart from God, free from God's interference. That is the real horror: hell is a self-imposed isolation.

Just what you want to be, you will be in the end.

Popular, But Wrong

If we are to speak intelligently about hell, therefore, we must jettison the popular but false mythology about both heaven and hell and hold carefully to what the Bible actually teaches. We do not reach our "eternal destiny" at the instant of death. Death is not immortal life — it is *death*.

Part of the problem is that many people wrongly believe that "immortal" means "disembodied." This idea originated not in the Bible but among Greek philosophers who considered not only the physical body but the entire physical universe to be inherently evil, despicable, and unredeemable. They therefore believed the "immortality" (literally, "undying life") we should desire could only be obtained in a disembodied, purely "spiritual" existence somewhere other than in a material world.

That whole worldview rejects the goodness of creation expressed in Holy Scripture. The Greeks' notion of immortality therefore never squares with the Bible. It is true that in death we will experience a time of disembodiment. But that is not immortal *life*, it is death. Death, I have said, leads to eventual blessing, but *is not itself* the blessing. When you hear someone mourn the loss of a relative or friend by saying "They're in a better place," the truth is, they're not. They're dead. Death is not human life, it is a sub-human, half-human existence. As even the Old Testament writers saw, it is only a kind of shadow-life where our whole person has been sundered and only a part survives. This is why the popular mythology that believes heaven is our *final* destiny is false. Heaven is not our "eternal home," God is. Heaven, according to Scripture, is merely the temporary resting place of the righteous dead, the "Paradise" Jesus speaks of in the parable of the rich man and Lazarus (Luke 16), the Paradise to which Jesus himself went *in death* prior to his resurrection (Luke 23:43). Scripture understands "heaven" as a place of peace for those who know the hope of resurrection, but it was never understood in the apostolic period as the final destiny of the redeemed.

God made us for something better. In Christian theology, immortality means the undying, everlasting life of *the whole person,* body and spirit, the person as God first made us. This is not possible until the resurrection when we are restored, body and spirit, to a full humanity like that of our risen savior (1 John 3). Christ promises not just eternal life now but a true immortality that brings back together our God-given spirit in a God-made body (1 Corinthians 15:38, compare Genesis 2:7). What Jesus is in his humanity, we shall become. That is the promise of the New Testament. And anything that promises less is either a half-gospel, or a false gospel.[7]

But remember God's timing. This final restoration of life does not happen at death. The restoration of all things comes only at Christ's return to this world for the resurrection and final judgment at "the last day" of this present age of history.[8]

God's Love Prevails

Hell is necessary because God's love must prevail along with his justice, even at death. God is love and he loves sinners despite their sin. He does not, as the wording of our sixth question would imply, randomly "condemn" anyone to hell. He sent Jesus to defeat hell. Jesus suffered a most brutal death to set right the relationship between God and his children.

So let us not go squeamish. Just as God's love prevails for those who will accept it as a gift, his love also requires that he leave evil and cold-hearted people to their chosen destiny. God allows them hell because they, too, were made co-rulers. They have the power to separate themselves forever from his love and grace, and that is what many choose.[9]

This may always seem objectionable to sensitive minds for it suggests an element of cruelty. It is, nevertheless, just one more instance of God's permissive will. Ask: would it be less cruel for God to entirely strip such persons of their own will? We cannot have it both ways. Either we — and God — honor these choices, or our humanity is gone.

Although we must accept the awful reality of hell, we must not lose sight of the glorious alternative. For those who choose Christ, for those who will obey him, the resurrection will bring a restored, fully human, and everlasting life, serving God as faithful stewards, co-rulers over his world. No more tears, no more pain, no more suffering, and the last enemy, death, finally defeated. His plan of Shared Sovereignty will not fail. Once we have learned obedience, it will finally prove itself right.

Our sixth question is answered. How could a loving God "condemn" anyone to an eternal hell? He doesn't, and won't. We build the walls of our own spiritual prisons — many are doing that right now. God gives us the means to break out. But God will, out of love, ultimately make a final separation of sheep from goats. For to do otherwise would not only be unjust, it would be an offense against love.

<u>Endnotes</u>

1. An excellent discussion of hell is found in a book I have already referenced, C. S. Lewis' *The Problem of Pain,* from which the lead line of this chapter is taken. Many may not know that Lewis also created an allegorical tale about heaven and hell in his short book, *The Great Divorce.* The insights found in both are worth every reader's time.

2. For a more in-depth discussion of these topics see my book *New Heavens, New Earth* (2002). For other discussions of the biblical understanding of "the last things" (Christian eschatology), I heartily recommend N. T. Wright's excellent treatment in *Surprised By Hope* (2008) and J. Richard Middleton's *A New Heaven and a New Earth* (2014).

3. It is true that those who hold to the Calvinist heresy argue that God does send souls arbitrarily to hell for no reason other than his own "inscrutable will." For a critique of the Calvinist view, see Appendix B.

4. Universalism is the view which says that because God is infinitely loving he cannot send anyone to hell. Therefore, whatever "heavenly" state of existence any good person may reach is the same place to which God will send all evil souls, regardless of their lives or actions.

5. Sadly, the prevalence of Calvinism in some modern churches leads many Christians to wrongly believe that God pre-condemns (damns) certain people to hell through no fault of their own — a falsehood abhorrent not only to the New Testament but to all of Holy Scripture. When Jesus warns us to fear him who has power to cast both body and soul into hell, his warning *presumes* that we can do something about it. He warns so that we will change course. It is why he calls us to "repent" (literally "to turn") and change our path. Repentance is a choice. The Calvinist must face the fact that a God and Messiah who had predetermined everyone's ultimate destiny would not bother with such warnings. The warnings would be not only needless, but deceptive and even insidious. Again, see Appendix B.

6. THE PROBLEM OF PAIN by CS Lewis © copyright CS Lewis Pte Ltd 1940 (Chapter 8, "Hell"), used by permission. The phrase is often misquoted as "The gates of hell are locked on the inside."

7. It is true that while in heaven, that temporary place of rest before the resurrection, our spirit survives death in a disembodied state, but this is not full immortality. Otherwise God would not have planted that first Tree of Life in Eden. True immortality is not, as the Greeks speculated, our natural state, or origin; it is purely a gift from God. Restoration to our full humanity in an age to come is God's plan, set out in the New Testament. We must remember this because only then do we see the true tragedy of "the second death." Like all evil, that "lake of fire" is a place God tolerates but does not desire for us. He has made us for better.

8. For a few examples see John 5:28-29, 6:39-44, 12:48; 1 Thessalonians 4:13-17, 5:2; 1 Corinthians 5:5, 15:51-52.

9. One tragedy of this final hell is that those who end there are not unaware of the beauty of the restored creation, the new heaven and new earth, where the redeemed of God dwell in his close presence. The redeemed now see Jesus face to face; the wicked outside the gates see his face, too, but continue to turn their own way.

Thirteen

Evil is widespread yet still seems to increase by the day. Why does God allow it to continue? This bring us to our seventh, final question: "Why doesn't Jesus just come back — today — and stop all this evil, and death, and destruction? He promised to return. Why is he waiting?"

Perceptive readers will see that I have already answered this indirectly. God has a long-range plan for his world that includes the restoration and perfection of creation. This work requires our participation as his stewards and co-rulers. It demands a complete purging of sin and wickedness, and a voluntary surrender of rebellious mankind to our one Lord.

But as we know, God allows us great sway in managing our lives and the broader affairs of mankind. He can interfere at any moment he chooses to directly accomplish his will, but in general leaves us to follow our chosen path.

Does this mean God is no longer involved, or ignoring us entirely? No. The Bible records instance after instance when God has stepped in directly to act, or aid us. The incarnation of his son Jesus was certainly the most obvious and direct "interference" in human history because the arrival of the incarnate Son of God changed the entire course of history. Now, roughly a third of the world's population follows Jesus as Lord. As a result, the world is less self-focused than would otherwise be true. Christ continually directs our attention back to the word and will of our true Father, and this continues to move the path of history on a much different course than we would have chosen on our own.

Still, history runs on and we naturally wonder how long God will let it. Well, the basic answer is, he intends it to go on forever.

That is the whole point of the New Testament's promises. God's plan is not an end of history but a new "age" of history to follow this one, a restored creation in which redeemed humanity will live forever. Recall the answer I gave to the question, "How long do you plan to live?"

But we also know that the New Testament — and the Old — speak of a clear end to this *present* age of history, this epoch in which we live, this time of the Church which the apostles of Jesus called "the last days."[1] God allows this period to run its course, but only he knows the moment when that course will suddenly and forever turn — with the return of Jesus.

We should not think his delay has been pointless, or fruitless. Certainly, much beauty and great good has come from mankind over the generations since the incarnation. But we have reached a point where our technological advances have made life not only much easier but more dangerous. While technology has put into our hands great weapons against things like disease, it has put into the same hands the means of mass destruction on a scale we don't even want to think about.

In other words, the longer God allows man to run amuck in this present age of history, the greater danger we face that we will do more damage than good to his overall creation, and ourselves.

How much will he tolerate? When will he say, "Enough"?

The answer to that question — not surprisingly — can also be learned from what God has revealed in the record of Scripture. Part of the answer is in Paul's first letter to his coworker Timothy, referenced in the previous chapter:

> First of all, then, I urge that supplications, prayers, intercessions, and thanksgivings be made for all people . . . This is good, and it is pleasing in the sight of God our Savior, *who desires all people to be saved and to come to the knowledge of the truth.* For there is one God, and there is one mediator between God and men, the man Christ Jesus, who gave himself as a ransom for all (1 Timothy 2:1-6; *emphasis* added).

God loves all he has made, and he *desires* that all people would turn to him and receive the gift of eternal life. This is the clear, central message not only of the New Testament but also of the Old. For in the second book of the Bible, God makes it clear that his "calling" is not just for a few, it is for all people. The "special" calling of Israel was for them to be "a priestly people, a holy nation" (Exodus 19:6)[2] with a purpose: to manifest the love and laws of God *to the whole world.* God was never interested only in redeeming (salvaging) one particular nation or people. Israel was chosen to be God's *instrument* drawing other people groups back to their common Father, a "servant nation" that would be a beacon to all others:

> It is too light a thing that you should be my servant to raise up the tribes of Jacob and to bring back the preserved of Israel; I will make you as a light for the nations, that my salvation may reach to the end of the earth (Isaiah 49:6).

God's call to humankind ever since the Fall of Adam was a global call, intended for everyone: for you, for me, for all. God made this foundational truth known to the great Israelite forefather, Abraham. God tested Abraham by asking him to offer his son and heir Isaac on an altar of sacrifice, knowing he would stop Abraham from carrying out that brutal act of child sacrifice. But because Abraham proved his unwavering love and obedience, even in what surely seemed an ungodly and irrational request, God tells Abraham that his obedience is the seed through which the whole world would one day be blessed:

> By myself I have sworn, declares the LORD, because you have done this and have not withheld your son, your only son, I will surely bless you, and I will surely multiply your offspring as the stars of heaven and as the sand that is on the seashore. And your offspring shall possess the gate of his enemies, and *in your offspring shall all the nations of the earth be blessed,* because you have obeyed my voice (Genesis 22:16-18; *emphasis added*).

God restated the same promise to Abrahams' son Isaac, the son whose life God spared on that mountain top:

> Sojourn in this land, and I will be with you and will bless you, for to you and to your offspring I will give all these lands, and I will establish the oath that I swore to Abraham your father. I will multiply your offspring as the stars of heaven and will give to your offspring all these lands. And in your offspring *all the nations of the earth shall be blessed,* because Abraham obeyed my voice and kept my charge, my commandments, my statutes, and my laws (Genesis 26:3-5; *emphasis added*).[3]

God's promised blessing for all the nations was fulfilled in the sending of his own son Jesus as the sacrifice for the forgiveness of mankind's sin. This, too, had been foreshadowed cryptically when Abraham took his son Isaac to that mountain top:

> When they came to the place of which God had told him, Abraham built the altar there and laid the wood in order and bound Isaac his son and laid him on the altar, on top of the wood. Then Abraham reached out his hand and took the knife to slaughter his son. But the angel of the LORD called to him from heaven and said, "Abraham, Abraham!" And he said, "Here I am." He said, "Do not lay your hand on the boy or do anything to him, for now I know that you fear God, seeing you have not withheld your son, your only son, from me." And Abraham lifted up his eyes and looked, and behold, behind him was a ram, caught in a thicket by his horns. And Abraham went and took the ram and offered it up as a burnt offering instead of his son. So Abraham called the name of that place, "The LORD will provide"; as it is said to this day, "On the mount of the LORD it shall be provided" (Genesis 22:9-14).

"The Lord will provide." The pledge to bless all nations was fulfilled in a way Abraham could never have seen nor imagined. For "the place of which God had told him" was a mountain "in the land of Moriah" which in later generations would become the site of a city named Jerusalem where Jesus, the "lamb of God," would one day be slaughtered.[4]

But before that happened, there would be a very long delay, a delay during which the Jewish people became impatient. They began to doubt that God would ever act, that he would ever come to set things right in this broken world.

Why did God delay his promise to Abraham for over a thousand years? In part because he was letting mankind try to run the world, and bear their own constant failures. All that time, however, God was preparing the world to recognize the true "sacrifice" when he arrived. Many of Jesus' own countrymen failed to recognize him when he appeared on the scene; a good many *did* recognize him but realized he was a threat to their power. They had him destroyed — or so they hoped.

In a similar way, we Christians may wonder why God delays, holding off Christ's final return to earth. His patience with us, his children, is a major part of the answer. He desires all to be saved, although it is very apparent many will not accept that offer. Many refused the offer even when Jesus stood right in front of them; many will still refuse the offer when Jesus stands before us again.

Even as our impatience simmers, we should be grateful that God's patience is beyond what we can imagine. From his divine viewpoint, observing our actions and constant misbehavior from outside of time, he possesses the unique advantage of not only knowing where we are headed but knowing how and when he himself will bring his plan for human history to its fulfillment.

Part of that plan is the work of his Church, the Body of Christ around the world, bringing the Gospel of Jesus to all nations. This takes time, and God knows exactly how long. What seems to us an intolerable delay is the exact period of time God will use to accomplish his purpose. As St. Peter found, even the earliest Christians had to be reminded of this:

> Remember the predictions of the holy prophets and the commandment of the Lord and Savior through your apostles, knowing this first of all, that scoffers will come in the last days with scoffing, following their own sinful desires. They will say, "Where is the promise of his coming? For ever since the fathers fell asleep, all

things are continuing as they were from the beginning of creation." For they deliberately overlook this fact, that the heavens existed long ago, and the earth was formed out of water and through water by the word of God, and that by means of these the world that then existed was deluged with water and perished. But by the same word the heavens and earth that now exist are stored up for fire, being kept until the day of judgment and destruction of the ungodly. But do not overlook this one fact, beloved, that with the Lord one day is as a thousand years, and a thousand years as one day. *The Lord is not slow to fulfill his promise* as some count slowness, *but is patient toward you, not wishing that any should perish, but that all should reach repentance* . . . Since all these things are thus to be dissolved, what sort of people ought you to be in lives of holiness and godliness, waiting for and hastening the coming of the day of God, because of which the heavens will be set on fire and dissolved, and the heavenly bodies will melt as they burn! But according to his promise we are waiting for new heavens and a new earth in which righteousness dwells (2 Peter 3:1-13, *emphasis added*).

God could step in and stop evil today, this moment. He delays. Jesus could return this evening. He waits. God knows evil has been with us since our first parents; it will be with us to the last child. Stopping evil, however, is not his only consideration. The broader consideration is how to turn people back to himself, the one God. That is the work of the Gospel in which we are each called to engage. God's redemption of humankind through the incarnation, death, and resurrection of his own child, the true son of Adam, will overcome every evil for those who will learn obedience, to love what he has commanded (John 14:15).

Through the centuries of the Old Testament period, God taught the Jews the importance of love, obedience, and willing sacrifice. They learned the lesson, yet they were not faithful in living it. In Jesus, God made the one sacrifice that could be effective for us all. God himself provided that sacrifice. God, in a real sense, offered himself — the innocent victim and holy warrior — for the sinner.

God's Patient Plan

To this day, this is a truth that offends sinful man, men and women who want to claim credit for their own goodness and believe their "good life" should save them. It won't. One thing will: the gift and sacrifice of Jesus.

This lesson takes many of us a lifetime to finally learn. Thankfully, God is *very* patient. He is not in a hurry to bring down the final curtain on this present age of history. I wish he would hurry up, but that is because I am selfish and impatient. I want to see God's plan made clear to the whole world. I want God to act decisively, now.

Gratefully, God is more patient than me.

Like Peter, St. Paul reminds us that we often misread God's silence and patience:

> Or do you presume on the riches of his kindness and forbearance and patience, not knowing that God's kindness is meant to lead you to repentance? But because of your hard and impenitent heart you are storing up wrath for yourself on the day of wrath when God's righteous judgment will be revealed (Romans 2:4-5).

We should never presume that God's forbearance means he is ignoring our misconduct. As Peter and Paul both tell us, God is patient for one reason, so that we would turn and repent. We also do well to remember what St. Gregory once said, that the God who has promised forgiveness to all who repent has not promised a tomorrow in which to do it.[5]

We may find too late that God's patience, like our own, has its limit. Indeed, there is a very sobering moment when Jesus teaches the crowd something that we ought never to forget:

> "Do you think that these Galileans were worse sinners than all the other Galileans, because they suffered in this way? No, I tell you; but unless you repent, you will all likewise perish. Or those eighteen on whom the tower in Siloam fell and killed them: do you think that they

were worse offenders than all the others who lived in Jerusalem? No, I tell you; but unless you repent, you will all likewise perish" ...

He went on his way through towns and villages, teaching and journeying toward Jerusalem. And someone said to him, "Lord, will those who are saved be few?" And he said to them, "Strive to enter through the narrow door. For many, I tell you, will seek to enter and will not be able. When once the master of the house has risen and shut the door, and you begin to stand outside and to knock at the door, saying, 'Lord, open to us,' then he will answer you, 'I do not know where you come from.' Then you will begin to say, 'We ate and drank in your presence, and you taught in our streets.' But he will say, 'I tell you, I do not know where you come from. Depart from me, all you workers of evil!' In that place there will be weeping and gnashing of teeth, when you see Abraham and Isaac and Jacob and all the prophets in the kingdom of God but you yourselves cast out. And people will come from east and west, and from north and south, and recline at table in the kingdom of God. And behold, some are last who will be first, and some are first who will be last" (Luke 13:2-5, 22-30).

This passage should be taped up by every doorway in our house for those days when we become complacent. If we are Christians, we should memorize and repeat it often, especially when we smugly start to think we have moved to the head of the line.

God made a global promise to all the world through Abraham, and as Abraham's spiritual offspring, the Church bears that call and must do its part:

> "And this gospel of the kingdom will be proclaimed throughout the whole world as a testimony to all nations, and *then* the end will come" (Matthew 24:14; *emphasis added*).

This prophecy tells us part of what must take place before Jesus will return, and we find our "marching orders" at the end of Matthew's gospel when Jesus speaks to his disciples after his resurrection:

"All authority in heaven and on earth has been given to me. Go therefore and make disciples *of all nations,* baptizing them in the name of the Father and of the Son and of the Holy Spirit, teaching them to observe all that I have commanded you. And behold, *I am with you always,* to the end of the age" (Matthew 28:18-20; *emphasis* added).

Although Jesus left us physically not long after that, he did not abandon us. He is with us through his Holy Spirit, as he promised, to the end of this present age. Then, and only then, will he physically return to accomplish his final purposes: the final judgment, his renewal of the whole creation, and the establishment of his kingdom among all who will bow to him in love.

Luke's Gospel tells of the same promise:

Then he said to them, "These are my words that I spoke to you while I was still with you, that everything written about me in the Law of Moses and the Prophets and the Psalms must be fulfilled." Then he opened their minds to understand the Scriptures, and said to them, "Thus it is written, that the Christ should suffer and on the third day rise from the dead, and that repentance for the forgiveness of sins should be proclaimed in his name *to all nations,* beginning from Jerusalem" (Luke 24:44-48; *emphasis* added).

He Will Return

Jesus — as King — will return. The New Testament is not vague or unclear on this point. So, as God's people, we have work to do. The truth is, we should spend less time wondering about the possible date of his appearance and be busy doing what he has commanded. We are still his stewards, his co-rulers; we do better to be about our Father's business and spend less time mentally dictating our preferred timetable.

It seems to us, from the human perspective, that God is not in a hurry. But our "time" does not constrain him. A thousand of our years is no different than an instant in the divine eyes. Jesus blinks, and centuries pass before him. When we feel frustrated at God's apparent delay, and the fact that he continues to allow evil to thrive

— and sometimes rule — we need to be on our knees asking that he will give us the kind of patience we ourselves have received from him. There were many days in my life when, had God "brought down the curtain" on my life, I would have been the sorrier. Let us give our fellow men and women the same patience.

We rightly long for the return of Jesus. But the fact is, most of us will likely hit the gate of death first. So be it. Our goal is to know and serve Jesus as far as we can right now and leave the future in his very capable hands. Those hands, which still bear nail marks, know how to handle evil, even when we don't.

The next horrid news story will come. The next human or natural catastrophe will happen when we least expect.[6] Such events will always shake us; hopefully they will always warn us of the awful destructive force of evil. We are still in training as co-rulers. Our very patient Lord continues to train us in love and righteousness even in the midst of evil and suffering. Though I long for his return, I am not anxious for him to show up unexpectedly, as we know he will (Matthew 24:43; 1 Thessalonians 5:2; 2 Peter 3:10).

God delays. Jesus continues to warn us. Are we paying attention to the signals?

No Time To Be Lost

God is patient, but there is no time to be lost. Today could be the last for any one of us.[7] Tomorrow could be the unexpected day of his return. If you are not yet part of the Christian work of carrying God's love and blessing to all the nations, why not?

Does God need your help? No. Does he want your help. Yes. You, too, are one of his co-sovereign rulers in this world. Your individual life may touch very little of its history; still, you will touch many lives. How many will not hear God's good news in Jesus if you don't do what you can? God has put real power in your hands. What are you doing with the life he has given *you?*

At times we may despair because the task is so great. We struggle to change even ourselves. How can we expect to change the world? When we fall into that pothole, we might consider this encouragement that Peter wrote to the young churches of his day:

> Like newborn infants, long for the pure spiritual milk, that by it you may grow up into salvation — if indeed you have tasted that the Lord is good. As you come to him, a living stone rejected by men but in the sight of God chosen and precious, you yourselves like living stones are being built up as a spiritual house, to be *a holy priesthood,* to offer spiritual sacrifices acceptable to God through Jesus Christ . . . But you are *a chosen race, a royal priesthood, a holy nation,* a people for his own possession, that you may proclaim the excellencies of him who called you out of darkness into his marvelous light. Once you were not a people, but now you are God's people; once you had not received mercy, but now you have received mercy (1 Peter 2:2-10; *emphasis* added).

We are living stones, God's true temple, "God's people." The Church is God's Israel in this present age. He entrusts us with the work of bringing blessing to all the nations. We have come far, we have often failed, there is still much to do. But staring up at the height of the mountain will never encourage us to start climbing. Small steps, though, will eventually carry us to the top.

Endnotes

1. There is much confusion about this phrase today. In the New Testament, the writers are clear that "the last days" of this present history are not in the future but the present: those last days began with the birth, death, and resurrection of the one by whom and through whom all things were first made (John 1; 1 Peter 1:20; 2 Peter 3:1-3; Acts 2:17; Hebrews 1:2).
2. "Now therefore, if you will indeed obey my voice and keep my covenant, you shall be my treasured possession among all peoples, for all the earth is mine; and you shall be to me *a kingdom of priests and a holy nation."* These are the words that you shall speak to the people of Israel. So Moses came and called the elders of the people and set before them all these words that the Lord had commanded him. All the people

answered together and said, "All that the Lord has spoken we will do" (Exodus 19:5-7).

3. Similar examples of this "global promise" are found spread across the Old Testament: Psalm 67:2, 72:17; Isaiah 66:18; Jeremiah 3:17.

4. The mountain where Abraham almost sacrificed Isaac was in "the land of Moriah." Moriah as a place name is mentioned only one other time in the Old Testament, by the Chronicler who referred to "Mount Moriah" (2 Chronicles 3:1) as the site of the first Jerusalem, the mountain on which "The City of David" and Solomon's temple were built — and by which, at a place outside the wall named Golgotha, the heir of David, Jesus of Nazareth, was crucified. God told Abraham that he himself would "provide the sacrifice" on that mountain. At the crucifixion of Jesus, God fulfilled that ancient promise.

5. Gregory likely borrowed this from St. Augustine of Hippo who said, "God has promised forgiveness to your repentance, but he has not promised tomorrow to your procrastination."

6. As I was finalizing this book, the Covid-19 pandemic hit.

7. I was recently reminded of this — painfully. While still completing a major edit of this book, I was in a serious rollover accident in a blizzard in which I might have been killed.

Fourteen

I have answered the seven questions posed in the first chapter. In Chapter Eight, I summarized the answers to the first three. Let me summarize here the answers to the last four:

4. Our fourth question: "If God allows something terrible to happen to me personally, doesn't that show he really doesn't love me or never cared about me in the first place?" No. God gave his son's life to demonstrate his unfailing, eternal love for you. "Bad things happen to good people" because bad things happen to all people. We can begin eternal life in this present life, but we still share the common troubles of sinful, broken humanity. God does not insulate us from those troubles. Many we bring on ourselves. Though difficult, they can help us learn to rely on his grace.

5. The fifth: "Why do we have to die?" To enter God's kingdom requires a willing choice, a decision to "be born over again" and accept eternal life in Christ. Ultimately, we must give up our present, corruptible body. Death does not end our life. It frees us from the corrupted flesh of this present world so that we can receive an immortal body in the resurrection, a body no longer subject to pain, disease, or death.

6. The sixth question asked, "How could a loving God condemn anyone to an eternal Hell?" God does not "condemn" anyone to this fate; God "assigns" them this destiny because they have chosen it. "Hell," both at death and after the resurrection and final judgment, is where God isolates them from fellowship with himself, for *that is their desire*. God compels no one into his kingdom. He must therefore provide a place for those who reject him. Like eternal life, hell can begin in this present life.

7. The last question was, "Why doesn't Jesus just come back — today — and stop all this evil, and death, and destruction? He promised to return. Why is he waiting?" The short answer is, God is patient, not wanting anyone to perish in hell forever. He shows kindness and mercy by allowing us to limp along so that more people over the generations have the opportunity to hear the good news of Jesus. God is growing his kingdom. At the time God chooses, Jesus *will* return to fully establish that kingdom in a new creation.

My answers to all seven questions have been focused through the lens of long pastoral experience. They give me hope, as I hope they will for each reader, knowing that God's sovereignty overarches our own, not only for this life but for the world yet to come.

Others may arrive at different answers. I hope they share them. The answers I have given are rooted in Holy Scripture. I could cite thousands of other passages that are relevant to these questions but to do so would have been to ask the reader to essentially read the whole Bible. Of course, I hope every reader does that anyway. Because if you begin reading with an understanding of Shared Sovereignty, everything you read from Genesis on may take on new light and deeper meaning.

But be careful not to misunderstand what I have said about Shared Sovereignty. We must never jump to the false conclusion that we are the master of nature. As I have tried to make clear, we are merely its stewards. Nature has one Master, the one who is ultimately sovereign. Modern man's problem is that so many appoint themselves as the supposed master of all things. They do exactly what the serpent invited Eve to do, to become their own god. Our role as co-sovereigns is never exercised rightly, or effectively, unless we keep ourselves under obedience to the one who made it all and entrusted to us a certain role.

None of what I have offered is a sugar pill. The answers I have given do not "smooth things over" between us and God. We will continue to be upset and experience doubts whenever life's tragedies overwhelm us. In some ways, the answers I have given may tempt some readers to rebel against God even more. As evil and suffering continue to strike us, our tendency is so often to seek a scapegoat. We grew up learning to be blame-shifters, so our "gut" emotional response to evil — especially personal suffering — may still be to blame God. As the friend I mentioned in Chapter Three suggested, if God has the power to stop tragedies and doesn't, shouldn't he have to shoulder the blame?

It may be a natural response, but once we understand Shared Sovereignty and accept our role as stewards in co-ruling God's world we can move beyond that knee-jerk reaction of blaming God. I discussed how our world would crumble into chaos if God interfered in human affairs every few minutes. Any semblance of human freedom would vanish like smoke in a strong divine wind. So God restrains his power to allow us to exercise the roles he has given us. We can critique his methods, but the truth is, most of us don't want to surrender the freedom we have to become subhuman machines who never do wrong because God manipulates our every thought and controls every action.

My hope is that each reader will ponder what I have offered and prayerfully apply these answers to his or her own experience. Evil will not disappear tomorrow so you will have plenty of opportunity. But remember that while God permits evil, he never ignores it — or its perpetrators. He has shown that he can and does deal with evil. Scripture also makes plain that those who perpetrate it will be held to account. Many people fear the reality of our ultimate, final judgment. For me, it is one of the things that gives me genuine hope. When I see how the wicked seem to thrive in this present world, I take a breath and remember that their judgment will not delay forever.

Our Real Pursuit
One of my main goals with this book is to help the reader grow spiritually in his or her relationship with God, a relationship that requires trust. We will have made no progress at all, though, if we rest our entire spiritual pursuit on rational answers to what are deeply emotional questions. In the end, our real hope is to turn

prayerfully to God for answers in each situation. Our solution to any spiritual dilemma is to know God better, to love him more, and better obey his will. It is necessary — indeed it is essential — to express our doubts, to ask life's difficult questions with honesty, and not dodge the answers.

When those answers are difficult to digest, we still must not shrink from pursuing them. We are building our relationship with an all-powerful God. We should not be surprised if his spirit, his presence, and his ways sometimes overwhelm us, or confuse us. Indeed, if we don't get overwhelmed at times we are probably worshipping a false god. Our knowledge, understanding, and even *awareness* of evil are very tiny in comparison to God's wisdom. His understanding and wisdom will forever be beyond our own (Isaiah 55:9); we will not fully comprehend the mysteries of how his will operates and all he does to combat evil on our behalf. As is true even in a human relationship, there is a huge element of the unknown and of trust demanded from us.

So, we must never be ashamed of our questions, or shrink from our doubts. God himself has placed such a mind and heart within us. He knows that heart, he interplays with that mind. He will not love us less because we sometimes harbor doubts. If our love for him is genuine, he will not fault our mental slights and weaknesses because evil has overwhelmed us. His "shoulders" are broad enough to bear us up. They are the shoulders that hung from the cross. We need never fear his rejection. "All that the Father gives me," Jesus promised, "will come to me, and whoever comes to me I will never cast out" (John 6:37). He wants us to approach him with confidence, not fear.

Our daily endeavor and lifelong pursuit should be thoughtful but prayerful Christian living. Such a life cannot be sustained merely by intellectual debates about God, the universe, evil, or ourselves. Christian living is not the product of "man's search for God" but *the result* of God's unwavering pursuit of us, his very rebellious creatures.

Life In The Holy Spirit

If we have surrendered our life to Christ, the Spirit of God is dwelling within us. We must daily bow to him. This is the path to spiritual maturity. We are, from beginning to end, his workmanship (Ephesians 2:10). Genuine, faithful Christian living involves not just the *knowledge* of who Jesus Christ is but the daily willingness to submit to his lordship, even when catastrophic, world-altering events happen. The most catastrophic, world-altering events of all time were his crucifixion and resurrection. He is capable of helping us through any challenge.

Christianity is frequently mischaracterized by those who have never lived it. It is thought to be "pie in the sky by and by" only by those who have never tried to carry on a serious Christian life. As G. K. Chesterton once said, "The Christian ideal has not been tried and found wanting; it has been found difficult, and left untried."[1] Those who actually commit to living out the Gospel know that faith is not "blind obedience" in the face of contrary evidence; faith is the deep trust we discover in bowing before God's incomprehensible love, even in the face of the most terrible suffering and tragedy. We are able to bow because we know what Jesus endured on the cross. And if we want to see the cost of man's wickedness, we need only look at that bloodstained wood.

So when pain, suffering, or tragedy hit us, we must not cower. Evil will try to stare us down. We will defeat it only when our eyes stay fixed on Jesus. When I sometimes tremble at the forces of evil around me, I remember how Jesus was tempted by Satan in the wilderness, at the very beginning of his ministry (Matthew 4; Luke 4). Jesus knows what we face, for he has faced it before us. He challenges us to take up our cross and follow him daily. So far, most of us have not been nailed to one.

As his disciples, we know the cross did not end the life of our Lord. Instead, it brought to light what God has planned for all who love him: "the regeneration" of God's world where humanity will grow to the perfection to which God calls us (Matthew 19:21, 5:48). Speaking of that age, Jesus told the first disciples:

> "Truly, I say to you, in the new world ["in the regeneration"], when the Son of Man will sit on his glorious throne, you who have followed me will also sit on twelve thrones, judging the twelve tribes of Israel" (Matthew 19:28).[2]

I cite this because it reveals something crucially important: God's plan for Shared Sovereignty is not for this present world only. It is inherent in his design for creation and humankind. We must never neglect to shoulder the responsibilities God has given us, for we will carry those responsibilities in that world yet to come (Hebrews 2:5). Our daily battle with evil in all of its forms is part of Christian faith and living, until evil is conquered and finally abolished.

Our combat with evil is empowered by God's overwhelming and unrelenting love for us; our courage to fight is born of our grateful reception of his singular gift: Christ's sacrifice on the cross. In bending our knee to the Son of God as our true sovereign, we find true strength to stand against evil.

Yet some knees cannot be bent. Humankind as a whole continues to resist God's rule; not content with the power he has given us, they seek to usurp his, too. In St. Stephen's only recorded sermon — which got him stoned to death — he chastised his fellow Jews for their hardness of heart: "You stiff-necked people, uncircumcised in heart and ears, you always resist the Holy Spirit. As your fathers did, so do you" (Acts 7:51). What was true of his countrymen remains true of many today. Some hearts grow so hard that they can no longer be turned. Their bearers tread along the spiritual death march of selfishness, trying to turn the world into an image of themselves, not only resisting God's grace but anxious to blame him for all the evils we ourselves create.

To come under the lordship of Jesus, to be "in Christ," means we must first turn around. The biblical meaning of "repentance" is to turn about, to do a one-eighty, to turn back to God. This means a new beginning, but it requires that we quite literally die to our old self and hardened heart. St. Paul put it this way:

I have been crucified with Christ. It is no longer I who live, but Christ who lives in me. And the life I now live in the flesh I live by faith in the Son of God, who loved me and gave himself for me (Galatians 2:20).

Apart From Christ, There Is No Hope

Sadly, the seven questions we have considered have often been weaponized by those whose hearts are hard, those who wish not only to question God but want to indict him "for crimes against humanity." It is an attitude not far from that of Adam and Eve as they hid in the garden trying to think up an excuse for their own behavior. Human nature — our old nature — has changed very little over so many generations.

More sadly, hearts hardened against God cannot experience his love. And apart from God's pursuing love, there is no hope for any person. Christ said plainly he is the only pathway to the God (John 14:6). Many false gods, false messiahs, and political leaders over the centuries have claimed otherwise; fine claims, but none have died on a cross.

If your own heart has become hardened, I hope what I have offered in this book will make it pliable again. I hope these chapters will soak into your soul in such a way that the next time suffering or catastrophe strikes, you will hold confidence in God and in Christ Jesus to help you overcome it. "Be faithful unto death," Jesus promises, "and I will give you the crown of life" (Revelation 2:10). He has made you his co-ruler. Our life in Christ is not to be about ourselves first, but about how we share God's power and love with others. God did not need to make the world, or us. He made us for no other reason than to shower his love on us.

That must be the core of our own life. It is the purpose of Christian living. None of us will ever be fully up to the task. All of us will stumble when personal suffering hits. But just as a knowledge of God's greatness can overpower us, the power of his love can undergird us in those times of pain or fear. Go to an online Bible sometime and do a word search for "do not fear." You will be amazed. When evil rears before us, God does not want us to cower but to have confidence in him. Jesus affirmed this at his Passover meal with his disciples just before his crucifixion: "I have said these things to you, that in me you may have peace. In the world you will have tribulation. But take heart; I have overcome the world" (John 16:33).

If you were to ask the average Christian today if they would be willing to undergo martyrdom for their faith, most would say something like, "Oh, I could never do that! I am not that strong." But in fact, every Christian has already laid his or her life down; they have laid it at the foot of the cross:

> Do you not know that all of us who have been baptized into Christ Jesus were baptized into his death? We were buried therefore with him by baptism into death, in order that, just as Christ was raised from the dead by the glory of the Father, we too might walk in newness of life. For if we have been united with him in a death like his, we shall certainly be united with him in a resurrection like his. We know that our old self was crucified with him in order that the body of sin might be brought to nothing, so that we would no longer be enslaved to sin (Romans 6:3-6).

The good news — the *great* news — in Jesus is that freedom from sin means freedom from fear. We will each someday die, but we need not die spiritually. We need no longer fear what lies ahead because we have already "passed from death to life." Eternal life, remember, begins not at death but, as Paul just said, at our baptism. Far from being "pie in the sky by and by," life in Christ means new life *here and now,* free from the fear of evil, even when it attacks us personally.

If at times we slump back into fear or wallow in anxiety about all the evil in the world, we are forgetting that God has put power into our hands to help stop it. If we fall into the game of blaming God for human evil, questioning God about why he allows it, this is not a failure of our intellectual capacities but of our hearts. We are, under the cloak of being morally indignant, trying to avoid our own responsibility as his co-rulers.

It is not just that God allows evil; we do, too. We are the ones who allow evil "to run free" when we don't stand against it or combat it, when we "give in" and simply tolerate what we have the power to stop. If that battle causes you pain, bear it. In doing so, you share in and demonstrate the divine intolerance of evil. You call it what it is, and you help assuage the problem of evil as best you personably can.

No, you will not stop evil entirely. But you can stop what is under your control. If *every* person could restrain evil in his own heart, the world would be very different. At least we would slow or delay the effects of evil. Better that than doing nothing.

Like it or not, God has placed a heavy responsibility on each of us. Blame him for that, if you wish, but we are not helpless. The weight of evil often seems intolerable. Jesus found out the hard way, on the cross.

But there is Good News. He has overcome this world. And when we bring ourselves under his lordship, we advance the power of his kingdom over the reign of evil.

So we can confidently say, "The Lord is my helper;
I will not fear; what can man do to me?" — *Hebrews 13:6*

Endnotes

1. G. K. Chesterton, *What's Wrong With The World,* Part 1, Chapter 5.
2. When Jesus speaks of the disciples "judging" the tribes of Israel, we must not take this to mean judging or condemning for wrongdoing as in a modern court of law. The Old Testament concept of the "judge," as in the Book of Judges, was that of the national or tribal leader, the one who acted as governor and sovereign in the absence of a king (at that time the Jews had no king except God), although such "judges" did sometimes rule in determining guilt or innocence in cases of alleged wrongdoing. Jesus' point is that his disciples will "sit on thrones" acting as overseers, governors of peoples and nations.

See what kind of love the Father has given to us, that we should be called children of God; and so we are.   — *1 John 3:1*

Final Thoughts

When St. John wrote the words above to the young churches he served, they were in a time of tremendous persecution. Evil was rampant, then as now. John's words prompted these few final thoughts.

In Christ, we have been given an opportunity for a fresh beginning in our relationship with God, children of the new birth. While awaiting God's new creation, we can each become such ourselves (2 Corinthians 5:17-18). God originally made us to share his own nature, "children" who reflect his own image, his creativity, and his sovereign rule over what is, start to finish, *his* world. What a remarkable privilege, one we too often abuse.

But we sacrificed that birth right by choice, by choosing sin over God's love. Not Adam, not Eve. All of us. As God's stewards and co-rulers we have often failed, personally and collectively. Even God's "chosen" people of the Old Testament "did what was evil in my eyes and chose that in which I did not delight" (Isaiah 66:4). A central theme of this book is that it is our own moral failing that brought evil down on our heads. We are not free to condemn God because he allows evil, since it is *our abuse* of the power he granted us that causes evil.

Running in our moral nakedness to hide behind a bush in our modern "Eden" — just as Adam and Eve found — will not wash. Seeking an excuse for evil and pointing the finger back at God will not stand. Though we shirk our personal and moral duty, God "makes clothing" for us by giving us his moral law, by making us aware of what he expects and requires of each of us. We can plead ignorance; it will always be feigned ignorance. For even pagans know of God's justice, and know right from wrong (Romans 1).

At the arrival of Christ in our world, the ultimate son of Adam, we are allowed to see what *godly* humanity actually looks like. And he looks a lot like ourselves, except for sin. God's pursuing love constrains us to be better than our fallen selves; his goal is to turn each of us into a Christ-like man or woman, a little god not unlike the Son of God. But this requires our consent, for he will not compel us. It requires our work, our love, our cooperation. But it is the only medicine that will save us from despair in the ugly face of evil. To recapture a sense of God's deep and unrelenting love for each of us — yes, even for those in hell — is the only armor that can shield us in the midst of suffering, when evil strikes and that ice sheet of creeping hopelessness overtakes us.

I shared a few of my experiences in the opening chapter. Consider your own experience. We have all faced problems, horrible times, and sometimes catastrophe. We may want to hide in ivory towers; but most of us live in mud huts. Evil surrounds and threatens us from nearly every side and angle, and can not only oppress us but overwhelm us. What I have written here I offer in the hope that it will touch you in your spiritual core and enable you to think more clearly about these very real, very troubling questions that burden us. If you have, as I sometimes have, wandered from God, I pray this book will turn your face back toward him and help you fall back in love with the one who made you. If you have not yet met him, I pray he will catch you in some dark alley of your life and pull you back from the one thing that is worse than physical death. The world has one Savior. You don't need to look for him, because he is looking for you.

It is possible that this book will just upset you and turn you further away from God. That is your choice.

The deep spiritual alienation of our era coupled with advanced technology means that we face, perhaps more than prior generations, a very heavy burden as co-sovereign rulers of this world with God. If the horrors of the 20th century taught us anything it is that in the 21st humankind is in greater danger than ever of not only physical self-destruction but spiritual self-destruction. In the spiritual vacuum that marks much of modern, secular societies, the threat of spiritual death for many grow worse each day. It has become an epidemic. As God's stewards, we have an obligation to our fellow humans to bring the good news of Christ into their lives. I have pleaded that you might take your part. I hope you will.

Love can always surmount tragedy. In first chapter, I mentioned the tragic death of my sister Mimi and the devastation it wrought on her young family. I am happy to report that Lee, her widowed husband, did a spectacular job raising their son and daughter. Lee is one of my heroes, a champion of the first order, stronger by far than those ridiculous, cartoonish superstars you see parading across the big screen. Against the most difficult odds, he and their children weathered a storm I would never want to face. They show that self-sacrificing love beats out all the competitors, imitating Christ-like love at great cost.

In a world marred by self-centered egotism, more and more unfettered from the commands of the One who made us, I do worry for the coming generations. Unless our present societies can bring themselves back under obedience to God's right commands, evil will grow worse. This can be no surprise. When you drive God out of a society, you end with a godless society. Ironically, it is often those farthest from God who demand that God should act to stop evil, that "he should step in and do something!" They don't seem to understand that if he steps in, he will be stepping on *us*.

I have never believed we humans can create a Utopia on this present earth, however well-intentioned we pretend to be, but I know that God's overarching plan for us is a *restored* creation where his Lordship and his will are daily obeyed, as many of us ask in the Lord's Prayer. That day can only come by God's grace. Christians, today as throughout the Church's history, must live with one foot firmly planted in this present world and the other planted deeply in that further creation we cannot yet see. Good news again: Christ has gone ahead. If anyone is impatient for that new world and a final end of human evil, it is him.

When and exactly how his kingdom will arrive in its fullness, God alone knows. We are called to seek it, to desire it, to help give it birth, but to desire and seek him above all else. Christ knows evil more deeply than we ever can. He continues to push history forward toward *his* goal, toward a world whose joys and beauty we cannot begin to imagine.

Thankfully, he can.

So we do not lose heart. Though our outer self is wasting away, our inner self is being renewed day by day. For this light momentary affliction is preparing for us an eternal weight of glory beyond all comparison, as we look not to the things that are seen but to the things that are unseen.

— *2 Corinthians 4:16-18*

Appendix A
Why Should We Pray?

Why should we pray, and how can prayer work?

These are common questions I encountered doing pastoral ministry. They are very legitimate concerns, in particular for anyone stuck in a worldview where they believe God has "foreordained" every event in history (see Appendix B). Some people believe God controls absolutely everything that happens, so they are left wondering why we should bother to pray at all.

Understanding the biblical principle of Shared Sovereignty, however, we must consider prayer knowing that God not only gives us the power to make decisions, but that he has laid a direct commandment on us to rightly carry out our role as stewards in his world. Prayer is an essential part of that role, and of our underlying relationship with God. But this still leaves some questions floating about.

Does God need our advice? Of course not. Are we going to tell him something he does not already know? No. So again, why pray?

Let us examine two points.

First, God commands us to pray. But there are different types of prayer, the most fundamental of which is praise and adoration of God. This prayer asks nothing, and seeks nothing. It is prayer that shows our love of God for his own sake. Prayer can sometimes involve direct confession of our sins to God. Here, we are not "pleading our case." We merely want to be open with God, to show our awareness of our failings, and to ask his forgiveness. We know we cannot bargain for forgiveness. God offers it to us freely, a part of our salvation.

But much of our prayer in focused on what is usually called intercession or petition. In this, we ask God for some specific guidance, or some specific good. And we have the pledge of Jesus that whatever we ask "in his name" that is in accord with the Father's will, will be granted by God (John 14:13; Mark 11:24; Matthew 21:22). Prayer offered in faith — that is, trusting that God will both listen and grant what he desires — is essential if we are to grow in the life of the Spirit.

Second, Jesus specifically taught his disciples to pray, not just by his words but by his own example. He would often slip away to a quiet place to spend time with his Father, and pray, and he encourages us to do the same (Matthew 6:6). If Jesus, the Son of God incarnate, prayed to his Father, even though he already possessed deep insight to God and the nature of the world, it shows that there is both power and purpose in prayer. For Jesus prayer was both a form of communion with God but also a way of discerning his own course. The most poignant example are the prayers Jesus uttered the evening before Good Friday, just before his arrest.

At his final supper before the resurrection, Jesus offered a long prayer for his disciples and for all who would come to believe through their future witness. That night in the Garden of Gethsemane, Jesus prayed — in great agony — to discern what he must do. He prayed that he would submit his own will to that of the Father, knowing this meant he would face a very painful death the following day.

This, then, is why we should pray. We pray because Jesus taught us to, and he demonstrated that this intimate communication with our common Father is absolutely central to our relationship with God. Some might think that because Jesus was much more closely tied to his Father that he did not need to "consult" on how to conduct himself. But Scripture assures us that Jesus shared our "weaknesses," the one "who in every respect has been tempted as we are, yet without sin" (Hebrews 4:15).

The real point is that for Jesus, as for us, prayer is the essential but simple process of keeping in close touch with our Father in heaven, maintaining the intimacy which God desires with us and which he wants us to desire with him.

When We Ask

We are told to pray for ourselves and for others. This kind of prayer, called intercession, means we share our own needs as well as those of our fellows before God and ask him to care for us. Does this suggest God does not already desire our best? No. Does it mean God does not plan to supply any need unless we ask? No, again. Jesus clearly said that God already knows all that we need and will fulfill those needs, but that our first priority in prayer should be on seeking God's lordship, personally and as his people:

> "Therefore do not be anxious, saying, 'What shall we eat?' or 'What shall we drink?' or 'What shall we wear?' For the Gentiles seek after all these things, and your heavenly Father knows that you need them all. But seek first the kingdom of God and his righteousness, and all these things will be added to you" (Matthew 6:31-33).

By constant personal prayer we "stay in touch" with God. Such intimacy will change our approach to each day and help us place our reliance on his grace and mercy over our own power and wisdom.

Genuine prayer should be heartfelt, like personal communication with a close friend. When we gather in a large group in church, we may pray with formal written-out prayers and beautiful phrases so that we can pray as one, but we also can — indeed must — pray in the simplicity of our own thoughts and words, as we would speak with anyone we are close to. The most essential thing in prayer is that we express truth to God: honesty about ourselves (genuine humility); complete honesty about our failures and sin (confession); and a willing desire to follow him in all things as far as we are able.

I once read the quip, "Many wish to serve God, but only in an advisory capacity." Though funny, it is too often true. But God does not ask us to pray because he needs our advice or doesn't already know all our needs. He commands us to pray because *we need* to be mentally and spiritually open to him at all hours, day or night, awake or asleep. (Yes, rest can be prayerful if we approach it and consecrate it with prayer.)

We express our needs to God because this changes how we then receive gifts from his hand. When we submit ourselves in prayer, we do two things. First, we are expressing what we need or desire. But second, and more importantly, we say that if God's answer is "No," we accept that answer as his wisdom. We always think we need a lot; we desire even more. But much of what we claim we need is not truly necessary to our life. Some of what we want may be harmful. By bringing our needs to God in prayer, we ask in humility, knowing that whatever his answer is it will be the best one at that moment.

Prayer To The True Lord
A further reason we must pray is because it is an integral part of what I have discussed as the central theme of this book: Shared Sovereignty. Since God made us his stewards of creation, his co-rulers, he has placed power into our hands and the permission to use it. But also, as I mentioned in Chapter Eight, this means he has placed his trust *in us.*

This is a foreign concept to many, that God chooses to trust us. But trust is the essence of any relationship; it operates equally in our relationship with God. Every relationship is a two-way street. You cannot maintain for very long a friendship where one party trusts the other but that trust is not mutual. The relationship will break down. If a husband trusts his wife to be ever-faithful, but she does not similarly trust him, how will that marriage thrive? It won't.

In the same way, in giving us power over his creation and its many creatures, God has placed a tremendous trust in us to do our work in accord with his design and wishes. Of course, we abuse that trust on a regular basis. Every time you or I commit even the simplest sin, we violate the trust God has placed in us. Fortunately, he does not usually react as a jilted spouse. (He does sometimes, and examples are famously recorded in the Old Testament.[1])

Constant In Prayer

St. Paul encouraged the Church to "Rejoice in hope, be patient in tribulation, be constant in prayer" (Romans 12:12). Similarly, he exhorts us to "Rejoice always, pray without ceasing, give thanks in all circumstances; for this is the will of God in Christ Jesus for you" (1 Thessalonians 5:16-17). That does not mean — as some long-winded preachers seem to think — that we never take a breath or never sleep. It means simply that prayer is the continual vocation of the Christian: to live prayerfully, bringing every moment of praise and intercession before God that we can.

When the disciples asked Jesus to teach them to pray, he didn't say, "Don't bother." He taught them a simple prayer that many Christians have repeated over the centuries. His "Lord's Prayer" is an outline, an example of how we should form our prayers, remembering that we are stewards of God's world. It we cease praying, if we stop communication with the one we serve, what is likely to happen? We will run off on our own tangents, and soon run off the rails. Many of us learn this the hard way.

Regular prayer is not about asking God for favors, it is about constantly seeking his guidance, trying to discern his will in a particular life situation, then tuning our will toward his. Holy Scripture is our essential guide, here. But it is not always simple to apply it to our daily situation. We are promised, though, that the Holy Spirit will help us understand Scripture and all that Jesus taught us if we read it prayerfully, asking God to open our minds to what he is saying through its pages (John 15:26; 16:13).

Many Christians have had experience of this. They have found that the very same passage of Scripture can "come alive" in different ways on different days, depending in part on what is going on in their life at that moment. "For the word of God is living and active, sharper than any two-edged sword, piercing to the division of soul and of spirit, of joints and of marrow, and discerning the thoughts and intentions of the heart" (Hebrews 4:12). The Bible is not a collection of dead men's sayings. It is the living Word of God written, and through it God speaks to our immediate situation in ways that will often amaze us. "Prayerful" reading of Scripture simply means that when we open each book, we ask God to open our heart, mind, and spirit to its meaning so that we can hear his voice through its pages.

Hired By God

Consider an analogy: imagine that you have just been hired as the Operations Manager for a major manufacturing plant. The owner hands you your credentials, passwords, and key cards, pats you on the back, and says, "Go run my factory. By the way, you are not allowed to speak to me ever again. Best of luck."

No good owner would do this. The new manager will need advice and direction from time to time. At times, the manager may have some good advice for the owner on how to improve the manufacturing process or improve the product. Communication is not only vital but indispensable.

So it is with us. When we consider the principle of Shared Sovereignty, we see why prayer is possible, but also why it is essential. God has, so to speak, put us in charge of his factory. He designed it from scratch and built it; he alone knows how best to operate it. But he has placed us in charge of day-to-day operations. It is therefore critical that we have ongoing conversation with him. The "machinery" in the plant includes our own spirit and body. Early on in life, we may not know how to operate these correctly. The owner does. But we should not presume that he will just jump in and take charge anytime we find ourselves in the deep end of the pool. We need to ask. He is not that owner who pats us on the back and says, "Good luck." He is the owner who says, "Ask for whatever you need." Though anxious to help, he waits for us to ask so that he does not "step on" his children or the duties he has given us.

That is why prayer is key. God could run the world all right without us, but that is not the world he made. As we have seen in answering our seven key questions, he refrains from constant interference so that we can learn. He also knows that mistakes, especially the big ones, are often our best teachers.

God hangs back but he never abandons us. From the beginning he has been speaking with us — if we will pay attention. That was the early relationship we see between he and Adam and Eve in Eden, before sin. And he has given us his revelation through Holy Scripture, the record of thousands of years of interaction between God and humanity. We ignore it all to our peril; we grow when we immerse ourselves in its pages.

Where Scripture gives no immediate or clear answer, prayer often can. But we must not just talk; we must listen. As in any communication, listening is the more important half of the equation. We often miss "a word from God" because we have not paid attention, or were too busy to listen.

The profound thing about prayer is that God keeps the communication channel open at all times. There is never a moment, never an instance, when we cannot seek him out in prayer. It is a key part of our job as his stewards, his plant managers. C. S. Lewis perfectly expressed why prayer works in his short essay entitled "Work and Prayer":

> We know that we can act and that our actions produce results. Everyone who believes in God must therefore admit (quite apart from the question of prayer) that God has not chosen to write the whole of history in His own hand. Most of the events that go on in the universe are indeed out of our control, but not all. It is like a play in which the scene and the general outline of the story is fixed by the author, but certain minor details are left for the actors to improvise. It may be a mystery why He should have allowed us to cause real events at all; but it is no odder that He should allow us to cause them by praying than by any other method. Pascal says that God 'instituted prayer in order to allow His creatures the dignity of causality.' It would perhaps be truer to say that He invented both prayer and physical action for that purpose.[2]

Lewis sums up my central point well. As co-sovereigns, we should be in constant, intimate communication with the owner if we are to run his "factory" properly. When we lose touch, we create the next disaster.

Prayer works because God has entrusted it to us as one means of us acting to influence the course of events not only around us, but in us. I believe that when we want God to "interfere" in the world, he may often do it through those who are listening to his wishes through prayer. We are stewards but also instruments. He can and does use us to accomplish his goals in particular situations. We will be unable to help if we are deaf to his voice.

When Prayers Conflict
There will, of course, invariably be times when our prayers and those of others conflict. Our hearts and lives run in so many directions that this is bound to happen. What does God do?

Let us say, for example, that my dear old Uncle Charlie is very ill. (I don't have an Uncle Charlie, but let's say.) I am very fond of Uncle Charlie. He sometimes acts like an old codger but he is dear to me. He is so sick that the doctors say he will die within days. I pray earnestly, asking God to spare him, and not only that, but to heal him so that I can enjoy a few more years with him around. What I don't know is that Uncle Charlie is tired of the long-term pain he has suffered, he feels old and feeble, his spiritual house is in order, and he wants to let go. He is praying earnestly that God will give him a speedy and relatively easy death.

Who should God listen to? Does he respect my love for Uncle Charlie? Will he intervene miraculously to heal Charlie enough so he can survive, albeit in further pain, for another two or three years? Or does God listen to Charlie?

Prayers will often conflict like this. We must trust God's judgment over our own. He is seeing all these needs and hearing our prayers in the very same "moment" (as we would put it, though it is not quite accurate of a supreme being that exists completely outside of time). Surely his wisdom is far greater than ours.

I am not God, but were I, I would grant Charlie's prayer over mine. Charlie is the real concern, and he is not afraid to die. And God doesn't have to actively kill Charlie; he need only let the death process run its course.

Does that mean God ignored my prayer, or some possible good that might have come to me if Uncle Charlie had survived? Yes, God has. In this case, Charlie's need is much greater than my own. A just God will honor that, in part because Charlie loves God and is not afraid of impending death.

Even though our prayers will often conflict like this, God still tells us to pray. He will always answer, though we will not always like his answer. He will answer in one of several ways, often in the way we least expect. He may answer "Yes." Quite often he will flatly say "No." That is because, 1) prayers of someone else may be in direct conflict with our own; or 2) God sees some greater good in saying no because we will learn something important in the process. In Uncle Charlie's case, for example, I may be forced to learn that physical death is not (by far) the worst thing that can happen to a person. I may also come to see that my prayer was mainly self-serving. It was not so much about Charlie not dying as it was about me retaining his friendship.

Lastly, God may answer "Not yet." His timing will always be better than ours. He may wish to grant something we deeply desire, but he knows we are not spiritually or emotionally equipped to handle it yet. A classic case might be an instance of two young people very much in love. Their "hearts desire" may be for an early marriage; God sees it ending in an early divorce. He may say "Not yet," not intending to prevent the marriage forever but preventing it until the young couple has matured enough individually and in relation to each other so that they can develop a marriage that will last through their lifetime. (Yes, that does still happen.)

Prayer is work. Indeed, it can be demanding and time consuming. It is part of the work God has entrusted to us as his co-sovereign stewards. Our primary prayers should be prayers of worship and adoration, thanking God for nothing else but his love, his goodness, and his mercy. It is fundamentally an expression of our trust in him and our desire that we might become worthy of *his* trust. All prayer should flow from that starting point, and toward that end.

> *And it is my prayer that your love may abound more and more, with knowledge and all discernment, so that you may approve what is excellent, and so be pure and blameless for the day of Christ, filled with the fruit of righteousness that comes through Jesus Christ, to the glory and praise of God.*
> *— Philippians 1:9-11*

<u>Endnotes</u>
1. Two examples will suffice: Ezekiel 16:15-22; Hosea 1:2; 2:8-13.
2. From the essay "Work and Prayer" in, GOD IN THE DOCK by CS Lewis © copyright CS Lewis Pte ltd 1970, used by permission.

He was foreknown before the foundation of the world but was made manifest in the last times for the sake of you.
— 1 Peter 1:20

Appendix B

Calvinism & Predestination

I have made several references to Calvinist thought in the body of this work but have deferred a detailed discussion of Calvinism to this appendix, for two reasons. First, Calvinism is a contentious subject far outside the primary scope of the book. Second, the claims of Calvinism run directly contrary to basic biblical truths highlighted throughout the book, in particular the principle of Shared Sovereignty. Having read this book, the reader is now in a better position to recognize the problems inherent in Calvin's predestinarian worldview.

My Purpose

I do not pretend this appendix to be an exhaustive rebuttal of Calvinism in all its forms. There are so many variations of Calvinist thought today that it would be a fool's errand to try to address them all. (This would require not a simple Appendix but one or two volumes.) For example, I have listened to self-identified "moderate" Calvinists minimize or even deny one core tenant of Calvinism, Calvin's belief in the "predestination" of all individuals to salvation or damnation — what should more precisely be called "divine determinism."[1] So, in the current environment, any consideration of Calvinist thought may provoke conflicting reactions from those who hold differing views of what they think "Calvinism" is.

I offer this appendix for one reason: I recognize that anyone coming to the present book from a Calvinist worldview may suffer a massive theological headache over the biblical principle of Shared Sovereignty. Though biblical, this principle violates fundamental ideas the Calvinist has been taught to believe, and holds sacred. Shared Sovereignty begins from the revealed truth that God has endowed every human with freedom of choice; for many Calvinists, this will upset the cart carrying all their apples.

My goal here is simple: to briefly review Calvin's teaching on predestination and contrast it with what biblical Christianity has always held. I will mince no words: I believe Calvin's predestinarian view is wrong because its central premises are false.

Who Was Calvin?

John Calvin (Jehan Cauvin, 1509-1564) was not trained as a clergyman but as a humanist attorney. A native of France, he broke from the Roman Church around 1530 AD and moved to Switzerland where he joined several fellow Frenchman in the growing Reformation movement in Geneva. His principle theological work was *Institutes of the Christian Religion* in which he addressed a wide range of subjects controversial at the time.[2] One, the issue of "predestination" of souls to salvation or damnation, became the contentious centerpiece of Calvin's theology.

Calvin held a radical form of divine determinism. Briefly expressed, he believed that God is utterly sovereign over all creation and everything that happens only happens because God *directly* wills it. God thus *controls* even the "apparent" choices and actions of every person. Calvin held that God's will is irresistible and absolutely sovereign: it cannot *in any way* or *to any extent* be challenged or resisted.

If the reader doubts this interpretation of Calvin, I would simply refer him to The Westminster Confession, a 17th century attempt to make sense of, and codify, Calvin's thought. Chapter Three (Section I.) of that Confession claims that "God from all eternity did, by the most wise and holy counsel of his own will, freely and unchangeably *ordain whatsoever comes to pass"* (emphasis mine). The section does go on to allege "yet so as thereby neither is God the author of sin, nor is violence offered to the will of the creatures, nor is the liberty or contingency of second causes taken away, but rather established." These latter four phrases are directly and unforgivably negated, of course, by the primary assertion that God causes *everything* that happens. It is as if those who drafted the Confession thought that simply holding their intellectual breath long enough would cause the stench of the contradiction to dissipate, and somehow (miraculously) transform nonsense into reason.

Their mention of "second causes" refers to Calvin's attempt to solve the dilemma that his system created: because his deterministic logic would make God the ultimate cause of all sin and evil, Calvin tried to absolve his error by distinguishing between God's will as the "proximate" (primary) cause of all events versus what he termed the "remote" or "secondary" cause, that is, a human person's "choice" that seemed to precipitate the same event. Thus, Calvin argued, one and the same event could be determined (ordained) by God as its true "proximate" cause to be a "right" and "good" thing, yet *the very same event* could be caused "secondarily" by a person intending it to be something wrong or sinful.

Calvin was essentially saying that one event could be both good and evil at the same time, depending on one's viewpoint. This view would have us erase any final distinction between good and evil. His extended logic ignores the fact that certain moral choices and actions are evil and wrong objectively, regardless of the first, second, or contributing causes.

By this convoluted reasoning, Calvin attempted to evade the logical outcome of his arguments that must, in the end, lay all sin at the doorstep of God's inviolable, irresistible will. But Calvin's reasoning merely creates a false dichotomy and introduces a new level of complexity into the dilemma. (He was apparently not a fan of Ockham.) The problem is that in Calvin's worldview, humans have no *actual* freedom of choice in any meaningful sense. They simply execute God's overriding will in all things, for God's will — so Calvin believed — cannot be obstructed even to the slightest degree.

The fatal error of Calvin's view is that when we dutifully follow his path to its inevitable end we are forced to the conclusion — Calvin's denials notwithstanding — that God *directly wills* all sin and evil to occur. Calvin believed that God does not — indeed *cannot* — permit anything contrary to his own will. If true, then God, as the "proximate" (primary) cause of *all* that happens, becomes the ultimate source and purveyor of all evil. This assertion, of course, violates God's love, divinity, and justice, and transforms God into a demon.

Saved, Or Damned
One unfortunate corollary of Calvin's determinism is that he believed the eternal destiny of every individual man or woman is also predetermined solely and sovereignly by God. Their destiny, he asserted, has *nothing whatsoever* to do with their life, thoughts, decisions, or actions. Those who are saved from eternal death are chosen for salvation by God alone, apart from anything they think or do. This claim forced Calvin to the logical corollary: the person who is damned to eternal punishment is likewise damned by God's sole, predetermined choice. Their damnation has nothing to do with anything they have thought, or done, or not done.

Put simply, Calvin claimed that God "sovereignly predestines" some to be saved and others to be damned, and those so chosen are *incapable of resisting or altering* their final destiny. The saved cannot *not* be saved; the damned *cannot* in any manner be saved. Their destinies were determined solely by God before they were conceived or born.

Calvin makes this case in Book III of his *Institutes* (Chapters 21-23), arguing that "Predestination, by which God adopts some (people) to hope of life and adjudges others to eternal death, no one, desirous of the credit of piety, dare to absolutely deny" (Chapter 21).[3] Calvin claims God's "election" of who will be saved or damned is not based upon the person's thoughts or deeds; he then goes further to insist that it is "preposterous" to think that God's election has anything to do with his foreknowledge of their lives:

> Predestination we [that is, Calvin] call the eternal decree of God by which he has determined in himself what he would have to become of every individual of mankind. For they are not all created with a similar destiny, but eternal life is foreordained for some and eternal damnation for others. Every man, therefore, being created for one or the other of these ends, we say he is predestined either to life or to death (Chapter 21).

You did not misread. Calvin said that God *specifically creates* some persons for the sole purpose of damnation. Calvin called this doctrine "gratuitous election" (Institutes, Chapter 23) and he refuses to waver. Every person's destiny is "foreordained" by God before he makes that person, and, as just mentioned, that foreordaining has nothing whatsoever to do with God's foreknowledge of how the person will conduct himself in life. Indeed, The Westminster Confession defended Calvin's view: "By the decree of God, for the manifestation of his glory, some men and angels are predestinated unto everlasting life, and others foreordained to everlasting death" (Chapter 3, Section III).

Calvin built some of his argument on quotations from St. Augustine, in particular an essay entitled "On Rebuke and Grace":

> ... Augustine further writes, "It is beyond all doubt, therefore, that the will of God, who has done whatever he has pleased in heaven and in earth, and who has done even things that are yet future, cannot possibly be resisted by the will of man so as to prevent the execution of his purposes since he controls the wills of men according to his pleasure" (quoted by Calvin from "On Rebuke and Grace," XIV).

Calvin apparently took this to mean that God controls every decision of every person's will. But Calvin was selective in what he quotes from Augustine, to support his own views. He avoids passages like this from Augustine's same essay:

> It is to be confessed, therefore, that we have free choice to do both evil and good; but in doing evil everyone is free from righteousness and a servant of sin, while in doing good no one can be free, unless he have been made free by Him who said, "If the Son shall make you free, then you shall be free indeed" ("On Rebuke and Grace," Chapter II).

If we give St. Augustine a full and fair reading, we discover that far from believing God controls every decision we make, Augustine knew we often go *against* God's will and his plan for our lives. Indeed, early in his famous *Confessions*, Augustine wrote, "'Woe to the sins of men!' When a man cries thus, you show him mercy, for you created the man but not the sin in him" (Confessions, 1.7.11).

How could Augustine be certain that we can resist God? The answer is simple: his own life was his best evidence. For years, he had been caught up in the Manichean sect, a heretical group of dualist Christians who claimed there was a battle between an unalterable "good" and "evil" will in each person. Addressing their error, Augustine described his own experience: God does not "control" our wills in the sense of causing every thought, or decision, or action; rather, he *influences* our wills to draw us back to himself out of the sin we ourselves create:

> My heart and my memory are laid open before you, who were even then guiding me by the secret impulse of your providence and were setting my shameful errors before my face so that I might see and hate them (Confessions 5.6.11).

He describes how God drew him toward Christian faith, not against his will, but by "goading" it:

> But you, 'my refuge and my portion in the land of the living' [Psalm 142:5], goaded me thus at Carthage so that I might thereby be pulled

away from it and change my worldly habitation for the preservation of my soul (Confessions, 5.8.14).

Further in *Confessions,* Augustine reflects on how complex the exercise of our human will is, and how, as in his own case, the will can become chained by habitually indulging in sin so that we come to feel divided against ourselves:

> The enemy held fast my will, and had made of it a chain, and had bound me tight with it. For out of the perverse will came lust, and the service of lust ended in habit, and habit, not resisted, became necessity. By these links, as it were, forged together — which is why I called it a chain — a hard bondage held me in slavery. But *that new will* which had begun to spring up in me freely to worship you and to enjoy you, my God, the only certain joy, was not able as yet to overcome my former willfulness, made strong by long indulgence. Thus my two wills — the old and the new, the carnal and the spiritual — were in conflict within me, and by their discord they tore my soul apart (8.5.10; *emphasis* added).

His point is clear: his former, corrupted will was not influenced by God but by Satan. As the time of his conversion to Christ drew closer, Augustine described how his will was torn and perplexed:

> Who am I, and what is my nature? What evil is there not in me and my deeds; or if not in my deeds, my words; or if not in my words, my will? But you, Lord, are good and merciful, and your right hand reached into the depth of my death and emptied out the abyss of corruption from the bottom of my heart. And this was the result: now I did not will to do what *I willed*, and began to will to do *what you did will*. But where was my free will during all those years and from what deep and secret retreat was it called forth in a single moment . . .? (9.1.1; *emphasis* added).

The passage is poignant and clear: Augustine had allowed his will to become chained by sin; but God's grace drew him away from sin and set him free so that he *could now choose* to conform his will to God's. Even then, however, God did not (as Calvin would argue) "control" Augustine's will in an absolute sense. Augustine had to make that decision to turn to Christ and abandon his former life.

God's Will And Ours

So, what *did* Augustine mean in the passage from "On Rebuke and Grace" which Calvin later quoted: that God's will "cannot possibly be resisted by the will of man *so as to prevent the execution of his purposes* since he controls the wills of men according to his pleasure"?

Based on his own experience, Augustine could not have been suggesting that God controls human wills in an absolute sense, "ordaining" (determining) every decision you and I ever make, or that God's will was irresistible. Augustine's own rebellion disproved this. So, his statement that God "controls the wills of men according to his pleasure" can only be understood to mean that God *influences* our wills by his own in order to "goad" or direct us toward the right goal. Augustine's primary point is that our decisions that obstruct God's will cannot *"prevent the execution of his purposes"* in the broader sense. That is, God's purposes for his creation will ultimately prevail despite our individual rebellion and resistance. We are co-sovereign, but God is ultimately sovereign. His overarching plan for humankind and the larger creation will be accomplished in the long term, despite the interference of our wills, our decisions, and our sinful actions (Romans 7-8). We can resist God; we know we do. We can *obstruct*, but we cannot finally defeat his will.

In looking back at his own life, it is plain that Augustine did not believe in what Calvin would later characterize as God's "irresistible will." Augustine's own experience disproved such an idea. He resisted God's will for years. God goaded him and called to him, but God never compelled him. Augustine had to make the choice to follow. His *Confessions* describe in elaborate and painful detail — for page after page — how he resisted this surrender to God up to the last moment.

Moreover, Augustine did not hold that each person's eternal destiny was "foreordained" and unalterable because he described how even an "elect" Christian, already saved by God's grace, could backslide and turn away:

> If, however, *being already regenerate and justified*, he relapses *of his own will* into an evil life, assuredly he cannot say, "I have not received," because *of his own free choice to evil* he has *lost the grace of God* that he had received. And if, stung with compunction by rebuke, he wholesomely bewails, and returns to similar good works, or even better, certainly here most manifestly appears the advantage of rebuke ("On Rebuke and Grace," Chapter 9; *emphasis* added).

Yes, Augustine believed it possible for a person to turn back from salvation in Christ by his own bad choices and again rebel against God. Calvin clearly missed this truth, as do some present-day Christians.[4] The quotation just given, ironically, again comes from Augustine's same essay, the essay Calvin tried to use to argue that God totally controls every decision we make.

If a person does not look too closely, Calvin's arguments may seem well-intentioned, defending (so he believed) the dignity and sovereignty of God. But once we understand the revealed reality of Shared Sovereignty, we see that Calvin's system misreads the entire record of Scripture and the fundamental relationship God established in the beginning between himself and humankind. Calvin would have us believe that God *directly causes* everything that occurs to occur. Consider the absurdity: if I were a Calvinist, I would have to insist that God is presently causing me to write this book, including this particular Appendix proving that God does *not* directly cause everything that occurs — an intractable conundrum if ever there was one.

To maintain Calvin's view that God *directly* causes everything, we would have to isolate ourselves from fact and reality, erase the whole biblical narrative, and dismiss the principle of Shared Sovereignty. But by understanding the reality of God's "permissive will," we know that God can and *does* allow certain things to occur that are contrary to his own will. To the Calvinist, such a breach of God's sovereignty can only be jeered at. Indeed, to Calvin the very idea of Shared Sovereignty would be repugnant, a violation of God's irresistible, absolute will. From Calvin's view-point, no human could act as a co-sovereign with God. The very suggestion would probably seem to Calvin to be a sacrilegeious slight.

Calvin was not a stupid man, nor haphazard. He seems to have genuinely struggled with what he perceived to be the logical dilemma between an all-powerful, sovereign God alongside his creatures who seem to be making choices at the same time. Calvin resolved the conflict, in an unbending fashion, by attributing every event — and every person's ultimate destiny — to God's implacable, unalterable, and irresistible will.

Calvin thus hung himself in his own logical noose: if God is irresistibly sovereign, it is impossible for anything to happen unless God determined "in advance" that it will happen; but if that is true, one cannot exclude evil (try as Calvin did). God must directly cause every good, but also every evil.

The Tragic Irony Of Calvinism
Here, then, is the great irony in Calvin's predestinarian system, and its principal defect: in trying to *defend* the sovereignty of God, Calvin failed to recognize the true *magnitude* of his sovereignty. That is, Calvin failed to allow for the fact that it is *God himself* who *sovereignly creates* his human (and angelic) creatures in a manner that allows each of them to *share* his sovereignty, in limited measure, as his co-workers and co-creators in this world, allowing them a significant degree of control over their own lives and destinies, and over the world around them, even while God moves his own plan and purposes for his world and each creature forward.

Recognizing the reality of Shared Sovereignty is simply a matter of giving due credit to Scripture as true. If we will stand back and look, we cannot fail to see that the whole, underlying narrative of Scripture describes this "give and take" nature of man's relationship with God. So, for example, when it comes to the decision to accept or reject God's sovereign act of saving grace through the cross of Christ, God has allowed his human creatures complete *individual* sovereignty as to their own eternal destiny.

Why this reality remained a mystery to Calvin remains a mystery to me. Both the Old and New Testaments routinely tell of God's call for his creatures to make choices which will affect their own lives and future destinies, and which often affect the lives and destinies of those around them. Yes, we might argue *ad infinitum* about the effects of sin on our ability to make those choices, or about how "free" or "bound" our choices are because of the warping defects of our sin, or of the "sin nature" inherited from our parents. Yes, there seems little question that the stain and effects of deep sin in our souls and personalities does affect how we consider our choices, and how we carry them out.

Having said that, however, I am not prepared to make the fatal leap others have made to the erroneous conclusion that our "will" is therefore either entirely ineffective, or utterly destroyed by sin. That view might be argued were it not for the fact that it is God's prevenient (leading) grace that enables us to respond to his gift and call in Christ (John 6:44) in the first place, nor does it credit the promise that the grace of God continually pours over those of us who are now "in Christ" (Romans 5:3-5) to preserve us from uncontrolled obedience to sin.

God is perfectly able (for he is God) to work his own will and to move his sovereign, over-arching plan for history forward while still allowing his rational creatures to make individual choices day-to-day, hour-by-hour. Like a coach (an inerrant coach) alongside a football field or basketball court, God can easily take into account the decisions and actions that we — and our opponents — make, while still implementing his own plan, so that the final outcome of the "contest" will be the outcome he desires. Our stupidity, choices, and failures may alter events somewhat, for a time, but they will not finally obstruct God's plan.

Further, God's "timing" is always perfect. Here again, Calvin and his predestinarian followers fall short because they fail to see the larger picture from God's vantage point instead of their own. When they speak of God "*pre*destining" some person to life or death, they are speaking in a manner that shows their vantage point is restricted within our human perception of time and space. But in the most basic, truest sense, God does not "*pre*-destine" anything. God has no past-tense, and no future-tense, no "time" in which he "did" something in the "past," or made some determination about someone's "future" destiny. God *is*. God *acts*. When we say God "*fore*saw" my future or destiny, we are speaking only from our own viewpoint, and are locking God — perhaps unwittingly — into the time-structure in which we ourselves must operate. In truth, though, God "*fore*-saw" nothing: God *sees* our actions and decisions as realities that, from his vantage point, have no past or future. We see a decision we make "at present" that may alter our "future." God knows both as present and related realities.

And here we approach what was perhaps the real core of Calvin's error.

God In Relation To Time

A central problem in Calvin's thought, and in all predestinarian systems, is that they grow out of a complete misunderstanding of the *relationship* of God, who exists in himself entirely outside of time, with his "space-time" creation. To cut around Calvin's apparent logical dilemma of "divine determinism" and his subsequent assumption about the predestination of all souls, we must first arrive at a clear understanding of God's relationship with what *we perceive* as the structure and framework of "time."

As a form of divine determinism, Calvinism fails because it misunderstands this relationship: how God-in-himself acting in eternity (that is, *outside* of time) *interacts* with his creatures, and how he expresses and exercises his will *within* time. Calvinism is maimed by two fatal assumptions:

1. It misunderstands how God, *from our perspective,* "foreknows" a thing, because it perceives God's knowledge of that thing or event as if *what* God knows is trapped "inside" of time.

2. Then, perceiving our relationship with God only from within our own time-perspective, the determinist presumes that because God "foreknows" an event before it occurs *in time* that his very knowledge of the event *directly causes* it to happen in that precise way.

A simple example may help. If I am about to throw a bowling ball down the bowling alley, since God sees "beforehand" that it will end in the gutter, God forces me (according to the predestinarian) to throw it in such a way that it *must* end in the gutter — because he has seen it do so before it "actually happens" in the space-time world in which I live.

Although many Christians might not express their idea of "God's will" in this way, the widespread influence of Calvinist thinking causes many secretly (and fearfully) to hold such a view. It is wrong. Here is why.

Taking A God's-Eye View

If we can try to mentally suspend the constraints of our perception of the "time-sequence" of events that constantly "go on" (notice the present-to-future assumption of that phrase), and instead try to approach the question from God's side, events will appear differently. If we can try to see an "event" from his divine point of view in eternity (that is, outside time), it is actually incorrect to say that God "*fore*knows" something, because the "fore-" only has meaning "inside" of time. Within himself, God does not *fore*-know the thing or event, he simply "knows." This, indeed, is why we call him "omniscient," which means "all-knowing": God knows all things at once, in "the same instant" as it were, not "before" or "after" as we perceive things. God is "eternal" not because he has "lived a long time" but because he himself is not "in time" at all. His existence is not "measurable" in that way, he just "is." We must also recognize, however, that while God made time and is not "trapped" within it, he can *enter* or *inhabit* or *interact* with time — as indeed he did most perfectly in the Incarnation of Jesus — even while his own divine existence is outside of and beyond time.

Our problem, of course, is that this kind of perception strains our minds and we constantly lapse back into thinking within our normal time-structured framework. So, we say that God "foreknows" events. But this is to mischaracterize God's own reality. Certainly, *from our perspective* he "knows it before we do," but this is only true from our sphere within the "passage" of time. For God himself, there is no fore-knowing or post-knowing. He simply knows: to God, all reality is "present tense." Thus, for example, our Lord says "Now he is not God of the dead, but of the living, for all live to him" (Luke 20:38). Notice the tense of "all live."

On one level, this is not too difficult to see, but we must allow our minds in a sense to "drift" and imagine we are somehow "outside" time with God. If we try that, we can form at least a partial picture. Normally, you and I see events as they *occur* and *pass* in time; but God sees those events as a *singular reality*. God constantly interacts with time and space, but he is bound by neither. When we, his time-bound creatures, say that God *pre*determines, or "*pre*destines," or "*fore*ordains" some thing or event, we are introducing our time-structured perception into his eternal, non-time-limited acting. Simply put, God does not *pre*-determine, he determines. We become aware of his decisions and actions from within time, so we say "he knew before-hand," but to him there is no "before-hand."

Seeing God's "eternal" viewpoint, however, becomes more complicated when we speak of how God's eternal will and decisions interact with our time-based wills and decisions. I have already touched on the key issue: does God's "knowledge" of an in-time event *cause* the event? Does God's "knowing" a decision that I make "inside" time *determine* my decision?

To comprehend how his will and ours relate and interact, it is helpful to draw a mental picture of what happened at creation: when God creates the space and time universe, he has made a new, different *level* or *kind* of existence (if we may crudely put it that way) that is both separate and different from his own personal existence, yet it is a manner of "existence" *in which* he can make himself present and in which his own knowledge and will can operate. From beyond time and space, he interacts with creatures and events they cause within the space-time continuum. In other words, God engages our moments of life, our "now," from the *outside*. But his *interaction* with us does not *trap* or *contain* him in time or space: he engages with events as they (for us) "transpire"; but for him, they do not "transpire," they simply "are."

It is from within this "divine" viewpoint that we must understand the magnitude of what St. Peter says in the words that lead this appendix. For the "interaction" of God with his creation —his divine intervention in our history — is most perfectly defined, summed up, and spelled out in the "event" we call the Incarnation of the Son of God. At the Incarnation, the eternal, non-time God personally *steps inside* his creation (thus into time) to inhabit and share, in a very concrete manner, the life of humanity through the divine-human personhood of his Son. God unites to himself the full humanity of a *particular* human being, Jesus of Nazareth, but Jesus Christ the Son of God has, from God's perspective, "always" existed as a perfect union of the divine and the human natures.

This may stretch and bend our minds, but it is essential that we understand this. While the Father continues to interact with creation from "outside," Jesus the Son also now simultaneously interacts with the same creation from "inside," from *within* time. Thus, the Incarnation of the Son is not "an event that happened" at some point, then ended: the eternal Son is known with the Godhead as Incarnate from before all time — from before time itself was made. Indeed, the whole point of the Resurrection of Jesus is that the Incarnation *cannot* in any sense "end" because it was always true. Christ "ascends" to the Father not as a dead, disembodied man but as the Risen Lord, still fully divine and fully human, embodied and glorified. Even when, for some hours, his body lay dead on a slab of stone, it did not stop being a reality of the Incarnation — which is why the empty tomb is so significant.

You may want to take a deep breath here, for God does not stop with this amazing conjunction of time, space, and eternity. Just as every other human being God creates, once created, will continue to live forever, in the same way the *humanity* of Jesus Christ which clearly had a beginning moment in time, in the womb of Mary, has been eternally united with the Godhead, and will now never cease to exist within space and time. "Christ is risen!" is not just a nice Easter chant: it is *the complete explanation* of everything God has done, and is doing, in creation as a whole:

> In him we have redemption through his blood, the forgiveness of our trespasses, according to the riches of his grace, which he lavished upon us, in all wisdom and insight making known to us the mystery of his will, according to his purpose, which he set forth in Christ as a plan for the fullness of time, to unite all things in him, things in heaven and things on earth (Ephesians 1:7-10).

In other words, the Incarnation of the Son of God is not a "one-time" event that begins, then ends. It is a *continuing reality* that runs alongside God's eternity, from our perspective, "forever." Christ is born among us, he dies, and is buried. But the Incarnation did not thus end. He is resurrected with his full human nature; his human spirit and body are reunited with the Godhead of the Son. He stands "now" at "the right hand of the Father" not as a disembodied spirit but as a fully glorified son of Adam. God does not just "foreknow" his Son in regard to his human birth and life: he *knows* him perfectly, in all eternity, both his divinity and his manhood (John 1). "How" that relationship of Father and Son operates both inside and outside time "at the same time," so to speak, is an operation our brains will never exactly take in.

Here again, we experience what Tozer called "trying to pour the ocean into a teacup." The nature of the interactions between God and ourselves can turn our poor brain tissues to gelatin. We are so fully constrained to *see* and *experience* everything from inside time that we have to forcibly bend our "time awareness" in order to step beyond it and imagine God's perspective; but it is only in doing so that we can overcome the errors of the predestinarian argument. What we must simply hold onto is this: when we say God "foreknows" something, we are saying something about our-selves, and nothing about him. We are trying to speak of his omniscient knowledge and unbounded will from within our own time-structures, and seeing events only from our side of the window. For us, from our side of that glass, it is "true" that God *fore*-knows. He knows something "before" we do, for the simple reason that he "always" knows it. But we must force ourselves to remember that the "it" for God has no before or after.

The unbounded God transcends his creation, that "different" existence he creates and sustains, yet he maintains his own manner of interacting with *what* he made.[5] This is why Genesis describes God walking in the garden with Adam and Eve. This is not just poetic imagery: in a real manner beyond our minds, God himself — pre-incarnate — is present *within* his creation from the beginning, while continuing to exist in his full personal essence outside of it (John 1:1-3).[6] It is because God maintains this "separation" between himself and the created order that he can *know* things and events while also *allowing* his self-determining creatures to make independent decisions and carry out their own actions without himself causing those decisions or actions. We see our actions and decisions happen along our time-structured sightline. They are real decisions and real actions. The fact that the omniscient God simultaneously knows these actions does not cause them nor control them. As we said in Appendix A, God has given us "effective" power over our lives and our world such that constant prayer is an essential part of our human vocation and "labor."

Time And Eternity

Because of our time-limited minds and perspective, we have a tendency to consider God's actions, like our own, in a linear fashion, but this is only because of our limited sightline. For us, events move along in "the present," then become our "past," and we can speculate about an unknown "future." God, however, knows all three time realities simultaneously (Revelation 1:17-18; 4:8) as continually present to himself.

If we can hold these seeming paradoxes in our feeble brains (yes, this requires an act of juggling), the question of God *pre*-determining some event will fade and we can see how he can interact with us on this different *level* of existence within his creation while still allowing us our freedom, and while remaining apart from us in his own existence. He can "observe" us doing things, making decisions, and carrying those decisions out without himself *causing* them.

Within the process of time, then, God interacts with us based on our wills, our choices, and our actions. He responds — *in time* — accordingly. That is what the whole record of Scripture shows. He does not "preempt" human choices or events merely by seeing them from outside of time, nor does he cause them. He has not, as Calvin implied, made us puppets, but his co-rulers. This being so, we must reject the false view that God imperiously saves or condemns individuals without regard for their actions. The "pre" in predestine has only to do with *our* perception of time; it does not mean God has "*pre*ordained" every event, for that would make creation not only useless, but love impossible. When St. Paul tells us God "predestines" those whom he "foreknew" (Romans 8:29) he is correct: both words express reality *only* from the human side of the window, as the "sequence" of things affects us.

Just as St. Peter assures us Christ himself was "predestined" as Messiah before creation itself, in a similar way God *knows* (present tense) each of us *before* we are first created in the womb, both our origin and our destination (Jeremiah 1:5); yet his knowledge does not thereby control our actions. From our vantage point, God *fore*knows our entire life from now into forever. And to say that God has a *plan* for my life — what he desires for me — means that God will continually goad and guide my heart and my will in such a way that he draws me toward himself. But contrary to Calvin's error, God has not chained me before he made me, and he is not dragging me to some particular place or outcome. As I come to know God in the way he knows me, through deepening, perfecting love, his love and grace toward me can overcome my staunchest rebellion — but only if I am willing to give him a crack in the door, and even half an inch inside.

In short, when God interacts with us in time, he acts *alongside* us as his co-workers, not as our Puppet Master. The Incarnation of his Son reveals this perfectly. When we consider the full biblical record in its integrity, we see how God's loving grace operates side-by-side with our own wills. This causes no dilemma for God. The one who made us first of all loves us. As I have said more than once, love demands there be no compulsion in his relationship with us. Yes, we may get frustrated or angry that God allows so much evil and suffering, but we must recall that there is a reason. God is patient. The early-Christian apologist Justin Martyr, writing in the second century, put it very clearly like this:

> Among us the chief of the evil demons is called the serpent and Satan and the devil, as you can learn by examining our writings. Christ has foretold that he will be cast into fire with his host and the men who follow him, to be punished for endless ages. God delays doing this for the sake of the human race, for he foreknows that there are some yet to be saved by repentance, even perhaps some not yet born. In the beginning he made the race of men endowed with intelligence, able *to choose the truth and do right,* so that all men are without excuse before God (First Apology, Ch. 28).[8]

God delays carrying forward his own plans for each of our lives, foreknowing that some will yet "repent." Indeed, an indispensable part of God's "predestining" grace is his patience: his desire that every person born will return to him as their true Father, and inherit the promise of eternal life. Sadly, those who have fallen into the sinkhole of Calvinism have lost sight of this beautiful truth.

Finding Clarity

I have tried here to suggest ways to hold in balance the realities of God's will and our wills operating side-by-side. We will never, though, be able to prevent our minds perfectly from falling back into our human time-space frame of reference: it outlines, shapes, and provides boundaries to every aspect of our daily lives, our thoughts, our feelings, and our decision-making. In other words, it is not second-nature, but first. This is why it is so crucial to remember the sequence St. Paul speaks of in that key passage in Romans which I have previously cited. I cite it here again because I am convinced that it is absolutely essential to understanding everything else Paul said about God's "calling," "election," and "predestination" of his "chosen" people:

> "And we know that for those who love God all things work together for good, for those who are called according to his purpose. *For those whom he foreknew he also predestined* to be conformed to the image of his Son, in order that he might be the firstborn among many brothers. And those whom he predestined he also called, and those whom he called he also justified, and those whom he justified he also glorified (Romans 8:28-30; *emphasis* added).

Paul speaks as from "our side of the window," knowing, as well as we do, that for the eternal God there is no "past" or "present" or "future." Paul puts this "sequence" in our time-space framework so that we can apply them to ourselves: "those whom God foreknew he also predestined." From his side of the window, God sees our decisions and actions, and acts accordingly. As Scripture repeatedly makes clear, God is both loving and just. He does not condemn us randomly or unjustly: he judges according to our thoughts, our decisions, and our actions, and "records" them in his "book." He is not The Grand Puppeteer. He is our loving Father.

"Knowing" us from beyond time, God can destine each of us (*pre*destine, from our point of view) to everlasting joy with him, or permanent separation from him. This is not arbitrary, or imperious, nor is it the exercise of what Calvin characterized as his "irresistible" will. God loves us. He wants an everlasting relationship of joy and fellowship with us through his Son, and he pulls out all the stops to make that possible. In the end, sadly, as we too often see, many refuse his offer, just as we often refuse the offer of love from our fellow human beings in this present life.

Yes, hell is real. If you should end there, it will not be God's doing. The God who formed each of us in the womb "calls" each of us to eternal life. He "desires all people to be saved and to come to the knowledge of the truth" (1 Timothy 2:4). The choice we will make, eternal life, or spiritual death, will be our own. Some say if you make the wrong decision, you can never turn back. I say you can. At this very moment.

Calvin's Error

When the Calvinist claims Holy Scripture proves that God's will is irresistible, he cuts the throat of his own argument, for the simple reason that the Bible records literally thousands of mankind's misdeeds which are so clearly *contrary* to God's will. If you want to make up an argument for divine Determinism, you are free to do so, but don't be so silly as to try to base it on the Bible.

If we credit Holy Scripture as true and take off self-imposed blinders, we cannot fail to see that God's foreknowledge does not dictate events "in time." His knowledge *operates* both inside and outside of time. If we lose that point, we will end in a fog. The sheer number of terrible sins recorded in Scripture alone should clear our mind of any false thought that a human (or an angel) cannot resist God's will. The whole of biblical history proves otherwise.

How, then, are we to understand God's "foreknowledge" in relation to actual, specific events? A simple illustration can show the truth. Suppose you are standing on top of a tall building and look down to see two cars racing toward the same intersection from different streets. They are about to collide. You can see it. You can "foretell" with near certainty that they *will* collide because the intersection is blind and the two drivers cannot see each other's approach. You scream out your fear to the friend standing by you. Then, the cars collide violently.

Thus, you foresaw the event, *and* you foretold it. Now ask: did you *cause* them to collide?

So it is with God's foreknowledge. He has made a world in which many independent creatures possess wills that both act and conflict. God can sit, so to speak, atop his tall building of eternity and see with certainty all that will take place. But his foreknowledge is independent of time and does not control our wills or behavior inside time. God can even foretell an event through a prophet, but that still does not *cause* the event. (Otherwise, why did God so often use his prophets to warn his people to *change course*?) God knows; but we control our own actions. He observes; but we are the ones careening toward the intersection.

Let's carry the illustration further. What is God to do? He may throw a large rock at both of us to get our attention; he may put up a very big stoplight — which we, the drivers, can still choose to ignore; or, he may let some terrible illness lay us low in bed that day to prevent us getting behind the wheel in the first place. But we could still jump in the car and drive. None of those "warnings" override our wills — the wills he himself gave us.

The great Christian preacher A. W. Tozer used this analogy. The world is like a great ocean liner, God's ship. God places each of us on the ship, which is headed from New York to London. As passengers, we are given freedom of choice. We are entirely free to move about the ship and do whatever we want — as the ship sails irreversibly on. We can do good to one another, or do evil. We can paint and polish the ship, or set it afire; but we cannot stop its forward progress. We may run amok on the ship our entire life, and sin, and cause havoc for our fellow passengers. But nothing we individually do will prevent the ship from reaching its predetermined destination. God is the captain, we are merely passengers. The sad fact is, some will end up overboard and be forever lost. So it is with our world: history will reach the goal God designed it to reach, despite anything you or I do along the way. We may even try to commandeer the wheelhouse and wrest control away from God — mankind has often tried, especially in "modern" times — but we will never succeed. The Captain will not be turned from his course.

This, I believe, is what Augustine meant when he said that God "controls" our wills in such a manner that we cannot finally obstruct his purposes. God allows us freedom but has set boundaries, like the confines of the ship, outside of which our wills have no impact. Within those boundaries, though, we are free to do as we choose. That God is ultimately in charge, that he is sovereign over history, does not mean he robs us of the freedom he himself gave. God is captain but we are "co-operators" of this ship. We can try to frustrate God's goal, but the ship will one day reach London.

Any system of predestination or divine determinism that denies this, that tries to deny human freedom *and responsibility,* cannot be squared with Holy Scripture. God does not randomly and irrationally choose our individual destiny, nor does he compel us into his kingdom. If he "compels" anything it is to require us to make a choice: to serve him, or rebel; to follow his will, or stubbornly hold to our own, even when it leads to terrible evil.

Sadly, Calvin's system turns God into the true villain, making him the ultimate cause of evil. Calvin's view would therefore lift us off the hook of sin. I have had Calvinists protest that, "No, if a man sins, it's his own fault!" But they cannot have it both ways: they cannot insist on a God whose will cannot be resisted or broken, then come back to earth and blame individuals for sin. Those sinners are — according to Calvin — merely acting out God's irresistible will.

Dance, parry, and evade as he may, the Calvinist must finally fall on his own sword.

Not A New Problem

I do not want to seem to cast all the blame for this confusion on John Calvin. Like a good prosecutor, he merely followed his misguided thinking out to its logical conclusion, as he careened over a theological cliff. His many lemmings have followed. And some believe that a few things Augustine wrote in his later years seemed to suggest that he really didn't feel he could have ultimately refused God's call on his life — which some would twist to imply an absolute "predestination" of his choices. But questions about predestination predate even Augustine. As early as the second century, Justin Martyr (quoted above) recognized the issue which had grown out of a misreading of certain passages in St. Paul (while ignoring Romans 8). The fatal error of attributing all events and all human action to the *direct will* of God, later embodied in Calvinism, was addressed and roundly rebuked by Justin:

> 42. ... But in our time Jesus Christ, who was crucified and died, rose again and, ascending into heaven, began to reign; and on account of what was proclaimed by the apostles in all nations as [coming] from him, there is joy for those who look forward to the incorruption which he has promised.
>
> 43. So that none may infer from what we have said that the events we speak of, because they were foreknown and predicted, took place according to inevitable destiny — I can explain this too. We have learned from the prophets, and declare as the truth, that penalties and punishments and good rewards are given *according to the quality of each man's actions*. If this were not so, but all things happened in accordance with destiny, nothing at all would be left up to us. For if it is destined that one man should be good and another wicked, then neither is the one acceptable nor the other blameworthy. And if the human race does not have the power by free choice to avoid what is shameful and to choose what is right, *then there is no responsibility for actions of any kind*. But that [man] walks upright or falls by free choice we may thus demonstrate. We [often] observe the same man in pursuit of opposite things. *If he were destined to be either wicked or virtuous, he would not be thus capable of opposites,* and often

change his mind. Nor would some be virtuous and others wicked, for then we would have to declare fate to be the cause of evils and [at the same time] to act in opposition to itself or to accept as true the opinion referred to above, that there is no real virtue or vice, but only by opinion are things considered good or bad; *which, as the true Reason shows us, is the greatest impiety and wickedness.* But we do say that *deserved rewards* are irrevocably destined for those who have chosen the good, and likewise their just deserts for those [who have chosen] the opposite. But God did not make man like other [beings], such as trees and animals, which have no power of choice. For he would not be worthy of rewards or praise if he did not choose the good of himself, but was so made, nor if he were evil would he justly deserve punishment, if he were not such of himself, but was unable to be anything different from that for which he was formed.

44. The holy prophetic Spirit taught us these things, saying through Moses that God said to the first-formed man, "Behold I have set before you good and evil, choose the good" (First Apology of Justin Martyr, c. 155 AD, Ch. 42-44; *emphasis* added).[9]

Justin makes an absolutely crucial distinction here: what God "predestines" is not our actions but *the reward or punishment* those actions deserve. This is entirely different from what Calvin would later allege, that God predetermines our every action and "choice" and saves or damns us arbitrarily *regardless* of our decisions or actions. Justin expressed what has always been the orthodox Christian view: that God predestines the *just* reward for our actions, good or bad, based upon his foreknowledge of how we will conduct ourselves in this life.

God Is Just

In other words, God is loving, fair, and just. The Old Testament prophet Jeremiah knew this, and saw how God would therefore judge even his own "elect" nation of Israel:

> For many nations and great kings shall make slaves even of them, and I will recompense them *according to their deeds and the work of their hands* (Jeremiah 25:14).

God had called the nation of Israel to glory, to be a light to the nations, but Israel failed. They suffered the consequence: the loss of their homeland, the loss of their national sovereignty, and captivity in Babylon. This was God's judgment on his "chosen people." (See also 1 Peter 4:17.)

Similarly, St. Paul understood God's inherent justice but also the power of our own choices. Like Augustine, Paul rebelled against God for years. He persecuted the young Christian Church; he stood by and approved when the innocent Stephen was stoned to death (Acts 7:58). Despite this, our seemingly ever-patient Lord called Paul in a dramatic, life-changing encounter. Yet it was Paul who had to make the decision: a decision to stop rebelling, and repent, and follow. So, Paul knew quite well that God does not "prejudge" us, arbitrarily assigning us heaven or hell on some divine whim. God is Justice itself, and his justice is perfect:

> Or do you presume on the riches of his kindness and forbearance and patience, not knowing that God's kindness is meant to lead you to repentance? But because of your hard and impenitent heart you are storing up wrath for yourself on the day of wrath when God's righteous judgment will be revealed. *He will render to each one according to his works:* to those who by patience in well-doing seek for glory and honor and immortality, he will give eternal life; but for those who are self-seeking and do not obey the truth, but obey unrighteousness, there will be wrath and fury (Romans 2:4-8; *emphasis* added).

Paul confirms this view in 2nd Corinthians:

> For we must all appear before the judgment seat of Christ, so that *each one may receive what is due* for what he has done in the body, whether good or evil (2 Corinthians 5:10).

". . . whether good or evil." St. Paul agrees with the rest of Scripture. God does not arbitrarily assign men and women salvation or damnation. God, justice himself, respects for good or ill what we have chosen and done with our lives. St. Peter agreed. Look at the opening verses of his first letter to the early churches:

> Peter, an apostle of Jesus Christ, to those who are elect exiles of the Dispersion in Pontus, Galatia, Cappadocia, Asia, and Bithynia, according to the foreknowledge of God the Father, in the sanctification of the Spirit, for obedience to Jesus Christ and for sprinkling with his blood ... As obedient children, do not be conformed to the passions of your former ignorance, but as he who called you is holy, you also be holy in all your conduct, since it is written, "You shall be holy, for I am holy." And if you call on him as Father who judges impartially according to each one's deeds ... (1 Peter 1:1-17; emphasis added).

Notice that: he calls them "elect" exiles "according to the foreknowledge of God the Father" because of their "obedience." Obedience is our decision that turns us from sin to return to God. I do not see how Scripture could be any clearer. These three passages alone shipwreck Calvin's system on the jagged reefs of his unbiblical, legalistic philosophy.

If we need further convincing (we should not), St. John records the same certainty in Revelation in his vision of the final judgment:

> Also another book was opened, which is the book of life. And the dead were judged by what was written in the books, *by what they had done* (Revelation 20:12; *emphasis* added).

Calvin was simply wrong. We are not divinely-constructed robots pushed here and there by an implacable, irresistible, and apparently merciless God. We share God's sovereignty — by his own choice. St. Paul is very clear about our role as co-rulers:

> Working together with him, then, we appeal to you not to receive the grace of God in vain. For he says, "In a favorable time I listened to you, and in a day of salvation I have helped you" (2 Corinthians 6:1-2).

"Working together with him" is a perfect statement of the principle of Shared Sovereignty that I have presented throughout this book.

We are God's co-workers, even in his work of redeeming his lost sheep, coaxing them back from the cliff of damnation. God called Paul to this ministry before he was born (Galatians 1:15-16) but Paul at first refused. Paul had to listen anew, and had to respond. A *calling* is not *compulsion.* Like Jeremiah before him, or Jonah looking for a fast ship going the opposite direction, Paul *resisted* God's call. In the end, he turned his heart toward God. He made a choice.

I can speak from similar experience, for even though I was called to the ministry at a young age and ordained as a young man, I abandoned that vocation for many years. God allowed me to do that. Did it make him happy? Doubtless not. But even when I returned to ministry it was because, again hearing his call, I chose to listen, and respond.

In a real sense, God calls not just clergy to a vocation, he calls every Christian. So, each has to make a choice. That is how, remember, the "new birth" works. As I pointed out before, we are all volunteers, not conscripts. But we must not be callous or lazy about his call. For as Jesus warned, there comes a day and a moment when the master of the house closes and bolts the door, and we can be left grumbling outside.

Summing Up

My fundamental objection to Calvin's predestinarian error is that it insidiously — and almost imperceptibly — relieves us of all moral responsibility for our choices. The Calvinist will not come right out and say this; many may not even recognize this fact. But as Justin pointed out, if we are mere pawns of divine fate, we cannot be held accountable for any actions, let alone our sins.

God, the Calvinist wants you to believe, chose your eternal destiny before he made you. Nothing you do, or can do, will alter that. Really, we have to begin to wonder why Calvinists would bother to preach the Gospel at all, or engage in any mission work. For if they are right, nothing they do will save anyone; the saved are already saved. Nothing they do will save a damned soul; those poor creatures were created only to be damned.

This sub-Christian thinking was rightly condemned as heresy when it appeared during the Protestant Reformation. Every Protestant body that preserved the basics of historic Christianity rejected it, and do so today. It is a philosophy (I will not label it theology) that overrules the whole of Scripture, and therefore must be excluded from Christian teaching. Sadly, it still spreads like a cancer in the Body of Christ. It is time for some radical surgery.

As I have shown in this book, God calls all men to repentance and his "desire" is that all should be saved, even while God knows — both in time, and in eternity — who will accept the gift. Many choose to reject it. But we do well to remember God's goal as St. Peter expressed it:

> The Lord is not slow to fulfill his promise as some count slowness, but is patient toward you, not wishing that any should perish, but that all should reach repentance (2 Peter 3:9).

Jesus said, "No one can come to me unless the Father who sent me draws him" (John 6:44). But each of us must respond to that call. From Genesis on, this is the heart of Scripture: God's loving call to his rebellious children, seeking out each who has become lost. It is also the very core of the Gospel of Jesus, who came into the world to call and save sinners, and who will leave ninety-nine sheep in the wilderness to find the one who has strayed. I must be blunt: if the Father had already made all decisions about our salvation — or damnation — then the entire ministry of Jesus becomes a sham.

If you have fallen into the bear trap of Calvinism, you should chew off your leg if necessary to get free (Matthew 18:8-9). God has called you. You have a choice. It is an everlastingly choice with eternal consequences.

Jesus himself was "predestined" before the foundation of the world to become our savior through his suffering and death (John 17:24; 1 Peter 1:20). Yet in the Garden of Gethsemane that night — at a very specific moment *inside* time — he, too, had to make the choice: "Yes" to the Father's will, or "No." Likewise, each of us was chosen "before the foundation of the world" from God's eternal perspective to become conformed to the image of his Son (Romans 8:29; Ephesians 1:4; Revelation 13:8). But we must be *willing* to abandon our rebellion and turn back to him.

Jesus made this very clear: "For I have come down from heaven, not to do my own will but the will of him who sent me" (John 6:38). The whole point of his incarnation is that the Son of God has reached down into creation, taken full human nature to himself, and raised it back to the Father. In this great saving act, by *the cooperation* of his will with the perfect will of the Father, we see the principle of Shared Sovereignty manifested most perfectly.

This is key if we will truly understand Jesus' act of submission in Gethsemane before his crucifixion. Holy Scripture assures us that Jesus was tempted as we are (Matthew 4, Mark 1, Luke 4) to violate his Father's will. Indeed, we are told that "we do not have a high priest who is unable to sympathize with our weaknesses, but one who in every respect has been tempted as we are, yet without sin (Hebrews 4:15).

Here is the final rebuke and overthrow of Calvinism: if Calvin was right, the Letter to the Hebrews is wrong. For if the Father was at all times utterly controlling Jesus' will, then Jesus could not possibly have been tempted. He would have been incapable of even considering temptation.

Hebrews is correct, and Calvin was wrong. Jesus was tempted. Look again at the excruciating evidence of those dark hours in Gethsemane just before his arrest as he literally sweated blood:

> ... he fell on his face and prayed, saying, "My Father, if it be possible, let this cup pass from me; nevertheless, not as I will, but as you will." And he came to the disciples and found them sleeping. And he said to Peter, "So, could you not watch with me one hour? Watch and pray that you may not enter into temptation. The spirit indeed is willing, but the flesh is weak." Again, for the second time, he went away and prayed, "My Father, if this cannot pass unless I drink it, your will be done" (Matthew 26:39-42).

"Your will be done." How often have we Christians prayed that in the prayer our Lord taught us? It must be made the essence and focus of every Christian life.

The anguish of those moments in the garden must never be reduced — as Calvin and other determinists would do — to Jesus mouthing empty words that were *predetermined* and therefore really meant nothing. Such a view is treachery against the human nature of Christ and would falsify the Gospel. His words and anguish were real, his prayer was painfully real, because Jesus knew he had the power to say "No." He had to choose: to conform his human will as Son of Man to his divine will as Son of God.

If that were not so, then those atheists today who accuse a wicked God of forcibly "murdering his son" would be telling the truth. Of course, Jesus contradicts them:

> "For this reason the Father loves me, because I lay down my life that I may take it up again. No one takes it from me, but I lay it down *of my own accord.* I have authority to lay it down, and I have authority to take it up again. This charge I have received from my Father" (John 10:17-18; *emphasis* added).

If this does not demonstrate Jesus exercising his will, in voluntary conformity to the Father's will, then I do not understand language.

Calvin and his followers were deeply mistaken. It distresses me that his false philosophy, a cancer in the Body of Christ, has led so many sincere Christians astray. But the truth and record of Holy Scripture must remain our foundation and guide, regardless of what the tradition of some man tries to claim to the contrary.

Once God has spoken; twice have I heard this: that power belongs to God, and that to you, O Lord, belongs steadfast love. For you will render to a man according to his work. — Psalm 62:11-12

Endnotes

1. The term "determinism" is used in a different sense by non-theistic "materialist" philosophers to refer to the impossible-to-break chain of

cause and effect which some believe is at work in the universe. One can (and many do) hold that kind of quasi-scientific "deterministic" view without ever thinking of, or speaking about, God. That is not what I am addressing here. This appendix is addressing only the theistic determinism held by John Calvin and his disciples.

2. Quotations from *The Institutes* are from the compendium *On The Christian Faith,* edited by the late John T. McNeill: The Liberal Arts Press, Indianapolis, 1957. The actual text of Calvin is Public Domain.

3. It was not unusual for Calvin to use this kind of veiled accusation against his opponents, implying that anyone who disagreed with him was impious.

4. Augustine's argument defeats those in our present day who argue for a doctrine of "eternal security," the notion that a Christian cannot fall from grace or lose his salvation. Jesus assures us that no one "can snatch" a disciple out of his hand, but nowhere does he say that we cannot turn and walk away of our own choice. The Gospel contains a number of instances where followers turn away and stop following Jesus. Perhaps the most obvious regards "the Twelve," one of whom betrayed him and eleven of whom abandoned him at his arrest.

5. Some will say that prior to creation God was not "acting" in any sense, merely (and fully) being. I have no plan to argue.

6. I understand that saying God is "outside" creation is itself a purely human perception again using analogical language. In any "real" sense God cannot be "inside" or "outside" time in the spatial sense. I use the analogy only because this is the simplest way for our minds to grasp what can otherwise not even be spoken of. In the same way, "eternity" is not "outside" time; it is an existence of its own in unique relationship with God which cannot be "measured" by its relationship to time.

7. This is what Lewis was expressing in the quotation cited in Appendix A regarding the effectiveness of prayer.

8. Cited from *Early Christian Fathers*, Volume 1: The Westminster Press, Philadelphia, 1953.

Appendix C

Demonic Beings And Evil

In the body of this work, I made reference to non-human evil powers and forces that affect humanity (Chapters Five, Six, Eleven, and Twelve), including several Scripture references to the devil or "Satan." As I said in an endnote to Chapter Seven, I chose to steer away from a more in-depth focus on the realm of demonic powers because, like the subject of Calvinistic Predestination (Appendix B), the subject of demonic power and influence in our world is a very complex area and very far beyond the scope of this present work. Indeed, the whole area of demonic power and influence could also easily command an entire volume on its own — likely a much longer volume than this present one.

I want to make very clear, though, that to say this present volume was not the place to address the full reality of demonic powers is not to simply dismiss the subject, or to class it as irrelevant or unimportant. It is a subject of very great importance, and I can assure the reader that I know quite well from personal experience that the realm of demonic power and its influence in the human sphere is widespread, and that unseen, personal demonic beings *influence* the thoughts and decisions of many people, non-Christian and Christian alike.

The key word, emphasized, is "influence." Demonic forces have deployed throughout God's creation since their first rebellion against God. When precisely, and how exactly, that rebellion took place, we do not know with certainty, because God has not revealed it to us in any great detail, nor did our Lord while he was directly among us (but see some of the Scriptural references below).

Still, a question many readers wonder about is, *How can demonic forces influence us?* The answer is not difficult, and on reflection will be apparent: this is possible because we ourselves are beings who share both a spiritual and a physical nature, and as such God has created us to continually operate in both the physical and the spiritual realms. In the spiritual realm we are, knowingly or unknowingly, in contact with demonic spiritual beings who may influence our thoughts or feelings and thus our subsequent actions. This is what St. Paul was warning about when he reminded us that we do not fight solely against human enemies:

> For we do not wrestle against flesh and blood, but against the rulers, against the authorities, against the cosmic powers over this present darkness, against the spiritual forces of evil in the heavenly places (Ephesians 6:12).

For the Christian, however, we must always remember that we have been clothed with the spiritual grace of Baptism, and its gift of the Holy Spirit within us, so we are able to put on the full armor of God that Paul speaks of in that same chapter. Being "in Christ," we have already overcome physical death (Romans 6) and have been brought into the Kingdom of light:

> He has delivered us from the domain of darkness and transferred us to the kingdom of his beloved Son, in whom we have redemption, the forgiveness of sins (Colossians 2:13-14).

Having acknowledged this, however, we must nevertheless understand — as both Paul and our Lord so clearly warned — that even though we are clothed in light and protected by the spiritual armor Christ forged for us on the cross, that does not mean we are *immune* from spiritual attack — just as Jesus himself was not immune, in the wilderness, and in Gethsemane. Demonic spiritual beings still can, and *still do,* attack us through our hearts and minds. They will tease, tempt, cajole, and ridicule us, and — pertinent to the present study — often seek to plant doubts in our minds about God's love or faithfulness. Further, as many mature Christians will testify, the greater holiness we seek or achieve, the more frequent and more trying these attacks will become.

Again, however, I want to emphasize the most important reality for the Christian: demonic beings can attack us, they can attempt to influence us, *but they cannot control us,* nor can they cause us to do anything against our will. Our decisions, as I have emphasized throughout this book, remain our decisions. Demons, of course, will like you to *think* that they are directly controlling you, because that will lend them a deeper influence over your mind or heart. But they do not, and they cannot, *control* you or your decisions or actions.

The reason this is so should by this time be plain to the reader: *God himself* constantly, because of his love, seeks to influence our thoughts, our feelings, and our decisions, but even *he himself* does not directly control us, as I have made plain throughout the book. In a similar manner, both godly and demonic spiritual beings (angels and demons) who inhabit the spiritual realm may seek to influence our thoughts or decisions, but God never allows them actual control. He himself has endued each of us with personal sovereignty in all matters that affect our spiritual nature, our spiritual life, and our spiritual destiny. So yes, God may allow demonic or angelic creatures to *influence* us, but never to directly control us.

I would suggest, however, that it is not so simple for those who reject God and his Christ, or who have not been clothed with the grace of Baptism. For them, without the direct protection of the Holy Spirit, I do believe that it is possible for them to allow themselves to fall under the more direct influence or even control of a demonic spirit, as we see in the very rare cases of true demonic possession.

Beyond this, I would highlight a few further realities that we know for certain from Holy Scripture about the demonic forces in the spiritual realm where we daily do battle.

Demonic "powers" or "authorities" are not only recognized in scripture as real beings, they are sometimes given specific names. One of the most common is our English transliteration of the Hebrew, "Satan." More correctly, this being is "the Satan," a name that derives from a Hebrew term that means "the accuser" or "the adversary."

Contrary to a lot of popular mythology, Satan is *not* some eternal "god." Far from it. Satan is very much a created being, like you and I. But he is not merely some amorphous, impersonal "power" or "force" as some "modern" scholars or theologians argue. He is a *personal* angelic being, a creature of God created in the invisible spiritual realm (invisible to us) to act as one of God's messengers, and to oversee parts of God's creation, in particular humankind and this earth, but who rebelled against God and perverted his own power and responsibilities.

Of course, the earliest and most prominent reference where Satan appears in Scripture (though not by that name but under the guise of the "ancient serpent") is in the temptation account in Genesis 3 that we considered in Chapter Five (see also Paul's references to that passage in 2 Corinthains 11 and 1 Timothy 2).[1] There are many other references to him, particularly in the New Testament, many directly from our Lord.[2]

Throughout this book, I have emphasized how our own human choices create and spread evil in the world. Having acknowledged that, though, we must be aware that while human wickedness is a primary source of evil and destruction in our world, humans may also be allied with unseen demonic beings whose influence we must never discount, nor underestimate.

There are a good many books available by biblically orthodox Christian writers that address demonic evil, and I would encourage the reader with further questions to seek them out.

Endnotes

1. This angel appears by the name Satan in the Book of Job (chapters 1-2) where he has been "patrolling" earth and mankind. There, for reasons

we are not told, Satan challenges God to cause suffering for the very righteous man Job, suggesting (like a good prosecuting attorney) that if God would withdraw His blessing from Job, Job will curse God and refuse to worship him any further. The book tells the entire story, including God's personal revelation of himself to Job toward the climax of the book. Elsewhere in the Old Testament, we are told Satan incited David to conduct a census of all Israel to try to bolster his army (1 Chronicles 21:1).

2. This same being, Satan, is mentioned repeatedly in the New Testament where he is consistently revealed to be an antagonist toward mankind, but most particularly an antagonist toward Jesus himself.

    a.   Satan is the person who tempts Jesus in the wilderness (Mark 1, Matthew 4, Luke 4), and Jesus often refers to Satan by name (Mark 3, 4). In Mark 8 (and the parallel in Matthew 16), Jesus rebukes Peter by calling him "Satan," placing Peter, at that moment, in the role of being an adversary to Christ's mission to bring his kingdom on earth.

    b.   In one place, Jesus speaks of witnessing Satan's "fall" from heaven (Luke 10), an event that may or may not refer to the account we read from Revelation 12 where St. John the Divine tells us about a war "in heaven" (the "heavenly places") when "that ancient serpent, who is called the devil and Satan, the deceiver of the whole world — he was thrown down to the earth, and his angels were thrown down with him" (Revelation 12:9). Thus, we come to see how Satan and other demonic beings are still at work in the spiritual realm of our world.

    c.   In Luke 22, Luke tells us that not only did Satan influence Judas' decision to betray Jesus (Luke 22:3; to which St. John also refers, John 13:27), but that Satan also influenced Peter's denial of Jesus shortly thereafter (Luke 22:31). In Revelation, St. John makes numerous references to Satan as an individual allied with evil in our world (Revelation 2, 3, 12, and 20).

    d.   St. Paul refers to Satan by name many times: Acts 28; 1 Corinthians 5 & 7; 2 Corinthians 11 & 12; 1 Thessalonians 2; 2 Thessalonians 2, and 1 Timothy 5.

About The Author

JOHN R. SPENCER holds a degree in English Literature from the University of Northern Colorado, where he was editor-in-chief of the campus literary magazine *NOVA,* and a Master of Divinity degree from Nashotah House Seminary near Milwaukee. He is a retired priest of The Anglican Church in North America.

His diverse career has included parish ministry, diocesan leadership, and 20 years in secular professions as a police detective, coroner's investigator, emergency medical technician, social worker, and community corrections supervisor.

He is the author of two other nonfiction works, *New Heavens, New Earth* (2002) and *The Other John* (2024), as well as the fictional *Solarium-3 Trilogy (Solarium-3, Haeven, and ReGeneration).*

He lives with his wife Candice in Wisconsin.

Also by John R. Spencer

Nonfiction
New Heavens, New Earth
The Other John

Fiction
Solarium-3, Haeven, ReGeneration
(THE SOLARIUM-3 TRILOGY)
ICEQUAKE!
Grand Slam

DeerVale Publishing

DeerVale™ is an independent publisher created to help new or independent authors bring their work into the marketplace of ideas. DeerVale books are available for order worldwide through most online book retailers and many local booksellers.

Faced with the obstacles of self-publishing, the high costs of many subsidy publishers, and no one to "get them in the door" of a traditional publisher, many writers feel stuck and simply give up.

DeerVale can help. We tailor publishing services to fit your needs. Since authors can handle some production work themselves (like hiring an editor or proofreader), we don't sell pricy "packages." We charge only for the essential services you actually need.

Unlike a vanity press, we don't publish everything submitted to us. We look for quality books we can support.

Visit our Submissions tab to learn more.

www.DeerValePublishing.com

www.ingramcontent.com/pod-product-compliance
Lightning Source LLC
Chambersburg PA
CBHW030547080526
44585CB00012B/296